Challenges and Opportunities of Educational Leadership Research and Practice

The State of the Field and Its Multiple Futures

A volume in
International Research on School Leadership
Alan R. Shoho, *Series Editor*

Challenges and Opportunities of Educational Leadership Research and Practice

The State of the Field and Its Multiple Futures

edited by

Alex J. Bowers
Teachers College–Columbia University

Alan R. Shoho
University of Wisconsin–Milwaukee

Bruce G. Barnett
University of Texas at San Antonio

INFORMATION AGE PUBLISHING, INC.
Charlotte, NC • www.infoagepub.com

Library of Congress Cataloging-in-Publication Data

A CIP record for this book is available from the Library of Congress
http://www.loc.gov

ISBN: 978-1-68123-274-4 (Paperback)
      978-1-68123-275-1 (Hardcover)
      978-1-68123-276-8 (ebook)

Copyright © 2016 Information Age Publishing Inc.

All rights reserved. No part of this publication may be reproduced, stored in a retrieval system, or transmitted, in any form or by any means, electronic, mechanical, photocopying, microfilming, recording or otherwise, without written permission from the publisher.

Printed in the United States of America

CONTENTS

Acknowledgments vii

1 The Multiple Futures of the Field of Educational Leadership
Research and Practice: An Introduction 1
Alex J. Bowers, Alan R. Shoho, and Bruce G. Barnett

SECTION I
EDUCATIONAL LEADERSHIP RESEARCH, THEORY, AND REFORM

2 Four Decades of Collective Leadership: The Connection Between
Leadership Theories of Action and Student Achievement 17
Chase Nordengren

3 Tensions and Contradictions in Approaches to Improving
Urban Inner-City Schools in the United States 55
D. Gavin Luter

4 Current Research on Arab Female Educational Leaders'
Career and Leadership: A Review of Extant Literature
and Future Directions for Research 87
Khalid Arar and Izhar Oplatka

SECTION II

METHODOLOGICAL CHALLENGES AND INNOVATIONS IN EDUCATIONAL LEADERSHIP RESEARCH

5 Challenges and Opportunities for Education Leadership Scholarship: A Methodological Critique 119
   Peter Goff and Maida Finch

6 Advancing Educational Leadership Research Using Qualitative Comparative Analysis (QCA) 147
   Katherine Marie Caves, Johannes Meuer, and Christian Rupietta

SECTION III

RESEARCH ON THE PREPARATION OF SCHOOL LEADERS

7 Viable and Effective Alternatives: Preparing Leaders for Non-Traditional Schools 173
   Kristy S. Cooper and Kate Rollert

8 Preparing Leaders in an Era of School Turnarounds: The Promise of University/District Partnerships as a Lever for Program Improvement... 199
   Chad R. Lochmiller, Colleen E. Chesnut, and Molly S. Stewart

SECTION IV

CONCLUSION

9 Mostly Unpunctuated Disequilibrium 225
   Carolyn J. Riehl

   About the Contributors.. 249

ACKNOWLEDGMENTS

The preparation of this book volume was a collaborative effort in which the co-editors wish to thank the many people who contributed their time and efforts to the volume. Particularly we wish to acknowledge and thank our colleagues who reviewed manuscripts for this volume and contributed their time and expertise as peer reviewers. Their timely and informative feedback, guidance, and suggestions to authors helped to strengthen the manuscripts throughout this volume. We are indebted to these colleagues and thank them for serving as peer reviewers.

Tom Alsbury, Seattle Pacific University
Dana Bickmore, Louisiana State University
Shelby Cosner, University of Illinois at Chicago
Karen DeAngelis, University of Rochester
Andrea Evans, Governors State University
Kristin Huggins, Washington State University
W. Kyle Ingle, University of Lousiville
Paula Kwan, The Chinese University of Hong Kong
Catherine Lugg, Rutgers, The State University of New Jersey
Ross Notman, University of Otago
Jessica Rigby, University of Washington
Elizabeth Farley-Ripple, University of Delaware
Martin Scanlan, Boston College
Cynthia Reed, Northern Kentucky University
Rick Reitzug, University of North Carolina at Greensboro
Mariela Rodriguez, The Unviersity of Texas at San Antonio
Angela Urick, The University of Oklahoma
Chris Willis, Bowling Green State Unviersity

CHAPTER 1

THE MULTIPLE FUTURES OF THE FIELD OF EDUCATIONAL LEADERSHIP RESEARCH AND PRACTICE

An Introduction

Alex J. Bowers
Teachers College, Columbia University

Alan R. Shoho
Unviersity of Wisconsin-Milwaukee

Bruce G. Barnett
The University of Texas at San Antonio

As the sixth volume in the *International Research on School Leadership* series, the contributing authors in this volume consider the history, challenges, and opportunities of the field of research and practice in educational leadership and administration in schools and districts. Ten years after the work of Firestone and Riehl (2005) and their contributing authors, our aim with the present volume was to summarize and update the work of the field, and provide a space to consider the multiple futures of educational leadership in schools and districts, as both challenges and opportunities. The first decade of the twenty-first century brought significant critiques, challenges, and competition to the research and practice of training leaders and administrators of schools and districts around the world. Congruently, the field experienced significant growth and change, as multiple new subdomains flourished and were founded. Thus, in this volume we were delighted to included excellent chapters from multiple authors that considered the duality of the challenges and opportunities of:

- The work of the field of educational leadership and administration research to date.
- The opportunities and challenges of new visions of leadership in traditional and non-traditional schools.
- The evolving state of research evidence in educational leadership and the increasing sophistication of multiple methodologies, including qualitative research, quantitative modeling, the ability to test theory, and the increasing opportunities brought on by the intersection of data, research, and practice.
- The preparation of educational leaders.
- And the emerging trends in the professional development of school leaders.

Throughout the volume, our colleagues from around the world provided chapters that speak to these central issues across the school leadership research domain, both as issues of the past, as well as visions of possible futures. Research on school leadership has historically been critiqued on issues of theory, methodology, research, findings, and application (Hailer, 1968). As one of the first citation analyses in education administration research, Hailer (1968) noted that the burgeoning field of educational administration at the time paradoxically suffered from these scholarly issues while at the same time had made great strides in providing new ways to understand and improve school leadership. Since that time, educational administration and school leadership research and preparation has come under continued critique (Edmonds, 1979; Hess & Kelly, 2005; Levine, 2005), while at the same time making significant strides in what is known about good school leadership (Bowers, Shoho, & Barnett, 2014; Boyce & Bowers, 2013; Hallinger, 2013; Hallinger & Heck, 2011; Krüger & Scheerens, 2012; Leithwood, Harris, & Hopkins, 2008; Leithwood & Louis, 2011; Robinson, Lloyd, & Rowe, 2008; Scheerens, 2012; Spillane, Halverson, & Diamond, 2004), especially for students in underserved and disadvantaged contexts. This continued conversation in the field is noted here in the present volume in Chapter 9 by Carolyn Riehl as "unpunctuated disequilibrium." Indeed, recent studies of the field of educational leadership and administration research have demonstrated that while researchers seem to work somewhat in isolation on significant problems of research, theory, and practice, a strong literature of research and theory has emerged over the last 50 years in the domain which has served to positively inform the research, policy, and practice of school leaders (Murphy, Vriesenga, & Storey, 2007; Richardson & McLeod, 2009; Wang & Bowers, in press).

The authors of the nine chapters in the present book volume took on this challenge of confronting the duality of not only including the past as we look to the future, but also the duality of the critique of the field in the midst of exciting and significant progress in our knowledge and understanding of leadership in schools. Here, in the first section of the book (Chapters 2, 3, and 4), the authors examine the interplay of educational leadership research and theory as it relates to reform in schools, especially as it relates to serving historically underserved populations globally. In section 2 (Chapters 5 and 6), the authors highlight the importance of methodological considerations in school leadership research as a means to understand theory and practice as well as providing interesting avenues that point to multiple exciting future possibilities through relying on current innovations noted within the chapters. Section 3, (Chapters 7 and 8) examines the research and practice of school leadership preparation, especially as it relates to university-district partnerships and non-traditional school settings. And in the final chapter, (Chapter 9), our capstone contributor provides a means to link the present volume with the past writings on these topics, while also providing a lens to view the exciting possibilities and promises of the multiple futures of the field of educational leadership research and practice.

SECTION 1: EDUCATIONAL LEADERSHIP RESEARCH, THEORY, AND REFORM

In Chapter 2, "Four Decades of Collective Leadership: The Connection between Leadership Theories of Action and Student Achievement," Chase Nordengren works to build a theory of collaboration and collectivity in schools as he synthesizes the research across multiple theories of leadership in schools, including instructional leadership, transformational leadership, teacher leadership, and distributed leadership. The central argument of the chapter is that the research on each of these theories, when examined together, demonstrates that they all focus on the collective context of leadership, as enacted through relationships between leaders (teachers and principals), leader actions, and student outcomes. Using a "theories of action" perspective, Nordengren conducted an extensive review of the literature on collective leadership through a systematic synthesis of the research to date. Through this process, Nordengren articulates a synthesis of three specific theories of action relating to the enactment of collective leadership in service to student achievement: targeting school improvement capacity, cultivating a culture of shared purpose, and redesigning teachers' work.

In the first theory of action, targeting school improvement capacity, Nordengren notes that collective conceptions of leadership are often framed as positively impacting student achievement and a school's ability overall to improve teaching and learning. This type of conception focuses on broad conceptions of school improvement, as well as conceptualizing school capacity through a systems lens, in which effects are more than direct, and are often mediated, moderated, and reciprocal. Second, cultivating a culture of shared purpose, Nordengren foregrounds the work of the large body of literature that places the culture of the school at the center of leadership practice. Here, conceptualized around the idea of collective leadership, and linked to the first theory of action on improving school capacity, school collective leadership focuses on a central shared purpose of improving teaching and learning, which in turn relates to the shared commitment and capacity of the organization. The third theory of action is centered on the issue of redesigning teachers' work. In this theory of action, the work of teachers is positioned as the central mediating variable between collective leadership and school achievement. Nordengren posits that the literature to date demonstrates that collective leadership consistently takes up the question of designing and redesigning teacher work, in an effort to adapt to multiple contextual and environmental demands of a school on teacher practice. The key synthesis here is that through the decentralized nature of collective leadership, teachers may be able to engage in deeper modes of work around school improvement through working together on alignment and coherence within and between classrooms.

In the end, through his synthesis throughout Chapter 2, Nordengren proposes the unifying concept of collective leadership as a means to bridge the multiple learnings across the current and recent theories in educational leadership. In this way, he provides a means to understand school improvement through a broader lens of teacher and leader collective action, taking into account the main perspectives of theories of leadership in schools that are central to the research literature to date.

In Chapter 3, "Tensions and Contradictions in Approaches to Improving Urban Inner-City Schools in the United States," Gavin Luter examines the challenges associated with trying to improve urban schools. To frame his examination, Luter looks at four approaches to addressing urban school improvement. They are comprehensive school reform, school choice, neighborhood/community, and place-based school reform initiatives. There are inherent tensions and contradictions to the various approaches for improving urban schools. What is not mentioned in the examination is the role of ideology and epistemology in these various approaches. In each of the approaches, there is an underlying philosophical theory driving its advocacy. For example, school choice advocates believe competition and student centered empowerment are the way to improve urban schools. In contrast, other approaches focus on the existing conditions within either the community or the school and attempt to improve those conditions to facilitate urban school improvement.

Luter's analysis revealed three emergent gaps in these approaches to urban school improvement. The first gap dealt with the implementation of place-based comprehensive community initiatives (PBCCI) efforts like Promise Neighborhoods (PN) and Choice Neighborhoods (CN). The second gap focused on the roles of the school district and the individual school in PBCCI. And the final gap derived from conflicting policy demands.

The implementation gap illustrated the challenges of coordinating multi-sector players to collaborate. The complexity of the multi-layers created a bureaucracy unto itself. As Luter noted, the scholarship on implementing any of the PBCCI is sorely lacking and needs to be addressed if we are to make any headway in what makes some approaches work and others not work. We may find out that it is not the approach, but rather the fidelity of implementation that is key to successfully helping urban schools to improve. It may be informative to the implementation challenge to examine the nature of the collaboration and determine if this is either fostering or hindering implementation of the PBCCI. A good resource to facilitate this examination would be Barnett, Hall, Berg, and Camarena's (2010) typology of partnerships for promoting innovation.

The next gap focused on the role of the school system in facilitating individual school improvement. As Luter discovered, there were no studies on how school systems actually help individual schools implement PBCCIs. This represents unexplored territory, ripe for in-depth study and analysis of the role school systems play in either fostering or hindering the progress of individual school improvement. Related to this, Luter highlighted the importance of the school leader working with their school community to initiate effective school reform.

And finally, Luter found there were a number of conflicting policy demands. He highlighted the lack of common metrics to determine progress, citing how states and the federal government look at student achievement as the end all, be all metric, while PN/CN metrics may be focused entirely on the services they provide. This illustrates the tension between short-term and long-term goals and how these goals are measured for success. As Luter notes, with the amount of money being spent on school reform initiatives, attention needs to be devoted to determining how all the facets and players intertwine to produce a successful outcome. Otherwise, we are likely to continue a "shot gun" approach where we hope something hits the target, yet we won't know for sure why or if it works in a systemic way. Or, as Jim Collins (2001) referred to in his book, *Good to Great*, can urban schools figure out what is required to be successful using a "hedgehog" approach or will we continue to use a "fox" approach where we grasp for straws, never knowing why something may or may not work. If we are to improve urban schools and help students in urban environments, we need research that focuses on processes tied to successful outcomes. Without it, we will continue to wade aimlessly in the ocean of urban school improvement.

Chapter 4, "Current Research on Arab Female Leaders' Career and Leadership: A Review of Extant Literature and Future Direction for Research," by Khalid Arar and Izhar Oplatka examines how various cultural and structural elements in Arab societies affect female school leaders. As growing numbers of females enter school leadership roles around the world, it is important to understand the realities women leaders encounter in different societies and cultures. Arar and Oplatka provide important insights to these lived experiences by examining the barriers Arab females experience in pursuing school leadership careers, the leadership styles demonstrated by these leaders, and the challenges they face in attempting to lead their schools. To address these three issues, the authors conducted an exhaustive review of existing empirical literature from 2000 to 2014 on this topic published in peer-reviewed journals written in English and Arabic. Their review examined 20 studies, consisting of 18 journal articles and two doctoral dissertations.

Their findings reveal important themes regarding Arab females' aspirations, leadership styles, and challenges in the principalship role. First, Arab females must overcome a variety of social and cultural barriers in their quest to become school leaders. On one hand, the strong patriarchal culture in Arab societies inhibits opportunities for women to engage in leadership roles, resulting in far longer time to obtain principalships than their male counterparts. Socio-cultural norms also pressure many women to maintain their homemaking and child-rearing roles. On the other hand, these obstacles negatively affect females' self-confidence and self-efficacy as well as their participation in secondary education, further hampering their career advancement. Second, the leadership styles Arab women demonstrate appear to be greatly influenced by the male-dominated societies in which they live. For example, many female leaders adopt a masculine or authoritative leadership style early in their careers; however, as they grow more comfortable in their roles, they shift to a more feminine style, emphasizing emotions, student learning outcomes, and participatory decision making more often than male principals. Finally, during their tenure as principals, many females face unique obstacles based on social and cultural norms. Many teachers of both genders prefer working with male school leaders; therefore, females are likely to encounter far more resistance to their goals, decisions, and ideas than males. Also, within many Arab communities, women

Multiple Futures of the Field of Educational Leadership Research and Practice ▪ 7

who seek to initiate professional development and teacher remediation face powerful opposition from local tribal families.

Arar and Oplatka conclude that gender leadership research in the Arab and Middle Eastern context is in its infancy with many promising areas for future studies, focusing on the positive aspects of their leadership. They suggest future investigations explore the factors that facilitate females' entry into and success in school leadership positions, uncover the lived leadership experiences and careers of successful female leaders, and examine the influence of Arab school leaders on their local communities and the broader society. We applaud these authors for identifying under-appreciated areas of research and look forward to seeing how their proposed research agenda unfolds in the future.

SECTION 2: METHODOLOGICAL CHALLENGES AND INNOVATIONS IN EDUCATIONAL LEADERSHIP RESEARCH

In Chapter 5, "Challenges and Opportunities for Education Leadership Scholarship: A Methodological Critique," Peter Goff and Maida Finch examine recent trends in quantitative studies on school leadership. In particular, they focus their investigation on the methodologies used and inferences drawn from their study. Specifically, they identify some of the potential benefits of conducting longitudinal versus the liabilities of cross-sectional studies. Their analysis illustrates how researchers can engage in deeper, more insightful inquiries if they were to use longitudinal studies to examine leadership effects.

Goff and Finch put forth a convincing argument for why educational researchers should be using more longitudinal studies rather the more commonly used cross-sectional studies. Unlike medical studies, educational research tends to use cross sectional, single site, and incident focused studies. This limits the impact and implications of educational studies. As noted by Goff and Finch, cross-sectional studies are easier and less expensive to conduct, but they also yield less robust and impactful findings.

This chapter is a major contribution to advancing the methodologies used to conduct school leadership studies. Rather than rely on single site studies, which have limited implications beyond their context, Goff and Finch provide the field with an invaluable argument for pushing the field to pursue more impactful and wider ranging studies across time and location.

To support their argument, Goff and Finch provide an example using a study involving leadership effectiveness as assessed using the 72-item Vanderbilt Assessment for Leadership in Education (VALEd) as the instrument and an adapted trust instrument from Hoy and Tschannen-Moran (1999). In their example, Goff and Finch examine the relationship between faculty trust in their principal and the principal's ability to practice learner-centered leadership. Intuitively, Goff and Finch hypothesized that as faculty trust in their principal increased, the principal's ability to practice learner-centered leadership involving classroom observations and meaningful post-observation de-briefings would be enhanced.

In order to test out their hypothesis, Goff and Finch used five models from ordinary least squared regression to clustered, fixed effects, two level HLM, to an SEM model. They examined these five models using three different specifications of leadership effectiveness and teacher-principal trust. What they discovered was with cross-sectional data, there was no way of knowing if a one-unit change in teacher-principal trust is a reasonable magnitude of change that occurs among teachers. With a longer time frame, lingering questions could be addressed. In addition, Goff and Finch note that cross sectional analyses were more susceptible to Type I errors, creating the illusion of a significant relationship when in reality none existed. And lastly, the results show that carrying out sophisticated analytical methods to analyze data does not compensate for weak research designs and data collection protocols. Although Goff and Finch's timeframe was only one academic year, the power of their method suggests that if scholars carried out longitudinal methodologies to multi-years, the results would likely yield more robust and meaningful results, conclusions, and implications for practice.

In Chapter 6, "Advancing Educational Leadership Research using Qualitative Comparative Analysis (QCA)," Kathrine Marie Caves, Johannes Meuer, and Christian Rupietta provide an overview and primer of the purpose and innovative application of the methodological process of Qualitative Comparative Analysis (QCA) as applied to studying educational leadership. As noted by the authors, QCA originated out of work in the 1980s, and has been applied in multiple domains previously, especially political science. In application to educational leadership issues, Caves, Meuer, and Rupietta eloquently detail how QCA is able to identify strong leadership practices and relate them directly to the impact of the school context on instructional improvement. QCA is a case-level analysis in which combinations of specific variables are aligned to outcomes and examined through a set of logic rules to provide specific recommendations for which effects are most likely working across contexts, and which are context specific. In this way, the authors present QCA as a means to bridge between qualitative case study analysis and specific recommendations about the most frequent practices in an organization that may be generalizable across multiple schools.

Caves, Meuer, and Rupietta note that QCA provides a means to analyze data in this novel fashion through focusing on a data minimization strategy that aligns directly to the goals of recent research on the educational leadership literature, including focusing on necessary and sufficient conditions, conjunctural causation in which multiple factors explain an outcome, equifinality in which multiple pathways lead to a desired outcome, and causal asymmetry in which the configuration of an outcome and its opposite are not mirror images. QCA provides these data analytic structures through a process of examining school case data to identify specific activities and processes occurring in the case in relation to specific outcomes. Throughout Chapter 6, Caves, Meuer, and Rupietta expertly guide the reader through the process and the application of the Boolean logic analysis procedure to identify each of the four issues of necessary and sufficient conditions, conjunctural causation, equifinality, and asymmetry. Then, the authors provide the case of "Ms. Barloetti superintendent of Circle County Schools" applying QCA to examine her organization in which hypothetical Superintendent Barloetti walks through each stage of QCA as she works to analyze the extent to which the district teacher training program is influencing student achievement in the district schools, focusing on the level of communication in the schools (measured through surveys), teacher participation in the training, and the socio-economic status of the school. Through the QCA process, the authors show that in the hypothetical case of Superintendent Barloetti, she is able to find that "... thus, schools with excellent communication and high SES will likely meet targets regardless of participation in teacher training, and those with training and excellent communication will likely succeed independent of socioeconomic context." Hence, in these ways, Chapter 6 provides one of the first detailed applications of QCA in educational leadership and administration research, and does so through an easy to follow application and example that aligns with real-world issues faced by educational leaders in schools and districts today.

SECTION 3: RESEARCH ON THE PREPARATION OF SCHOOL LEADERS

Kristy Cooper and Kate Rollert's study of preparing alternative school leaders is depicted in Chapter 7, "Viable and Effective Alternatives: Preparing Leaders for Non-Traditional Schools." Recently, more leadership preparation programs are emerging with the aim of developing leaders for specific contexts, such as turnaround schools and charter schools (Duke, 2014; National Alliance for Public Charter Schools, 2008). Cooper and Rollert contend that preparing leaders for the growing number of alternative schools serving disenfranchised students who struggle academically and socially in traditional schools is equally important, especially if our society wants to educate growing numbers of students who are "slipping through the cracks." They maintain that leading alternative schools requires a unique set of knowledge and skills, ones that are fundamentally different than those needed by leaders in traditional schools settings. Based on their review of resource guides and research guides as well as effective leadership and teaching practices in alternative school settings, they identify seven areas of distinct leadership knowledge and skills, ranging from understanding students' social and emotional needs to developing wrap-around services to providing targeted professional development.

After identifying these skill and content areas, the authors describe a continuum of leadership preparation options (which they call models) to prepare skilled and knowledgeable leaders for alternative schools. The first model involves developing a single course dedicated to leading alternative schools. The advantage of this model is that it would not require recruiting students; the course would become a requirement for all students in the preparation program. A second model, offering concentrations, expands the single course option by having students enroll in a series of courses devoted to alternative school leadership. This option would offer a multi-disciplinary perspective by incorporating coursework from psychology, sociology, curriculum and instruction, and program evaluation. Internships would provide opportunities for students to work for concentrated periods of time in alternative school settings. The final, and most comprehensive, model for preparing alternative school leaders would be to design an entire program dedicated to developing leaders for these school settings. Using a cohort-based learning format, students and faculty would establish networks with alternative school educators in the region. Recruitment would be more selective by targeting alternative school teachers, special educators, and social workers. This model would require creating partnerships between leadership preparation programs and local alternative schools. Besides identifying long-term internship sites for students, partnership school educators would help shape the curriculum and learning activities, similar to what occurred in the study conducted by Lochmiller and his colleagues reported in the next chapter, Chapter 8. Here, in Chapter 7, Cooper and Rollert provide a compelling argument for tailoring leadership preparation for a specific educational context, a trend we believe will become more prevalent in the future.

In Chapter 8, "Preparing Leaders in an Era of School Turnaround: The Promise of University/District Partnerships as a Lever for Program Improvement," Chad Lochmiller, Colleen Chestnut, and Molly Stewart reveal the internal dynamics and changes university faculty and programs experience when investing in school-university partnerships. They begin by identifying the advantages of school-university partnerships reported in the literature, highlighting trends for recruitment, selection, curriculum, and instructional delivery. They contend that partnerships have particular relevance for preparing principals for turnaround leadership, and describe a recently developed school-university partnership with this expressed aim. Using resources from the federal government's Race to the Top initiative, program developers created an accelerated preparation program that combined intensive internship experiences with university coursework. To obtain multiple perspectives on the partnership's formation and operation, program evaluators conducted interviews with university faculty and administrators, principals in the district who served as clinical instructors, mentor principals, and district administrators. The interviews focused on the operationalization of the partnership; however, specific attention was devoted to understanding ways in which the partnership influenced program content and delivery.

Interview analysis revealed significant ways in which the preparation program was impacted by the district participation. Initially, tensions arose between university faculty and district partners. University faculty expressed reluctance to accept school practitioners' knowledge base, believing they had little expertise in how best to prepare school leaders. School administrators, on the other hand, felt that program graduates lacked important knowledge and skills, particularly in helping teachers to work more effectively with struggling learners in turnaround schools. Over time, however, this balance of power shifted as district participants took more responsibility for shaping course content and aligning this information with the needs of their schools. By emphasizing practical and relevant learning experiences (as opposed to focusing on state standards and theoretical constructs emphasized by university faculty), district administrators, clinical faculty, and mentors began shaping the curriculum to become what they termed "the district way." Over time, university faculty realized their notions of leadership preparation were outdated and lacked the relevance sought by their district partners. These interactions also forced program developers to wrestle with their definitions and conceptions of key program concepts, especially the complexities of instructional leadership and school turnaround leadership. Over time, university faculty came to appreciate the contextual realities of turning around low-performing schools, realities they had heretofore not realized or been overlooked. Although a great deal is known about the *mechanics and operations* of forming and delivering school-university leadership development partnerships (Darling-Hammond, Meyerson, LaPointe, & Orr, 2010), Lochmiller and his colleagues shed new light on the *internal dynamics* between university faculty and district partners when engaging in collaborative preparation programs. Understanding these dynamics is critical if universities and districts want to develop more symbiotic partnerships that deeply connect theory and practice, an ongoing challenge in leadership preparation graduate programs (Levine, 2005).

SECTION 4: CONCLUSION

The capstone final chapter, Chapter 9, "Mostly Unpunctuated Disequilibrium: A Commentary on New Directions in Research and Practice in Education Leadership," by Carolyn Riehl concludes the book volume with a look back, a synthesis and a look forward. In this final chapter, Riehl first provides additional framing for the present book volume, following on ten years since the publication of the Firestone and Riehl (2005) book volume "A New Agenda for Research in Educational Leadership." The present work, in a way, is a successor to that work, but builds on, and builds beyond the work over the last decade in the research on educational leadership. In this chapter, Riehl first takes a historical lens to the field and the chapters here, and posits that educational leadership research, as a field, does not so much contain the "punctuated equilibrium" of other fields, which grow and develop not in consistent and stable ways, but rather through fits and starts, but rather that the field of educational leadership is an "unpunctuated disequilibrium" in that it is consistently contested and at odds, especially at the intersection of research, policy, and practice. However, throughout this final chapter, Riehl summarizes and synthesizes the chapters in the present volume as a means to demonstrate the evolving and positive outlook in the field of educational leadership research, which has made great strides in providing a robust and rich decade of proposing and testing novel and innovative theories and methods as a means to improve practice, both in schools in which leaders serve as well as in schools which train these same leaders. Through this lens, she then provides a thought provoking synthesis and framing of each of the chapters in relation to each other as well as the broader issues at play in the field of educational leadership today. As the final capstone chapter of the book volume, Chapter 9 provides a means to view the book volume as a synthesis across the chapters, and a lens to view the future of the domain.

REFERENCES

Barnett, B. G., Hall, G. E., Berg, J. H., & Camarena, M. M. (2010). A typology of partnerships for promoting innovation. *Journal of School Leadership, 20,* 10–36.

Bowers, A. J., Shoho, A. R., & Barnett, B. G. (2014). Considering the use of data by school leaders for decision making. In A. J. Bowers, A. R. Shoho, & B. G. Barnett (Eds.), *Using data in schools to inform leadership and decision making* (pp. 1–16). Charlotte, NC: Information Age Publishing.

Boyce, J., & Bowers, A. J. (2013). *Examining the evolving research on instructional leadership from 25 years of the schools and staffing survey (SASS).* Paper presented at the Annual meeting of the University Council for Educational Administration (UCEA), Indianapolis, IN.

Collins, J. (2001). *Good to great*. New York, NY: Harper Collins.
Darling-Hammond, L., Meyerson, D., LaPointe, M., & Orr, M. T. (2010). *Preparing principals for a changing world: Lessons from effective school leadership programs*. San Francisco, CA: Jossey-Bass.
Duke, D. L. (2014). A bold approach to developing leaders for low-performing schools. *Management in Education, 28*(3), 80–85.
Edmonds, R. (1979). Effective schools for the urban poor. *Educational Leadership, 31*(1), 15–24.
Firestone, W. A., Riehl, C. (2005). *A new agenda for research in educational leadership*. New York: Teachers College Press.
Hailer, E. J. (1968). The interdisciplinary ideology in educational administration: Some preliminary notes on the sociology of knowledge. *Educational Administration Quarterly, 4*(2), 61–77.
Hallinger, P. (2013). A conceptual framework for systematic reviews of research in educational leadership and management. *Journal of Educational Administration, 51*(2), 126–149.
Hallinger, P., & Heck, R. H. (2011). Conceptual and methodological issues in studying school leadership effects as a reciprocal process. *School Effectiveness and School Improvement, 22*(2), 149–173.
Hess, F. M., & Kelly, A. P. (2005). *Learning to lead? What gets taught in principal preparation programs*. Cambridge, MA: The Program on Education Policy and Governance.
Hoy, W. K., & Tschannen-Moran, M. (1999) Five faces of trust: An empirical confirmation in urban elementary schools. *Journal of School Leadership, 9*, 184–208.
Krüger, M. L., & Scheerens, J. (2012). Conceptual perspectives on school leadership. In J. Scheerens (Ed.), *School leadership effects revisited: Review and meta-analysis of empirical studies* (pp. 1–30). New York, NY: Springer.
Leithwood, K., Harris, A., & Hopkins, D. (2008). Seven strong claims about successful school leadership. *School Leadership & Management, 28*(1), 27–42.
Leithwood, K., & Louis, K. S. (2011). *Linking leadership to student learning*. San Francisco, CA: Jossey-Bass.
Levine, A. (2005). *Educating schools leaders*. New York: The Education Schools Project.
Murphy, J., Vriesenga, M., & Storey, V. (2007). Educational Administration Quarterly, 1979–2003: An analysis of types of work, methods of investigation, and influences. *Educational Administration Quarterly, 43*(5), 612–628. doi: 10.1177/0013161x07307796
National Alliance for Public Charter Schools. (2008). *Charter school executives: Toward a new generation of leadership*. The Working Group of Charter School Leadership, National Alliance for Public Charter Schools. Online at www.publiccharters.org.
Richardson, J. W., & McLeod, S. (2009). Where should educational leadership authors publish to get noticed by the top journals in the discipline? *Educational Administration Quarterly, 45*(4), 631–639.
Robinson, V. M., Lloyd, C. A., & Rowe, K. J. (2008). The impact of leadership on student outcomes: An analysis of the differential effects of leadership types. *Educational Administration Quarterly, 44*(5), 635–674.

Scheerens, J. (2012). Summary and conclusion: Instructional leadership in schools as loosely coupled organizations. In J. Scheerens (Ed.), *School leadership effects revisited: Review and meta-analysis of empirical studies* (pp. 131–152). New York, NY: Springer.

Spillane, J. P., Halverson, R., & Diamond, J. B. (2004). Towards a theory of leadership practice: A distributed perspective. *Journal of Curriculum Studies, 36*(1), 3–34.

Wang, Y., Bowers, A.J. (in press) Mapping the field of educational administration research: A Journal citation network analysis of the discipline. *Journal of Educational Administration.*

SECTION I

EDUCATIONAL LEADERSHIP RESEARCH,
THEORY, AND REFORM

CHAPTER 2

FOUR DECADES OF COLLECTIVE LEADERSHIP

The Connection Between Leadership Theories of Action and Student Achievement

Chase Nordengren
University of Washington

There is a paradoxical difference between evidence showing an indirect and sometimes weak relationship between leadership and student outcomes (Heck & Hallinger, 2009; Marks & Printy, 2003; Urick & Bowers, 2014) and the expectations of policymakers and the public that leaders can fix failing schools (Robinson, Lloyd, & Rowe, 2008). Explaining this difference has been a significant focus of leadership scholars over the last forty years, who have proposed a variety of models to understand who exercises leadership in schools, how they exercise that leadership, and how that leadership affects students (Hallinger, 2013). Models by themselves do not, however, describe the *what* and *how* of leadership practice: which practices of leadership are effective and, in particular, the link between these factors and theories of school improvement.

Authors in the field have begun to suggest that a "bewildering array of definitions" (Harris, 2003, p. 318) have prevented a deeper understanding of how leadership functions outside the models that attempt to categorize it (Mayrowetz, 2008; York-Barr & Duke, 2004). When leadership is "a social construction on the part of those experiencing it" (Leithwood & Jantzi, 1999, p. 681), the use of an explicit descriptor of leadership models is not necessary, nor even always expedient. Instead, scholars should consider means of examining studies *across* models, both to get a more complete picture of the state of the field and to understand common elements that transcend traditional model boundaries.

This chapter's purpose is to identify themes in recent educational leadership literature that cross boundaries between models of educational leadership, with an emphasis on new ways of thinking about how informal and formal leaders work together in schools. In doing so, it hopes to provide an introduction to recent scholarship in this arena, and also advance a conversation about how to better integrate models of leadership across diverse authors and contexts. It asks:

1. In literature on educational leadership written since the rise to prominence of collective models of educational leadership (roughly, the year 2000), how do authors conceptually understand leaders, leadership tasks, and student outcomes?
2. What are common "theories of action" in these literatures linking leadership tasks with changes in instruction and in student outcomes?
3. What are common features of these theories of action across leadership models?

Using a "theories of action" model, this chapter seeks to understand the commonalities underlying how collective leadership studies understand who leads, what behaviors leaders lead through, and the student outcomes that measure that success or failure. The chapter identifies three common types of theories of action across studies and three features of studies that are common throughout the educational leadership literature. The chapter concludes by arguing collective leadership serves as a bridge between mediated models of leadership and effects on student outcomes, exploring the implications of this idea for theory and research.

BACKGROUND

In this section, I argue four major models of educational leadership converge around the idea of collectivity. In turn, this convergence suggests the opportunity for work that seeks to integrate models, or understand models together, through "theories of action," or ways of describing how leaders, through leadership practices, cause impacts on student outcomes. While specific studies of school leadership, both quantitative and qualitative, may suggest a leadership model through which authors understand leadership, leadership models share important similarities that allow work among one scholarly tradition to have utility for scholars in other traditions.

Most leadership models now contend, at a minimum, that leadership is "a social influence process whereby intentional influence is exerted by one person [or group] over other people [or groups] to structure the activities and relationships in a group or organization" (Yukl, 1994, p. 3; see also Leithwood & Duke, 1999; Northouse, 2007). Models of leadership, therefore, address the questions of who ought lead, what they ought do to lead, and how these person or persons ought lead. As such, the relationship between leadership models and leadership as understood in practice is reciprocal and changing, and scholars should examine how accurately each reflects the other.

PROMINENT MODELS OF COLLECTIVE EDUCATIONAL LEADERSHIP

I use the term "collective leadership" here to encompass models of educational leadership that contain three common elements:

1. A unit of analysis: Collective leadership describes teams of leaders working together.
2. A unit of work: Collective leadership models focus on the routines or common practices leaders engage in, rather than the actions of individual leaders.
3. A unit of measurement: Collective leadership orients actors in the school towards the common goal of improving student outcomes.

I focus on four models that, I argue, contain collectivity: Instructional leadership, transformational leadership, teacher leadership, and distributed leadership. These four overlap in interesting ways, and, each in their own way, exhibit a growing or already well-developed focus on the collective nature of leadership practice.

Evolving Notions of Instructional Leadership

First, instructional leadership refers to several theories that discuss how leaders engage in the work of improving classroom instruction. Scholarship on instructional leadership has a long and diverse history. Beginning roughly from the period of the "effective schools" movement of the mid-1980s, scholars have sought to understand the role of principals in setting instructional priorities (Hallinger, 2005). Much of this early literature focused on firmly establishing what was expected of principals in terms of setting the vision for and intervening in activities traditionally reserved for teachers (Hallinger & Murphy, 1987). As the accountability movement took hold in the late 1990s and early 2000s, attention once again turned to how principals interacted with instruction, though this time with the desire to better meet more vigorous performance expectations placed on schools (Hallinger, 2005). The various models of instructional leadership may come, in part, from this long and multifaceted heritage.

The diversity of the instructional leadership literature may also stem from a recent focus within that literature on collaboration and collectivity. During the nascent stages of instructional leadership, which studied principals, literature focused on connecting leadership practices to student outcomes to the detriment of a focus on styles of leadership practice (Hallinger, 2005). The trend from "technological, rational planning" models of school improvement toward "cultural, collaborative approaches" (Sheppard, 1996, p. 328), observed by instructional leadership authors, encompassed several different interpersonal leadership styles. In turn, this shift may have also shifted the attention of authors toward the collaboration itself, including actors other than the principal in the leadership umbrella.

One understanding of instructional leadership—termed shared instructional leadership (Marks & Printy, 2003; Printy, Marks, & Bowers, 2009; Urick & Bowers, 2014)—explicitly addresses the role of teachers and other non-administrators in instructional leadership. These scholars begin from the principle that teaching and learning, as the "technical core" of schools and schooling, ought guide all of the short- and long-term objectives of schools as organizations (Marks & Printy, 2003). This process entails both principals mobilizing action toward improving student outcomes and teachers establishing the norms and culture through which other teachers act (Marks, Printy, & Bowers, 2009). The shared instructional leadership concept is in line with profiles of successful instructional leadership practice (Knapp, 2014; Murphy et al., 2007), and major critiques of the model by other scholars.

Though diverse, instructional leadership theorists share the belief that principals lead by defining and communicating goals, providing feedback on the teaching and learning process, and emphasizing professional development activities (Alig-Mielcarek & Hoy, 2005; Hallinger, 2005). Among some authors, these tasks also include setting a culture of high expectations, monitoring student data, and serving as a visible presence in the school (Hallinger, 2005). Instructional leadership theories still lend substantial, perhaps primary, focus to principals. Still, the focus on principals as collaborative agents has lent focus to collaborative processes, and what kinds of leadership may be exercised within them.

Transformational Leadership

The literature on transformational leadership in schools, begun in the 1970s, has focused largely on whether schools are good places to work and learn and, as such, has addressed a broader set of leadership goals and activities than the improvement of instruction. Under these models, principals are expected to understand and display the behaviors and dispositions necessary to build work environments supportive to teachers. It is incumbent on the leader in this case to promote the overall goals of the institution rather than the goals of the individual (Brower & Balch, 2005). Frequently, the model includes opportunities for teachers to collaborate on leadership activities to create a culture of shared responsibility and accountability.

Transformational leadership models across several literatures focus on the capacities and commitments of an organization's members (Leithwood, Jantzi, & Steinbach, 2009). Like instructional leadership, the introduction of transformational leadership implies schools are shifting away from the traditional model of leadership and changing "for the better" by increasing the purposes and resources of both leaders and followers (Leithwood, Jantzi, & Steinbach, 2009).

In recent years, authors (Hallinger, 2003; Marks & Printy, 2003; Urick & Bowers, 2011) have proposed reconciling instructional and transformational leadership models in various ways. Additionally, various reviews of literature (Robinson et al., 2008; Scheerens, 2012) have found that instructional leadership has a more significant impact on student achievement than transformational leadership. These findings may be associated with a decline in published studies utilizing this literature in recent years, as authors appear to transition into using other models to describe similar phenomena. Nevertheless, the term "transformational leadership" has a long history, and retains some salience among practitioners.

Teacher Leadership

Teacher leadership theories understand leadership beginning from the perspectives and needs of classroom teachers. Formally, the term "teacher leader" is used to refer to teachers with a variety of job arrangements outside of the classroom, from full-time formal coaching positions to occasional "drop-in" observation or advice-giving (Lord & Miller, 2000). In addition to these formal arrangements, teacher leadership scholars often seek to understand how teachers lead informally, including how practices such as modeling effective instruction serve a leadership function even if practitioners do not consider themselves leaders. An egalitarian view of teachers and teaching, combined with the newness of teacher leadership positions, has fed a line of scholarship separate from that focusing on leadership by principals (Neumerski, 2013).

Teacher leadership scholars have focused attention on these nonsupervisory, school-based leadership roles (Mangin & Stoelinga, 2008). While some authors in this space have focused on formalistic job responsibilities and roles—studying teachers who build professional development, critique lessons, and serve on committees (Lord & Miller, 2000)—others have taken an explicitly anti-hierarchical approach to understanding expertise and the building of relationships as key leadership practices (Firestone & Cecilia Martinez, 2007), while others have focused on how specific environments foster opportunities for, or even expectations of, teacher leadership (York-Barr & Duke, 2004).

Given its focus, scholars may consider teacher leadership a descriptive term for teachers who lead, rather than a model in its own right. However, like the other models in this section, teacher leadership scholars refer to a common, yet independent set of understandings about how leadership functions in schools, and share a unique conception of how leadership should function. Placing this literature in dialogue with other literature on collective leadership, while recognizing teacher leadership's limitations, represents the diversity of perspectives currently at play in educational leadership scholarship.

Distributed Leadership

Under a fourth strand of leadership scholarship, distributed leadership models argue that leadership is a situational, rather than permanent, quality of individuals and situations. Copland (2003) tracks the development of distributed leadership from the first human relations perspectives of the 1970s, which pushed against an assumed distrust of employees, through the development of transformational leadership (which focuses on the empowerment of staff), into Elmore's (2000) work, which focuses on re-aligning the center of authority in schools toward whole staffs. While the term distributed leadership is used in varying contexts (and at times to refer to relatively routine practices of delegation) I here refer to models that argue many individuals within a school can serve as leaders or co-leaders during particular times or in areas in which they have expertise (Spillane, Halverson, & Diamond, 2004). These authors reject the dichotomies of leader–follower and leadership–followership they see in other theoretical frames (Gronn, 2002).

By proponents, distributed leadership is seen as a key response to leadership studies that have left unanswered questions about the impact of leadership on instructional improvement (Harris, 2004). Empirical studies in distributed leadership look to "capture" leadership activities that other models might miss (Harris, 2004). In particular, certain authors within the distributed leader strand redirect focus from individual capacities toward the idea of a collective capacity for leadership, greater than the sum of its parts (Harris, 2004). This focus reflects an emerging consensus that distributed leadership is not merely the division of tasks among several persons but is a manifestation of the interactions that leaders and recipients have with each other (Timperley, 2005).

In distributed leadership theories, the situation is treated as the primary unit of analysis; distributed leadership attempts to understand how the cognition of actors is distributed by time, place, and socialization (Spillane et al., 2004). By focusing on interactions, "organizational routines and tools are a core defining element of practice" (Harris, 2008, p. 255). In this way, distributed leadership ties together knowledge, belief and action: "activity is a product of what the actor knows, believes, and does in and through particular social, cultural, and material contexts" (Spillane, et al., 2004).

Distributed leadership theories also highlight the importance of expertise, or the potential expertise of actors, in creating opportunities for leadership. In distributed leadership theory, expertise rather than hierarchy is a source of authority (Copland, 2003). Expertise is tied to a process of continual learning among teachers about curriculum and instruction (Harris, 2003). While this process can reinforce visions set by formal administrators, distributed leadership can also challenge authority in ways that make joint movement more difficult (Printy, 2007).

METHODOLOGY

This chapter seeks to identify and evaluate qualitative and quantitative studies that link collective leadership practices to student outcomes. In the context of collective leadership, I argue, it is possible to review works of literature across these multifaceted models of leadership by examining how researchers understand the relationship between leaders, leadership actions, and student outcomes.

Here, these understandings are termed "theories of action." A theory of action is a working hypothesis regarding how leadership practices and/or changes in instruction resulting from good leadership create observable improvements in student outcomes. I use the theories of action present in each study reviewed here as a means of understanding the way leadership functions in each instance (Hill & Celio, 1998), and to therefore find common features between studies with nominally different models of leadership. Theories of action, however, are not by themselves a replacement for leadership models or theories: Ultimately, they are primarily a tool for understanding studies together.

In constructing a basis for the review, I followed the eight criteria of successful systematic reviews of literature described by Hallinger (2003). Hallinger calls for reviews to have explicit goals (here, understanding the collectivity behind contemporary studies in educational leadership) and an explicit conceptual perspective (here, the idea of theories of action, which must be identified and explicated). These two orientations guided how studies in the review were sorted and what data was extracted from them (Hallinger, 2013). I conduced a "bounded search" (Hallinger, 2013) of literature, with an inclusive approach to sources of information, methods of leadership and conceptions of student outcomes, in studies from 2000 to the present. Beginning from the year 2000, this review seeks to pick up where Leithwood and Duke (1999) ostensibly left off. The period also encompasses major theoretical developments, including Gronn's (2002) early work on distributed leadership and the development of instructional leadership beyond the principalship.

Four separate strategies were used to gather studies:

1. The ERIC database was searched for abstracts containing at least one term for a leadership model that implied collective work ("distributed leadership," "teacher leadership," "instructional leadership," "leadership effects," "collaborative leadership," "shared leadership," or "collective leadership") and one term for student outcomes ("student achievement," "student learning," "student outcomes," "social outcomes," or "student performance").
2. All studies published from 2000 to the present included in Robinson, Lloyd and Rowe's 2008 meta-analysis were reviewed for inclusion.
3. Key theoretical literature on distributed leadership (Spillane, Halverson, & Diamond, 2004; Spillane, 2006; Mayrowetz, 2008; Gronn, 2002) was used as the basis for a Google Scholar reverse citation search to discover any empirical studies that utilized distributed leadership to describe leadership activities.
4. Key journals were identified and reviewed for any remaining relevant empirical studies. This search included the four key journals referenced in Leithwood and Duke's 1999 review of the history of leadership literature across the past century (*Education Administration Quarterly; Journal of School Leadership; Educational Management, Administration, & Leadership;* and *Journal of Educational Administration*) as well as two journals established after 1999 (*School Leadership & Management* and *Leadership & Policy in Education*). The previous three search strategies substantially incorporated work in other journals as well.

From this initial search strategy, 76 applicable studies were identified. These studies were placed in three groups, summarized in Table 2.1.

TABLE 2.1 Do Reviewed Studies (76) Conceptualize Leadership as Driven by Leadership Teams and Link Their Results to Student Outcomes?

Team of Leaders Without Link to Student Outcomes (29)	Team of Leaders With Link to Student Outcomes (26 in 29 Publications)	Focus on Teacher Perceptions of Principal Leadership (21)
• Beycioglu and Aslan 2010 • Curtis 2013 • Dean 2005 • Edge and Mylopolous 2008 • Eyal et al. 2004 • Feeney 2009 • Firestone and Cecilia Martinez 2007 • Gopalan 2004 • Hill 2009 • Huffman and Hipp 2000 • Hur 2011 • Ishimaru 2013 • Kelley 2011 • Kennedy et al. 2009 • Lambert 2006 • Lovett and Cameron 2011 • Margolin et al. 2000 • Margolis 2008 • Park and Datnow 2009	• Abbott and McKnight 2010 • Akopoff 2010 • Alexander 2010 • Angelle 2010 • Chang 2011 • Chen 2007 • Copland 2003 • Davidson and Dell 2003 • Droese 2010 • Fancera and Bliss 2011 • Foster 2005 • Grumdahl 2010 • Hallinger and Heck series (Hallinger and Heck 2010a; Hallinger and Heck 2010b; Heck and Hallinger 2009; Heck and Hallinger 2010) • Harris 2002 • Holland 2002 • Kim 2010	• Alig-Mielcarek and Hoy 2005 • Brown and Keeping 2005 • Cerit 2009 • Christianson 2010 • Deike 2009 • Donaldson et al. 2010 • Goldring et al. 2009 • Good 2008 • Griffith 2004 • Hulpia and Devos 2009 • Hulpia et al. 2011 • Jacobsen 2011 • Leithwood and Jantzi 2008 • Loder and Spillane 2005 • McDonald and Keedy 2002 • Murphy et al. 2009 • Shatzer 2009 • Shatzer et al. 2013 • Wahlstrom and Louis 2008

(continued)

TABLE 2.1 Do Reviewed Studies (76) Conceptualize Leadership as Driven by Leadership Teams and Link Their Results to Student Outcomes? (continued)

Team of Leaders Without Link to Student Outcomes (29)	Team of Leaders With Link to Student Outcomes (26 in 29 Publications)	Focus on Teacher Perceptions of Principal Leadership (21)
• Penuel et al. 2010 • Pitts 2009 • Printy 2007 • Printy et al. 2009 • Rogers et al. 2006 • Senesac 2010 • Sheppard et al. 2010 • Somech 2010 • Spillane et al. 2009 • Watson 2005	• Leithwood and Jantzi 2000 • Leithwood and Jantzi 2006 • Leithwood and Mascall 2008 • Leithwood et al. 2010 • Marks and Printy 2003 • Rivers 2010 • Seashore Louis et al. 2010 • Silins and Mulford 2004 • Terrell 2010 • Timperley 2008[1]	• Wells et al. 2010 • Williams 2006

[1] Study was discovered as part of the author's review of conceptual literature and not as part of general review methodology.

Studies were screened for relevance to the study (Hallinger, 2013) using two key elements. First, reviewed studies had to include non-principal actors (chiefly, teachers) who are treated as leading school-level improvement in tandem with principals. Second, studies had to make connections, direct or indirect, to student achievement. Broad discretion was given to authors to define the achievement variable of interest. Twenty-six studies (over 29 publications: four publications by Hallinger and Heck discuss the same data set) included multiple leaders and a link to student achievement; these met the criteria for review. Twenty-nine of the studies in the review included multiple leaders without a corresponding link to student achievement. The final group contains 21 studies that do not contain multiple leaders: these studies use distributed leadership or similar frameworks to understand how teachers perceive leadership by their principals.

In accordance with Hallinger (2013), I followed a specific strategy in extracting and collecting information from the 26 studies of interest. The intent was not to create a meta-analysis, in which the effect sizes of each of the studies are quantified. Instead, I used "narrative text, idea units [and] descriptions of studies" (Hallinger, 2013, p. 135) to extract the particular units of study design identified by Spillane (2006): who the leaders in the study were, how leadership was understood conceptually, the specific leadership style(s) or structure(s) under study, the means by which student outcomes were assessed or analyzed, and the general finding of the study. These units are presented in Table 2.2, the primary tool of analysis. From this matrix display, I drew conclusions through analytic tools such as understanding relationships between design features in the study, visible across the rows of the matrix, and contrasting and comparing the texts against one another (Miles, Huberman, & Saldaña, 2014), visible across the columns. From there, I was able to generate hypotheses about themes in the text and test those hypotheses by returning to the texts.

As a systematic review of literature, this chapter joins meta-analyses (Robinson, Hohepa, & Lloyd, 2009; Scheerens, 2012) that seek to understand the quantitative relationship between leadership and student outcomes. However, this chapter's purpose is to understand these relationships qualitatively, in order to clarify how leadership theory is applied, understood, and modified in each instance. Further while Scheerens' (2012) review focuses on measures of student outcomes and leadership variables, like this study, its focus on intermediate variables is primarily demographic, rather than seeking to understand the features of leadership examined in reviewed studies. This study therefore complements and extends this developing literature base.

TABLE 2.2 How Do Studies Including Both Teams of Leaders and a Connection to Student Outcomes (26 Studies Over 29 Publications) Understand Leadership?

Reference	Study Type	Leaders Under Study; Conception of Leadership	Changes in Leadership Structure or Style Examined	Variable(s) of Student Outcomes Examined	Finding
Abbott & McKnight 2010	Mixed methods longitudinal study, examining nine Title I schools over five years	Principals and teachers in secondary schools; Distributed leadership[2]	Multiple leadership meetings, including monthly instructional team meetings and biweekly teacher learning team meetings	Standardized test scores	Collaborative leadership schools showed stronger achievement than similar schools
Akopoff 2010	Qualitative multiple case study dissertation, examining three underperforming senior high schools	Principals, assistant principals & teachers; Distributed leadership	Professional learning communities, particularly group meetings	Program improvement status under NCLB and low California API score used as part of selection criteria	Inconsistent implementation negatively impacted program efficacy
Alexander 2010	Mixed methods dissertation, examining 109 multicultural teachers from two high schools in a southwestern state	Teachers with more than two years of experience; Transformative leadership (constructivist leadership)	Encouraged teacher creativity, shared decision making, and increased collaboration time	Teacher retention as strategy for student performance improvement	Constructivist leadership promotes teacher retention
Angelle 2010	Qualitative case study, examining one middle school selected by local flagship university	Principals, teachers and administrators; Distributed leadership	Teacher autonomy over decision making structures and planning time	Disciplinary data, value-added state test scores	Leadership practices support student achievement gains

(continued)

Four Decades of Collective Leadership ▪ 29

TABLE 2.2 How Do Studies Including Both Teams of Leaders and a Connection to Student Outcomes (26 Studies Over 29 Publications) Understand Leadership? (continued)

Reference	Study Type	Leaders Under Study; Conception of Leadership	Changes in Leadership Structure or Style Examined	Variable(s) of Student Outcomes Examined	Finding
Chang 2011	Quantitative correlational study, examining 1500 Taiwanese elementary school teachers	Teachers; distributed leadership	Teachers' perceptions of distributed leadership; academic optimism	Monthly student exams in four subjects	Distributed leadership has indirect positive relationship with student achievement via academic optimism
Chen 2007	Quantitative correlational dissertation, examining teachers and principals in schools in 57 districts over 15 Texas counties	Principals and teacher leaders; Distributed leadership	Principal leadership traits measured through teacher leader perceptions, including enabling the leadership of others	Texas statewide assessment data (AEIS)	Collaborative learning styles and enlistment of teacher leaders correlate with higher student achievement
Copland 2003	Mixed methods case study, examining 16 schools in Bay Area School Reform Collaborative	Principals and teachers; Distributed leadership	Teacher engagement in the analysis of student and school performance	Leadership capacity to advance continued school improvement	Inquiry-based approach aides staff in identifying key issues, sustaining reform over time
Davidson & Dell 2003	Mixed methods case study, examining three rural low income elementary schools	Principals and teachers; Teacher leadership (through Accelerated Schools Process)	Training in ASP values, inquiry process, coaching role, leadership cadres	Standardized test scores, student attendance rates, School Performance Score	ASP provides a process, leading to leadership action plans that improved test scores
Droese 2010	Qualitative case study, examining three schools	Teachers; Distributed leadership	Lesson Study model: Joint lesson planning and observation process	Pupils' academic self-concept, pupils' participation, student engagement	Lesson Study improves teacher-driven instructional improvement and student learning in mathematics

(continued)

TABLE 2.2 How Do Studies Including Both Teams of Leaders and a Connection to Student Outcomes (26 Studies Over 29 Publications) Understand Leadership? (continued)

Reference	Study Type	Leaders Under Study; Conception of Leadership	Changes in Leadership Structure or Style Examined	Variable(s) of Student Outcomes Examined	Finding
Fancera & Bliss 2011	Quantitative path analysis, examining 53 New Jersey high schools across state	Principals and teachers; Instructional leadership	Teacher perceptions of principal efficacy, including curriculum coordination and professional development	Collective teacher efficacy, school report cards	SES is a stronger predictor of achievement than instructional leadership or collective teacher efficacy
Foster 2005	Qualitative case study, examining two secondary schools involved in school improvement	Principals and teachers; Collective leadership	New outcomes-based curriculum, student advocacy program, cross-department cohort groups, etc.	Hopkins; focus on teaching-learning process	Leadership intervention leads participating teachers and principals to feel joint responsibility for student outcomes
Grumdahl 2010	Mixed methods, examining three elementary schools in one suburban district	Principals and teachers; Distributed leadership	Teacher participation in organizational change, use of data and professional development, via survey instrument and interviews	Superintendent perceptions of schools' academic improvement	TQM principles, strategic planning and supportive culture positively impacted the achievement gap
Hallinger & Heck 2010a, 2010b; Heck & Hallinger 2009, 2010	Quantitative longitudinal study, examining 192-198 elementary schools over a four-year period	Teachers; Collaborative leadership	Organizational structures and processes that support broad participation in decision making, via survey	Standardized test scores in reading and math	Data supports mediated and reciprocal effects models, where leadership drives change in school improvement capacity

(continued)

Four Decades of Collective Leadership ▪ 31

TABLE 2.2 How Do Studies Including Both Teams of Leaders and a Connection to Student Outcomes (26 Studies Over 29 Publications) Understand Leadership? (continued)

Reference	Study Type	Leaders Under Study; Conception of Leadership	Changes in Leadership Structure or Style Examined	Variable(s) of Student Outcomes Examined	Finding
Harris 2002	Qualitative multiple case study, examining 10 high-poverty improving secondary schools	Headteachers; transformational leadership	Headteacher leadership as mechanism for cultivating shared vision and values, professional autonomy	Empowering teachers leads to improved outcomes (via Silins and Mulford 2002)	Teacher leadership influenced collective problem solving
Holland 2002	Mixed methods case study, examining eight intentionally small schools in Chicago	Teachers; Distributed leadership (via PLCs)	Collective responsibility, shared leadership, focus on student care, professional community	Attendance rate, development of institutional ethos; school safety	Small high schools using leadership model had better attendance, stronger ethos of responsibility than other students
Kim 2010	Qualitative case study, examining two California charter schools identified for positive leadership practices	Principals and lead teachers; Distributed leadership	Teacher mentoring program, shared decision making, graduate leadership coursework for teachers	California API scores; teacher perceptions of student maturity, positive attitude toward learning and student collaboration	A positive correlation between leadership intervention and increase in standardized test scores
Leithwood & Jantzi 2000	Quantitative survey, examining 1818 teachers and 6490 students	Principles and teachers; Teacher leadership	Perception of teacher and principal influence on school culture	Student engagement via Student Engagement and Family Culture Survey	Principal leadership produces greater effects on student engagement, compared with teacher leadership

(continued)

TABLE 2.2 How Do Studies Including Both Teams of Leaders and a Connection to Student Outcomes (26 Studies Over 29 Publications) Understand Leadership? (continued)

Reference	Study Type	Leaders Under Study; Conception of Leadership	Changes in Leadership Structure or Style Examined	Variable(s) of Student Outcomes Examined	Finding
Leithwood & Jantzi 2006	Quantitative path analysis, examining 2290 teachers from 655 elementary schools	Principals and teachers; transformational leadership	Leadership styles that promote collaborative school culture, community relationships, via survey of teachers	British Key Stage 2 tests in numeracy and literacy	Leadership affected classroom practices but not achievement
Leithwood & Mascall 2008	Quantitative correlational study, examining 2570 teachers in 90 elementary and secondary schools	Principals and teachers; Collective leadership	Teacher work settings & conditions, as they influence teacher motivation	Student achievement data in language and math, averaged over three years	Collective leadership explains significant portion of variation in achievement
Leithwood et al. 2010	Quantitative correlational study, examining 199 schools through 1445 teachers	Teachers; Distributed leadership	Management of an instructional program	Grade 3 and 6 math and literacy province-wide testing	Four Paths model explains 43% of variation in student achievement
Louis et al. 2010	Mixed methods study, with data collected over six years from a survey 8,391 teachers and 471 school administrators and interview and observational data from a subset	District-level staff, administrators, principals and teachers; Multiple shared leadership perspectives	Leadership behaviors that direct organizational improvement, influence goal-setting and set the direction of staff	Student achievement data on state tests in literacy and mathematics, Adequate Yearly Progress Status	Broadly, collective leadership has a stronger influence on student achievement than individual leadership; school leaders influence achievement primarily through influence on teachers' motivation and working conditions

(continued)

Four Decades of Collective Leadership ▪ 33

TABLE 2.2 How Do Studies Including Both Teams of Leaders and a Connection to Student Outcomes (26 Studies Over 29 Publications) Understand Leadership? (continued)

Reference	Study Type	Leaders Under Study; Conception of Leadership	Changes in Leadership Structure or Style Examined	Variable(s) of Student Outcomes Examined	Finding
Marks & Printy 2003	Quantitative hierarchical linear modeling, examining 24 restructured schools across grade levels	Principals and teachers; Transformational and instructional leadership	Level of active leadership, as measured in teacher / principal collaboration on instructional planning and assessment	Student achievement in mathematics and social studies, as well as pedagogical quality as an indirect influence on achievement	Effect of transformational and shared instructional leadership correlates with significantly higher achievement and pedagogical quality
Rivers 2010	Quantitative correlational study, examining four South Carolina elementary schools	Principals, assistant principals and teachers; Distributed leadership	Leadership activities that create shared culture, responsibilities and practices, via Distributed Leadership Readiness Scale	Palmetto Academic Challenge Test data for 289 students in reading and math	Distributed leadership correlates with growth in reading and math
Silins and Mulford 2004	Quantitative path model, examining 96 schools in a collaborative research project	Principals and teachers; Transformational leadership	Leadership activities that support changes in school structure, intellectual stimulation for staff, individual support, and the expectation of high performance	Attendance, students' self-concept, participation in school	Teacher leadership is exercised in both formal and informal ways, and is predictive of organizational learning

(continued)

TABLE 2.2 How Do Studies Including Both Teams of Leaders and a Connection to Student Outcomes (26 Studies Over 29 Publications) Understand Leadership? (continued)

Reference	Study Type	Leaders Under Study; Conception of Leadership	Changes in Leadership Structure or Style Examined	Variable(s) of Student Outcomes Examined	Finding
Terrell 2004	Quantitative correlation, examining elementary schools in two urban school districts	Principals and teachers; Distributed leadership	Leadership activities that support the development of shared culture, mission, responsibility and leadership practices, via Distributed Leadership Readiness Scale	Reading and math pass rates on statewide assessments	No significant relationship between distributed leadership and student achievement
Timperley 2008	Mixed methods study, examining seven elementary schools involved in a school improvement initiative	Principals, literacy leaders and teachers; Distributed leadership	Opportunities for group interpretation of data and critique of teaching methodologies	Literacy scores upon school entry and one year after matriculation	The quality of distributed leadership depends heavily on which artifacts and routines of leadership are used

[2] Studies which focused on professional learning communities were classified as using a distributed leadership model. Professional learning communities (PLCs) are conceived in recent literature as a mechanism by which leadership is distributed (e.g., Hudson et al., 2013; Harris et al., 2007, 341).

FINDINGS

This review synthesizes and interprets contemporary research on collective leadership in K–12 schools. By specifically identifying the leadership practices at work in the included studies, this review differs significantly from previous work. By identifying together leadership models, leadership routines, and measures of student outcomes, this review depicts the theories of action under use in each study. This chapter also demonstrates that, outside individual models of leadership in each study, a general conception of collective leadership can serve as a bridge between mediated models of leadership and effects on student outcomes.

To answer its research questions, this review seeks common elements from the examined studies in order to understand how studies generally understand the relationship between leaders, leadership behaviors or actions, and changes in student outcomes. This section details similarities between reviewed studies in two respects: common theories of action, and common features of leadership activity. Each of these is described in detail below, along with representative examples drawn from the studied literature. This section concludes with a discussion of the limitations of this approach, and of attempts to reconcile diverse theories of action in leadership studies.

In concurrence with Harris (2004), I find relatively few studies measure the impact of leadership, either directly or indirectly, on student outcomes. In general, however, models that could explain a significant portion of the variation in student achievement, both qualitative and quantitative, hypothesized a clear theory of action connecting leadership activities with changes in classroom practice that impacted how students learn. In this case, the investigative power of studies was greatly enhanced by approaches that clearly understood leadership routines, and had methodological tools capable of investigating them. The remainder of this section parallels that emphasis, highlighting studies where the relationship between these three core elements was articulated in a clear but nuanced fashion.

The findings of this chapter are limited by the natural complexities involved in considering qualitative and quantitative work together across multiple contexts. This review produces no precise account of "what works"—or what does not—in the leadership of schools. Its methods cannot necessarily assess the quality of the studies it examines. What it endeavors to do instead is to understand the direction of the field as it is currently aligned: major trends in literature can both highlight areas of emerging effectiveness and shed light on corners of leadership work as yet unexplored.

THREE THEORIES OF ACTION CONNECTING LEADERSHIP AND STUDENT ACHIEVEMENT

Studies that demonstrate notable effects of leadership in this review show one or more of three types of theories of action at work: whole school change through the enhancement of "school improvement capacity," the cultivation of a culture of shared purpose, and/or the redesign of teachers' work. While each study maintains its own unique theory of action, often blending these types in different ways, a handful of the studies in the sample reflect trends and commonalities that appear across the literature sample. These commonalities in how leaders in studies, through behaviors, influence student outcomes, suggest a common structure between studies that, further, suggests ways in which leadership models are reconcilable with one another. Additionally, these theories are similar in scope and application to the factors identified in Scheerens' (2012) meta-analysis of similar work.

Targeting School Improvement Capacity

First, many studies utilize a theory of action in which leadership practices reciprocally influence "school improvement capacity," in turn improving learning (Hallinger & Heck, 2010; Heck & Hallinger, 2009; Heck & Hallinger, 2010). School improvement capacity refers to a school's ability to increase teacher learning and respond to learning problems (Hallinger & Heck, 2010a). The authors use nine factors of collaboration as their measure of leadership, including empowering staff, shared accountability and collaborative decision making focused on educational improvement (Hallinger & Heck, 2010a). Leadership is, under their conception, responsible for how an organization and its members deliberately change their practices to enact school improvement (Hallinger & Heck 2010b). In this way, the growth of school improvement capacity not only helps schools do something different, but something more.

One example of an approach using a theory of action with a focus on school improvement capacity is Copland's (2003) study of the Bay Area School Reform Cooperative. Copland uses a mixed methods case study that explores how 16 member schools, using distributed leadership, use data to improve instruction. The study outlines a clear theory of action: as teachers engage data, they increase their own and the school's overall leadership capacity to advance continued school improvement. Principals, in turn, shift their understanding of leadership to one "aptly reframed as leadership of inquiry" (Copland, 2003, p. 391). Key to Copland's conception of distributed leadership is practice that rests on expert, not hierarchical authority (Copland, 2003). Expert authority in part enables practices that are less likely to break down at the point of implementation (Copland, 2003). Additionally, it suggests a leadership team operates with more knowledge and capacity then any individual, reconciling the desire of policymakers for educational improvement via leadership with the inability of individuals to consistently act with extraordinary or heroic ability (Copland, 2003).

The large-scale longitudinal study conducted by Louis and colleagues (2010), which utilizes models that exemplify both distributed and instructional leadership, also relies on a theory of reciprocal growth in leadership like that in Copland. The authors collected over six years of data from a survey of 8,391 teachers and 471 school administrators, included interview and observation data from a subset, and correlated that data with state test results using a mixed methods methodology. Broadly, they find modes of collective leadership have a stronger influence on student outcomes than individual leadership. While they do not identify a single way to distribute leadership that is most effective, they find that "the more encompassing the goal, the greater the likelihood that multiple sources of leadership will be appropriate" (Louis et al., 2010, p. 282). Leveraging the capacity of expert leadership, Louis and colleagues demonstrate how leadership teams are able to undertake new responsibilities that lead to an increased focus on the goals and expectations of student achievement.

Other studies that exemplify targeting school improvement capacity include studies by Chen (2007), Grumdahl (2010), Leithwood et al. (2010), Marks and Printy (2003), and Silins & Mulford (2004). Throughout the literature, a focus on a "systems approach" (Grundahl, 2010) to improvement, or efforts to better identify routes through which schools enhance the skills of their members, such as Leithwood and co-authors' "Four Paths" model, or the discussion of leadership styles in Marks and Printy (2003), all speak of school improvement capacity's general proposition that the ability of collectives in schools to lead increases as leadership practices are enacted.

Cultivating Culture of Shared Purpose

A second set of theories of action considers the role of leadership in creating school cultures that unite staff around common goals. Culture is one of many active metaphors used to understand what an organization is and does (Smircich, 1983) and is particularly applicable to school leadership, where leaders are at least in part attempting to shift the focus of an organization's members toward a total emphasis on teaching and learning (Hallinger, 2003; Marks & Printy, 2002; Mayrowetz et al., 2007). In contrast with models that involve school improvement capacity, which refers to leadership changing what a school's members can do, cultural leadership involves changing what a school's members think about teaching and learning. Studies that utilize these models consider division among teachers on how best to improve student outcomes a major barrier to improving those outcomes.

Other research also highlights the central role that school culture may play in improving student achievement, and the role that leaders may play in building that culture. Kim's (2010) qualitative case study examined two California charter schools noted for their positive leadership practices. Kim finds a relationship between leadership interventions and improvement on standardized tests, but also gathers and analyzes data on student behavior.

Kim focused on the relationship between principal and teacher; specifically, how changes in that relationship change institutional structures and cultures (Kim, 2010). In particular, the author explored how institutionalized practices like mentoring programs, leadership team meetings, and other development programs supported an overarching mandate from the principal to shift school culture towards collaboration for learning improvement (Kim, 2010). Because teachers at one school studied were highly committed to this culture, teacher leaders made professional development a priority school-wide and made continuous learning about instructional improvement an expectation (Kim, 2010). This commitment in turn produced other changes in institutional practice, including participation in action research, more frequent collaboration among teachers, and greater teacher participation in hiring. By exploring student behavior factors in addition to test scores, Kim demonstrates how a culture of shared purpose impacts all members of the school community, providing an opportunity for teachers to exercise school-wide leadership towards a common culture of achievement impacted student maturity, collaboration and attitude (Kim, 2010).

Culture is discussed, to varying level of details, in several of the studies included in the review, including studies by Akopoff (2010), Alexander (2010), Angelle (2010), Droese (2010), Foster (2005), Harris (2002), Holland (2002), Rivers (2010), and Terrell (2010). Definitions of what constitutes a culture abound in the literature. In general, these definitions seek to differentiate and consider separately the thought of an organization (and that of its members) from its behaviors.

Redesigning Teachers' Work

A third theory of action regards the re-conception of teachers' work as a key mediating element between collective leadership and student achievement. Using theories of work design, Mayrowetz and co-authors (2008) conceptualize distributed leadership as a process that begins when teachers assume new responsibilities beyond their classroom, and administrators are forced to re-conceive their own job roles as a result (p. 70). Collective leadership entails by necessity changing the core tasks performed by teachers as part of their work. Whether a new distributed leadership model succeeds or fails, they argue, is largely dependent upon whether those teachers can make sense of their new work in their current context (sensemaking), whether the changes make teachers more excited about their work (identity) and whether the changes allow them to do their re-designed job better (learning) (Mayrowetz et al., 2008). Tasks that give teachers a strong sense of significance, identity, and autonomy best create fulfilling work, which leads to leadership.

Task identity (Mayrowetz et al., 2008), a key component of work redesign in schools, speaks to the additive function of collective leadership to school practices. Traditionally, teachers experience relatively little connection to the progress and outcomes of their students after the end of a school year. Under collective leadership models, teachers participate in the construction of a model for a school's success and supervise that model over time, in no small part by monitoring students as they progress through the school's grade levels. This process, of "crafting coherence" (Mayrowetz et al., 2008, p. 81) or translating the work of school improvement into workable changes in classroom activity (Harris, 2003) is a critical element of schools asserting more agency over the outcomes of their students.

A work design theory of action is articulated in Chang's (2011) quantitative correlational study, which explores the impact of distributed leadership among 1,500 Taiwanese elementary school teachers on student outcomes. Chang posits that teachers' academic optimism (in short, the belief held by teachers that their techniques are effective and that all students can learn) facilitates the establishment of effective learning environments. With these variables identified, Chang constructs a structural equation model connecting teacher perceptions of distributed leadership practice, academic optimism and student outcomes on monthly subject examinations, using established survey instruments with a strong basis in conceptual literatures. Chang describes these leadership schemes as planned: "decentralized" leadership "disperses leadership tasks through a systematic and planned scheme to the membership, makes more individuals follow the educational objectives, and provides opportunities for participating in the operation of the school" (Chang, 2011, p. 509).

Studies that explore the composition of teachers' work include studies by Abbott and McKnight (2010), Davidson and Dell (2013), Leithwood and Jantzi (2006), and Timperley (2008). These studies may discuss creating different job roles for teachers, or simply discuss incorporating new responsibilities or opportunities into teachers' work. Studies that address teachers' work, however, address a unique set of problems that are essential considerations for the field, including the challenges teachers encounter when they attempt to span organizational boundaries (Timperley, 2008), shifts in power that occur when teachers take on explicit leadership roles (Timperley, 2008), the need for strong district support for new teachers (Davidson & Dell, 2003), and other considerations that put the individual practice of leadership into a systemic perspective.

FEATURES OF LEADERSHIP THEORIES OF ACTION

In addition to similar theories of action, the reviewed studies also share some common features of effective leadership that cross between these boundaries. Irrespective of who leads, how they lead, and for what they lead, these features suggest what effective leaders focus on, think about, and prioritize. While leaders may have a variety of priorities, these three features are routinely highlighted in both quantitative and qualitative work reviewed here as critical components of a leaders' effectiveness and continual development. Common features include: the development of a common language among school staff, working on multiple levels of change simultaneously, and orienting the school organization's focus towards instruction.

Developing a Common Language

First, leadership theories of action often focus on how leadership practices create a common language to describe instructional practice. Instructional leaders are ultimately responsible for building culture (Hallinger, 2003). Key to the creation of a common culture is the use of a common language to describe practices: "language is culture, and vice versa" (City, Elmore, Fiarman, & Tietel, 2009, p. 34). Creating a joint understanding of how instruction works and how it needs to improve is a key prerequisite to mentoring, school-wide consideration of learning practices, or any other activity that seeks to make instructional activities a leadership issue. Through evaluation and mentoring, school leaders work together to create "sensemaking" (Louis, Mayrowetz, Smiley, & Murray 2009): An atmosphere in which teachers can describe their own and others' instructional strengths and weaknesses. A common vocabulary is required for such a discussion.

Research analyzed here suggests common language must become directly embedded in practice. Timperley (2008) undertook a mixed methods study of seven New Zealand schools involved in a school improvement initiative, using group instructional technique to improve student outcomes. Timperley showed quantitatively that literacy scores between schools were substantially different, then used an interview methodology to interpret the results of group meetings she observed. New vision statements are not in themselves sufficient to affect instructional improvement, Timperley finds;

instead, vision must be enacted through new practices. Those practices must be backed up, in turn, by ensuring the messages sent by leaders are consistent internally, with followers and with the content of artifacts such as how student achievement data is recorded and presented. Effectiveness was amplified in environments where consistency is emphasized and embedded in the analysis teachers undertake of their own and each others' practice. Leaders, then, are responsible for far more than setting an agenda: they are also responsible for recruiting and retaining the participation of other key school figures in the analysis of data and the development of responses to those findings.

For Timperley's schools, a common language serves as the building blocks that allow a diverse group of leaders to act on multiple issues at the same time without losing internal coherency. Common language also assists in resolving a tension in distributed leadership between taking advantage of a diverse set of skills on the one hand and creating a "greater distribution of incompetence" (Timperley, 2008, p. 220) on the other. A focus on boundary spanning and the activity of developing an organization-wide concept of instructional improvement helps multiple leaders focus on instruction specifically and close pre-existing gaps in teachers' "visions for and expectations of student achievement" (p. 220).

Studies that explicitly examined the development of common language included those by Chang (2011) and Droese (2011). However, developing common understandings undergirded by common language plays an implicit role in any number of studies in the review, particularly those that seek to change school cultures by targeting schools with heterogeneous views on student capabilities, or in any school where group analysis of learning problems is routine practice. These relatively few studies underline the importance of developing a common understanding of the problems of schools as prerequisites to more complete notions of collective leadership.

Multiple Levers of Change

Second, leadership theories of action often consider how leaders undertake multiple levers of change simultaneously. One of the key differences between instructional and transformational leadership as they are traditionally understood is their mechanism of change: Instructional leadership targets "first-order" variables that directly impact instruction, while transformational leadership influences "second-order" variables that regulate the capacity of others to make change (Hallinger, 2003). Authors featured in this review are, largely, interested in reconciling these two approaches: they seek to understand how these two variables work simultaneously.

Marks and Printy (2003) explore multiple levers of change, using a diverse data set—the School Restructuring Survey—to test their hypothesis that second-order changes are necessary but insufficient conditions for school improvement. Using a hierarchical linear model, the authors sort questions on the survey into those representing transformational leadership and those representing shared instructional leadership; the latter, they argue, emphasizes the practical need for principals to engage teachers when crafting instructional change. While the study's schools have widely variant scores on both leadership measures, Marks and Printy find no schools with high shared instructional leadership and low transformational leadership, implying the latter is a prerequisite to the former. High scores on both measures, however, explain 26% of the differences in pedagogical quality and 57% of the difference in student achievement between subject schools.

Other studies that describe first- and second-order leadership effects include those by Angelle (2010), Chen (2007), Copland (2003), Grumdahl (2010), Harris (2002), Holland (2002), Leithwood and Mascall (2008), and Louis et al. (2010). In many of these cases, authors attempt to characterize the effects leaders have on schools in general and study the relationship between these effects and student learning. Quantitative methods can provide valuable tools for understanding where leaders ought to, therefore, place the emphasis of their work. Cases, however, are equally informative, particularly inasmuch as they describe how the various roles of leaders interact with—and at times contradict—one another in the pursuit of school improvement.

A Collective Focus on Instruction

Finally, leadership theories of action often ensure that leadership practices are focused on instruction and improving student outcomes.

Through both an interpretation of the teacher leadership literature, and their own findings, Silins and Mulford argue teachers generally have little interest in leadership opportunities that do not include influence over curriculum and instruction (Silins & Mulford, 2002). The perceived benefits of transformational leadership—primarily, the organizational legitimacy that comes from the active involvement of teachers in decision-making—carries with it the implicit assumption that schools operate as learning organizations (Silins & Mulford, 2002). Even in high schools, where content knowledge is fairly diverse, Silins and Mulford find the strongest correlation between student achievement and group learning processes around instruction (Silins & Mulford, 2002).

Other studies that emphasize the importance of a collective focus on instruction include those by Abbott and McKnight (2010), Akopoff (2010),

Davidson and Dell (2003), Foster (2005), and the work of Hallinger and Heck (2009a, 2009b, 2010a, 2010b). As instructional leadership scholars have long understood, curriculum and instruction is the common ground on which teachers and principals come together to think and act on school improvement. A focus on instruction undergirds several group leadership practices common in education, such as inquiry teams, professional learning communities, and peer evaluation (Abbott & McKnight, 2010). Additionally, the prioritization of instruction by a principal or other non-instructional leader provides the space through which instructors can do the same (Abbott & McKnight, 2010). That focus on teaching and learning—what Marks and Printy (2003) call the "core technology" of schools (p. 377)—differentiates educational leadership from other forms of leadership and makes necessary places at the leadership table for career educators.

LIMITATIONS

Several elements of the approach to this review may limit its utility. First, the review's broad approach to understanding student outcomes may include several studies where the relationship between leadership and student outcomes is more opaque. While appropriate, therefore, for discussing how scholars apply leadership frameworks, this review may not be appropriate for determining which leadership style or approach is the best for students. Similarly, requiring that studies require clear conceptions of leaders, leadership behaviors, and student outcomes inherently excluded studies which meet part or none of the conditions of a "theory of action" as this study understands it. Finally, because this study allows theories of action and features of leadership to emerge from the literature, these ideas are naturally enlarged or constrained as this specific literature applies. These constructs may, therefore, not apply to other types of leadership studies, or be less effective in describing many of the studies excluded from the second stage of analysis.

Further, this chapter does not argue that collective leadership is the only or the best method of leading schools. That task is instead best left to large scale quantitative and mixed methods evaluations, some of which (Hallinger & Heck, 2010; Louis et al., 2009) are reviewed here. Much of leadership scholarship focused on collectivity, however, has sought to demonstrate not that collectivity ought to exist, but that it does. To the extent that diffuse sources of expertise and influence will inevitably exist in complex organizations like schools, understanding how those diverse sources can best work toward common ends is an essential and continuing task for leadership research in the years ahead.

CONCLUSIONS

This chapter explores the convergence of recent literature on educational leadership around collectivity: The notion that multiple individuals, across time and contexts, lead together to influence student achievement. Examining literature across models identified as instructional leadership, transformational leadership, teacher leadership, and distributed leadership, it identifies three key "theories of action," or ways of understanding the relationship between leadership and outcomes: targeting school improvement capacity, cultivating a culture of shared purpose, and redesigning teachers' work. This review also identifies three common features of these theories of action: developing a common language, exploiting multiple levers of change, and creating a collective focus on instruction. While relatively little research on collective leadership ties to student outcomes, studies that do form a set of common and coherent arguments regarding how leadership functions in schools that can be understood outside of individual models of leadership.

In keeping with a growing body of work over the last several years, this review finds that relatively few studies in the field connect leadership activities with student outcomes and, of those that do, wide variation exists in leadership's effects, in part based on how researchers understand leadership activities. Further clarifying how leadership functions, in theory and practice, can lay the groundwork for studies with more relevance to policymakers and practitioners. These should include both qualitative and quantitative studies that seek to get "inside" collective leadership practice, understanding how leaders do what they do in schools, and how those actions work together to form cohesive visions for and foci on instruction and school improvement. The theories of action and features of theories of action outlined here can provide a guide for researchers considering how to initially approach collective leadership environments to maximize the instances of leadership upon which they can collect data.

This review also suggests the need for work that more thoroughly explores how models of educational leadership work can be understood together. This work has already begun among some theoretical scholarship: integrated models such as "distributed images of instructional leadership" (Portin & Knapp, 2014), or "shared instructional leadership" (Printy & Marks, 2006), should become more common components of empirical work. However, the long term goal of theoretical work should be the integration, rather than the multiplication, of models for understanding school leadership. More than a decade later, a "bewildering array of definitions" (Harris, 2003, p. 318) still mark this field, complicating conversation between scholars and practitioners. Particularly as educational leadership scholars look to amplify the voice of practitioners, through methodological tools such as action research and increased participation for teachers and administrators in journals and professional conferences, overly subtle distinctions between models of leadership create a barrier to the democratization of this field of study.

For educational leaders, this chapter reiterates the need for strong and clearly articulated theories of action. In exemplary studies in this review, effective leadership programs clearly defined what constitutes a leader, what practices are employed by leaders, and how those practices are expected to improve instruction. A common focus on instruction and instructional improvement echoes throughout the studies examined here, and should continue to serve as a strong focus for educational leader preparation and for leaders themselves. These studies also suggest that this focus comes hand-in-hand with collective leadership, ensuring more of the adults in a school building have a voice in the organization's vision and operations. For leaders as well as scholars, collective leadership as an idea mediates what leadership models call for and changes in student outcomes.

Famously, leadership is said to change little about outcomes for students, outweighed by the effects of teaching and parenting. However, as demands both for school accountability and the further individualization of instruction increase, it is clear that future school leaders will be expected to do more with less, to steer school improvement even as they control relatively few of its products. The introduction of multiple leaders working together can decrease the burden of these demands, as well as potentially blur the line between leadership and instruction. This ambiguity can, and should, be embraced: As studies examined here demonstrate, good leading travels together with good teaching.

ACKNOWLEDGEMENTS

This work was completed while the author was conducting graduate work sponsored by the U.S. Department of Education, Institute of Education Sciences (#R305B090012). The author is, however, solely responsible for the paper's content.

REFERENCES

Brower, R., & Balch, B. V. (2005). *Transformational leadership & decision making in schools*. Thousand Oaks, CA: Corwin Press.

City, E. A., Elmore, R. F., Fiarman, S. E., & Tietel, L. (2009). *Instructional rounds in education: A network approach to improving teaching and learning*. Cambridge, MA: Harvard Education Press.

Copland, M. A. (2003). Leadership of inquiry: Building and sustaining capacity for school improvement. *Educational Evaluation and Policy Analysis, 25*(4), 375–395. doi:10.3102/01623737025004375

Davidson, B. M., & Dell, G. L. (2003). A school restructuring model: A tool kit for building teacher leadership. *American Educational Research Association* annual conference.

Elmore, R. F. (2000). *Building a new structure for school leadership.* Washington, DC: Albert Shanker Institute.

Firestone, W. A., & Cecilia Martinez, M. (2007). Districts, teacher leaders, and distributed leadership: changing instructional practice. *Leadership and Policy in Schools, 6*(1), 3-35. doi:10.1080/15700760601091234

Gronn, P. (2002). Distributed leadership as a unit of analysis. *The Leadership Quarterly, 13*(4), 423–451. doi:10.1016/S1048-9843(02)00120-0

Grumdahl, C. R. (2010). *How schools can effectively plan to meet the goal of improving student learning.* University of Minnesota.

Hallinger, P. (2003). Leading educational change: Reflections on the practice of instructional and transformational leadership. *Cambridge Journal of Education, 33*(3), 329–352. doi:10.1080/0305764032000122005

Hallinger, P. (2005). Instructional leadership and the school principal: A passing fancy that refuses to fade away. *Leadership and Policy in Schools, 4*(3), 221–239. doi:10.1080/15700760500244793

Hallinger, P., & Heck, R. H. (2011). Conceptual and methodological issues in studying school leadership effects as a reciprocal process. *School Effectiveness and School Improvement, 22*(2), 149–173.

Hallinger, P. (2013). A conceptual framework for systematic reviews of research in educational leadership and management. *Journal of Educational Administration, 51*(2), 126–149. doi:10.1108/09578231311304670

Hallinger, P., & Murphy, J. (1987). Assessing and developing principal instructional leadership. *Educational Leadership, 45,* 54–61.

Harris, A. (2003). Teacher leadership as distributed leadership: Heresy, fantasy or possibility? *School Leadership & Management, 23*(3), 313–324. doi:10.1080/1363243032000112801

Harris, A. (2004). Distributed leadership and school improvement: Leading or misleading? *Educational Management Administration & Leadership, 32*(1), 11–24. doi:10.1177/1741143204039297

Harris, A. (2008). Distributed leadership and knowledge creation. In K. A. Leithwood, B. Mascall, & T. Strauss (Eds.), *Distributed leadership according to the evidence* (pp. 253–266). New York, NY: Routledge.

Hill, P. T., & Celio, M. B. (1998). *Fixing urban schools.* Washington, DC: The Brookings Institution.

Hudson, P., Hudson, S., Gray, B., & Bloxham, R. (2013). Learning about being effective mentors: Professional learning communities and mentoring. *Social and Behavioral Sciences, 93*(21), 1291–1300.

Knapp, M. S. (2014). Introduction: The evolution of learning-focused leadership in scholarship and practice. In *Learning-focused leadership in action: Improving instruction in schools and districts* (pp. 1–20). New York, NY: Routledge.

Leithwood, K. A., & Duke, D. L. (1999). A century's quest to understand school leadership. In J. Murphy & K. S. Louis (Eds.), *Handbook of research on education administration: A project of the American educational research association*. San Francisco, CA: Jossey-Bass.

Leithwood, K. A., & Jantzi, D. (1999). The relative effects of principal and teacher sources of leadership on student engagement with school. *Educational Administration Quarterly, 35*(5), 679–706. doi:10.1177/0013161X99355002

Leithwood, K., & Jantzi, D. (2005). A review of transformational school leadership research 1996–2005. *Leadership and Policy in Schools, 4*(3), 177–199. doi:10.1080/15700760500244769

Leithwood, K., Jantzi, D., & Steinbach, R. (2009). *Changing leadership for changing times*. Buckingham: Open University Press.

Lord, B., & Miller, B. (2000). *Teacher leadership: An appealing and inescapable force in school reform?* Newton, MA: Commission on Mathematics and Science Teaching for the 21st Century..

Louis, K. S., Mayrowetz, D., Smiley, M., & Murphy, J. (2009). The role of sensemaking and trust in developing distributed leadership. In A. Harris (Ed.), *Distributed leadership: Different perspectives* (pp. 157–179). New York, NY: Springer Science.

Mangin, M. M., & Stoelinga, S. R. (2008). Teacher leadership: What it is and why it matters. In M. M. Mangin & S. R. Stoelinga (Eds.), *Effective teacher leadership: Using research to inform and reform* (pp. 1–9). New York, NY: Teachers College Press.

Marks, H. M., & Printy, S. M. (2003). Principal leadership and school performance: An integration of transformational and instructional leadership. *Educational Administration Quarterly, 39*(3), 370–397. doi:10.1177/0013161X03253412

Mayrowetz, D. (2008). Making sense of distributed leadership: Exploring the multiple usages of the concept in the field. *Educational Administration Quarterly, 44*(3), 424–435. doi:10.1177/0013161X07309480

Mayrowetz, D., Murphy, J., Louis, K. S., & Smylie, M. A. (2007). Distributed leadership as work redesign: Retrofitting the job characteristics model. *Leadership and Policy in Schools, 6*(1), 69–101. doi:10.1080/15700760601091275

Miles, M. B., Huberman, A. M., & Saldaña, J. (2014). *Qualitative data analysis: A methods sourcebook* (3rd ed.). Los Angeles, CA: SAGE Publications.

Murphy, J., Elliott, S. N., Goldring, E., & Porter, A. C. (2007). Leadership for learning: A research-based model and taxonomy of behaviors. *School Leadership & Management, 27*(2), 179–201. doi:10.1080/13632430701237420

Neumerski, C. M. (2013). Rethinking instructional leadership, a review: What do we know about principal, teacher, and coach instructional leadership, and where should we go from here? *Educational Administration Quarterly, 49*(2), 310–347. doi:10.1177/0013161X12456700

Northouse, P. G. (2007). *Leadership: Theory and practice*. Thousand Oaks, CA: Sage Publications.

Portin, B. S., & Knapp, M. S. (2014). Team-based leadership of instructional improvement in demanding school contexts. In *Learning-focused leadership in action: Improving instruction in schools and districts* (pp. 23–51). New York, NY: Routledge.

Printy, S. M. (2007). Leadership for teacher learning: A community of practice perspective. *Educational Administration Quarterly, 44*(2), 187–226. doi:10.1177/0013161X07312958

Printy, S. M., Marks, H. M., & Bowers, A. J. (2009, September). Integrated leadership: How principals and teachers share transformational and instructional influence. *Journal of School Leadership, 19.*

Robinson, V., Hohepa, M., & Lloyd, C. (2009). *School leadership and student outcomes: Identifying what works and why.* Wellington: New Zealand Ministry of Education.

Robinson, V. M. J., Lloyd, C. A., & Rowe, K. J. (2008). The impact of leadership on student outcomes: An analysis of the differential effects of leadership types. *Educational Administration Quarterly, 44*(5), 635–674. doi:10.1177/0013161 X08321509

Scheerens, J. (2012). *School leadership effects revisited: Review and meta-analysis of empirical studies.* (J. Scheerens, Ed.). London, England: Springer.

Sheppard, B. (1996). Exploring the transformational nature of instructional leadership. *The Alberta Journal of Educational Research, 42*(4), 325–344.

Silins, H., & Mulford, B. (2002). Schools as learning organizations: The case for system, teacher and student learning. *The Journal of Educational Administration, 40*(5), 425–446.

Smircich, L. (1983). Concepts of culture and organizational analysis. *Administrative Science Quarterly, 28*(3), 339–358.

Spillane, J. P. (2006). *Distributed leadership.* San Francisco, CA: Jossey-Bass.

Spillane, J. P., Camburn, E. M., & Pareja, A. S. (2008). School principals at work: A distributed perspective. In K. A. Leithwood, B. Mascall, & T. Strauss (Eds.), *Distributed leadership according to the evidence* (pp. 87–110). New York, NY: Routledge.

Spillane, J. P., Halverson, R., & Diamond, J. B. (2004). Towards a theory of leadership practice: A distributed perspective. *Journal of Curriculum Studies, 36*(1), 3–34. doi:10.1080/0022027032000106726

Timperley, H. S. (2005). Distributed leadership: Developing theory from practice. *Journal of Curriculum Studies, 37*(4), 395–420. doi:10.1080/00220270500038545

Urick, A., & Bowers, A. J. (2014). What are the different types of principals across the United States? A latent class analysis of principal perception of leadership. *Educational Administration Quarterly, 50*(1), 96–134. doi:10.1177/0013161X13489019

York-Barr, J., & Duke, K. (2004). What do we know about teacher leadership? Findings from two decades of scholarship. *Educational Research, 74*(3), 255–316.

Yukl, G. (1994). *Leadership in organizations.* Englewood, NJ: Prentice Hall.

REVIEWED STUDIES

Abbott, C. J., & McKnight, K. (2010). Developing instructional leadership through collaborative learning. *Journal of Scholarship and Practice, 7*(2), 20–27.

Akopoff, T. (2010). *A case study examination of best practices of professional learning communities.* Walden University.

Alexander, J. (2010). *An examination of teachers' perceptions regarding constructivist leadership and teacher retention*. Walden University.

Alig-Mielcarek, J. M., & Hoy, W. K. (2005). Instructional leadership: Its nature, meaning and influence. In *Educational Leadership and Reform* (pp. 29–51). Greenwich, CT: IAP.

Angelle, P. S. (2010). An organizational perspective of distributed leadership: A portrait of a middle school. *Research in Middle Level Education, 33*(5).

Beycioglu, K., & Aslan, B. (2010). Teacher leadership scale: A validity and reliability study. *Elementary Education Online, 9*(2), 764–775.

Brown, D. J., & Keeping, L. M. (2005). Elaborating the construct of transformational leadership: The role of affect. *The Leadership Quarterly, 16*(2), 245–272. doi:10.1016/j.leaqua.2005.01.003

Cerit, Y. (2009). The effects of servant leadership behaviours of school principals on teachers' job satisfaction. *Educational Management Administration & Leadership, 37*(5), 600–623. doi:10.1177/1741143209339650

Chang, I.-H. (2011). A study of the relationships between distributed leadership, teacher academic optimism and student achievement in Taiwanese elementary schools. *School Leadership & Management, 31*(5), 491–515.

Chen, Y. (2007). *Principals' distributed leadership behaviors and their impact on student achievement in selected elementary schools in Texas*. Texas A&M University.

Christianson, A. (2010). *A case study examining principal leadership behaviors that promote shared responsibility for English language learners*. Edgewood College.

Copland, M. A. (2003). Leadership of inquiry: Building and sustaining capacity for school improvement. *Educational Evaluation and Policy Analysis, 25*(4), 375–395. doi:10.3102/01623737025004375

Curtis, R. (2013). *Finding a new way: Leveraging teacher leadership to meet unprecedented demands*. Washington, DC: Joyce Foundation.

Davidson, B. M., & Dell, G. L. (2003). *A school restructuring model: A tool kit for building teacher leadership*. American Educational Research Association annual conference.

Dean, D. R. (2005). Thinking globally: The National College of School Leadership: A case study in distributed leadership development. *Journal of Research on Leadership Education, 2*(1), 1–62.

Deike, M. A. (2009). *The principal as an instructional leader within the context of effective data use*. The University of Texas at Austin.

Donaldson, M. L., Cobb, C. D., & Mayer, A. P. (2010). Contested terrain: Principal and teacher leadership at Grove Street Elementary School. *Journal of Cases in Educational Leadership, 13*(2), 29–38. doi:10.1177/1555458910372654

Droese, S. M. (2010). *Lesson study in the U.S.: Is it a mechanism for individual and organizational change? A case study of three schools*. University of Wisconsin-Madison.

Edge, K., & Mylopoulos, M. (2008). Creating cross-school connections: LC networking in support of leadership and instructional development. *School Leadership & Management, 28*(2), 147–158. doi:10.1080/13632430801969823

Eyal, O., & Kark, R. (2004). How do transformational leaders transform organizations? A study of the relationship between leadership and entrepreneurship. *Leadership and Policy in Schools, 3*(3), 37–41.

Fancera, S. F., & Bliss, J. R. (2011). Instructional leadership influence on collective teacher efficacy to improve school achievement. *Leadership and Policy in Schools, 10*(3), 349–370. doi:10.1080/15700763.2011.585537

Feeney, E. J. (2009). Taking a look at a school's leadership capacity: The role and function of high school department chairs. *The Clearing House, 82*(5), 212–219. doi:10.3200/TCHS.82.5.212-219

Firestone, W. A., & Cecilia Martinez, M. (2007). Districts, teacher leaders, and distributed leadership: Changing instructional practice. *Leadership and Policy in Schools, 6*(1), 3–35. doi:10.1080/15700760601091234

Foster, R. (2005). Leadership and secondary school improvement: Case studies of tensions and possibilities. *International Journal of Leadership in Education, 8*(1), 35–52. doi:10.1080/1360312042000299233

Goldring, E., Huff, J., Spillane, J. P., & Barnes, C. (2009). Measuring the learning-centered leadership expertise of school principals. *Leadership and Policy in Schools, 8*(2), 197–228. doi:10.1080/15700760902737170

Good, T. L. (2008). In the midst of comprehensive school reform: Principals' perspectives. *Teachers College Record, 110*(11), 2341–2360.

Gopalan, P. (2004). *Integrating districts in comprehensive school reform in the middle-grades: Lessons from middle start CSR. Policy.* New York, NY: Academy for Educational Development.

Griffith, J. (2004). Relation of principal transformational leadership to school staff job satisfaction, staff turnover, and school performance. *Journal of Educational Administration, 42*(3), 333–356.

Grumdahl, C. R. (2010). *How schools can effectively plan to meet the goal of improving student learning.* University of Minnesota.

Hallinger, P., & Heck, R. H. (2010). Collaborative leadership and school improvement: Understanding the impact on school capacity and student learning. *School Leadership & Management, 30*(2), 95–110. doi:10.1080/13632431003663214

Harris, A. (2002). Effective leadership in schools facing challenging contexts. *School Leadership & Management, 22*(1), 27–39. doi:10.1080/13632430220143024

Heck, R. H., & Hallinger, P. (2009). Assessing the contribution of distributed leadership to school improvement and growth in math achievement. *American Educational Research Journal, 46*(3), 659. doi:10.3102/0002831209340042

Heck, R. H., & Hallinger, P. (2010). Testing a longitudinal model of distributed leadership effects on school improvement. *The Leadership Quarterly, 111*(2), 226–252. Retrieved from http://www.sciencedirect.com/science/article/pii/S1048984310001293

Hill, V. (2009). *Evaluating a strategy for enriching the professional learning community of a secondary school through support for teacher leadership.* Cambridge, UK: teacherleadership.org.uk.

Holland, N. E. (2002). *Small schools making big changes: The importance of professional communities in school reform.* In Proceedings of the Annual Meeting of the National Association of African American Studies, the National Association of Hispanic and Latino Studies, the National Association of Native American Studies and the International Association of Asian Studies.

Huffman, J. B., & Hipp, K. A. (2000). *Creating communities of learners: The interaction of shared leadership, shared vision and supportive conditions.* Paper presented at the Annual Meeting of the American Educational Research Association (New Orleans, LA, April 24–28, 2000).

Hulpia, H., & Devos, G. (2009). Exploring the link between distributed leadership and job satisfaction of school leaders. *Educational Studies, 35*(2), 153–171. doi:10.1080/03055690802648739

Hulpia, H., Devos, G., & Van Keer, H. (2011). The relation between school leadership from a distributed perspective and teachers' organizational commitment: Examining the source of the leadership function. *Educational Administration Quarterly, 47*(5), 728–771. doi:10.1177/0013161X11402065

Hur, J. (2011). *Sustainability of professional development in a post-reform context: A qualitative study of shared leadership. Leadership.* University of Minnesota.

Ishimaru, A. (2012). From heroes to organizers: Principals and education organizing in urban school reform. *Educational Administration Quarterly, 49*(1), 3–51. doi:10.1177/0013161X12448250

Jacobson, S. (2011). Leadership effects on student achievement and sustained school success. *International Journal of Education Management, 25*(1), 33–44.

Kelley, J. D. (2011). *Teacher's and teacher leaders' perceptions of the formal role of teacher leadership.* Policy Studies. Georgia State University.

Kennedy, A., Deuel, A., Nelson, T. H., & Slavit, D. (2011, May). *Requiring collaboration or distributing leadership?* Phi Delta Kappan.

Kim, G. (2010). *Investigating promising school leadership practices in two California charter schools.* University of Southern California.

Lambert, L. (2006, Spring). Lasting leadership: A study of high leadership capacity schools. *The Educational Forum, 70,* 238–254.

Leithwood, K. A., & Jantzi, D. (2000). Principal and teacher leadership effects: A replication. *School Leadership & Management, 20*(4), 415–434. doi:10.1080/13632430020003210

Leithwood, K. A., & Jantzi, D. (2006). Transformational school leadership for large-scale reform: Effects on students, teachers, and their classroom practices. *School Effectiveness and School Improvement, 17*(2), 201–227. doi:10.1080/09243450600565829

Leithwood, K. A., & Jantzi, D. (2008). Linking leadership to student learning: The contributions of leader efficacy. *Educational Administration Quarterly, 44*(4), 496–528. doi:10.1177/0013161X08321501

Leithwood, K. A., & Mascall, B. (2008). Collective leadership effects on student achievement. *Educational Administration Quarterly, 44*(4), 529–561. doi:10.1177/0013161X08321221

Leithwood, K. A., Patten, S., & Jantzi, D. (2010). Testing a conception of how school leadership influences student learning. *Educational Administration Quarterly, 46*(5), 671–706. doi:10.1177/0013161X10377347

Loder, T. L., & Spillane, J. P. (2005). Is a principal still a teacher?: US women administrators' accounts of role conflict and role discontinuity. *Leadership, 25*(3). doi:10.1080/13634230500116348

Louis, K. S., Leithwood, K. A., Wahlstrom, K. A., & Anderson, S. E. (2010). *Investigating the links to improved student learning: Final report of research findings.* New York, NY: Wallace Foundation.

Lovett, S., & Cameron, M. (2011). Career pathways: Does remaining close to the classroom matter for early career teachers? A study of practice in New Zealand and the USA. *Professional Development in Education, 37*(2), 213–224.

Margolin, I., Ezer, H., & Karton, R. (2000). *Constructing a professional community of teacher educators during a curriculum-in-action process.* American Educational Research Association annual conference. New Orleans, LA.

Margolis, J. (2008). When teachers face teachers: Listening to the resource "right down the hall." *Teaching Education, 19*(4), 293–310. doi:10.1080/10476210802425628

Marks, H. M., & Printy, S. M. (2003). Principal leadership and school performance: An integration of transformational and instructional leadership. *Educational Administration Quarterly, 39*(3), 370–397. doi:10.1177/0013161X03253412

McDonald, D. H., & Keedy, J. L. (2002). *Principals as teacher leaders in the Kentucky education reform act era: Laying the groundwork for high-achieving, low income schools.* American Educational Research Association annual conference. New Orleans, LA.

Murphy, J., Smylie, M., Mayrowetz, D., & Seashore Louis, K. (2009). The role of the principal in fostering the development of distributed leadership. *School Leadership & Management, 29*(2), 181–214. doi:10.1080/13632430902775699

Park, V., & Datnow, A. (2009). Co-constructing distributed leadership: District and school connections in data-driven decision-making. *School Leadership & Management, 29*(5), 477–494. doi:10.1080/13632430903162541

Penuel, W. R., Riel, M., Joshi, A., Pearlman, L., Kim, C. M., & Frank, K. A. (2010). The alignment of the informal and formal organizational supports for reform: Implications for improving teaching in schools. *Educational Administration Quarterly, 46*(1), 57–95. doi:10.1177/1094670509353180

Pitts, V. M. (2009). Using social network methods to study school leadership. *International Journal of Research and Method in Education.* Northwestern University.

Printy, S. M. (2007). Leadership for teacher learning: A community of practice perspective. *Educational Administration Quarterly, 44*(2), 187–226. doi:10.1177/0013161X07312958

Printy, S. M., Marks, H. M., & Bowers, A. J. (2009, September). Integrated leadership: How principals and teachers share transformational and instructional influence. *Journal of School Leadership, 19.*

Rivers, S. D. (2010). *Leadership as a distributed phenomenon: A study of shared roles and 3rd grade student achievement.* Capella University.

Rogers, M. P., Abell, S., Lannin, J., Wang, C.-Y., Musikul, K., Barker, D., & Dingman, S. (2006, September). Effective professional development in science and mathematics education: Teachers' and facilitators' views. *International Journal of Science and Mathematics Education, 5*(3), 507–532. doi:10.1007/s10763-006-9053-8

Senesac, D. R. (2010). *Narrowing the achievement gap and sustaining success: A qualitative study of the norms, practices, and programs of a successful high school with urban characteristics.* University of Southern California.

Shatzer, R. H. (2009). *A comparison study between instructional and transformational leadership theories: Effects on student achievement and teacher job satisfaction.* Leadership. Brigham Young University.

Shatzer, R. H., Caldarella, P., Hallam, P. R., & Brown, B. L. (2013). Comparing the effects of instructional and transformational leadership on student achievement: Implications for practice. *Educational Management Administration & Leadership, 42*(4), 445–459. doi:10.1177/1741143213502192

Sheppard, B., Hurley, N., & Dibbon, D. (2010). *Distributed leadership, teacher morale, and teacher enthusiasm: Unravelling the leadership pathways to school success.* American Educational Research Association annual conference.

Silins, H., & Mulford, B. (2004). Schools as learning organizations—Effects on teacher leadership and student outcomes. *School Effectiveness and School Improvement, 15*(3), 443–466.

Somech, A. (2010). Participative decision making in schools: A mediating-moderating analytical framework for understanding school and teacher outcomes. *Educational Administration Quarterly, 46*(2), 174–209. doi:10.1177/1094670510361745

Spillane, J. P., Healey, K., & Parise, L. M. (2009). School leaders' opportunities to learn: A descriptive analysis from a distributed perspective. *Educational Review, 61*(4), 407–432.

Terrell, H. P. (2010). *The relationship of the dimensions of distributed leadership in elementary schools of urban districts and student achievement.* The George Washington University.

Timperley, H. S. (2008). Distributed leadership to improve outcomes for students. In K. A. Leithwood, B. Mascall, & T. Strauss (Eds.), *Distributed leadership according to the evidence* (pp. 197–222). New York, NY: Routledge.

Urick, A., & Bowers, A. J. (2011). What influences principals' perceptions of academic climate? A nationally represenative study of the direct effects of perception on climate. *Leadership and Policy in Schools, 10*(3), 322–348. doi:10.1080/15700763.2011.577925

Wahlstrom, K. A., & Seashore Louis, K. (2008). How teachers experience principal leadership: The roles of professional community, trust, efficacy, and shared responsibility. *Educational Administration Quarterly, 44*(4), 458–495. doi:10.1177/0013161X08321502

Watson, S. T. (2005). *Teacher collaboration and school reform: Distributing leadership through the use of professional learning teams.* Learning. University of Missouri-Columbia.

Wells, C. M., Maxfield, C. R., Klocko, B., & Feun, L. (2010, September). The role of superintendents in supporting teacher leadership: A study of principals' perceptions. *Journal of School Leadership, 20,* 669–694.

Williams, R. B. (2006). Leadership for school reform: Do principal decision-making styles reflect a collaborative approach? *Canadian Journal of Educational Administration and Policy, 53,* 1–22.

CHAPTER 3

TENSIONS AND CONTRADICTIONS IN APPROACHES TO IMPROVING URBAN INNER-CITY SCHOOLS IN THE UNITED STATES

D. Gavin Luter
Wisconsin Campus Compact
University of Wisconsin-Extension

INTRODUCTION

Improving urban inner-city schools within the United States (U.S.) is one of the most perplexing questions in contemporary educational research. At least two broad approaches emerged as paradigms shaping the nature of reform efforts: (a) building-based approaches such as comprehensive school reform (Slavin, 2008), and (b) place-based approaches that include interventions at the community and neighborhood-level (Jennings, 2012). The US federal government has supported both approaches, both separately (e.g., building-based approaches funded through No Child Left Behind,

NCLB, and place-based approaches by Full Service Community Schools, FSCS) and jointly (e.g., Promise Neighborhood, PN, Choice Neighborhoods, CN). Inherent tensions exist between these competing paradigms—tensions that are complicated by the political and competitive environment surrounding school reform (McGuinn, 2012). Additionally, the federal government's accountability system introduced the "public-school choice sanction" to create competitive forces between schools that further complicates the urban inner-city school reform landscape (West & Peterson, 2006, p. C48). To this end, this chapter examines the tensions and contradictions that exist between place-based and building-based approaches in the context of a school choice environment.

These tensions have largely been ignored by contemporary school reform and educational leadership literature. To better understand how local, yet federally funded, place-based reforms can exist in the same space as local school choice and federal standards and accountability policies, a more comprehensive framework is necessary. Such a framework (or frameworks) would offer a more complete picture of how these efforts were implemented, how they have existed on a daily basis, and how "on the ground" tensions have emanated from them. This analysis would provide a clearer understanding of the most impactful school reform approaches for low-performing schools, taking into consideration the local neighborhood context. The focus here is on the federal–local nexus in school reform.

This chapter takes readers through the evolution of approaches used by scholars and practitioners to address struggling urban inner-city schools. I begin by briefly providing an overview of the U.S. policy context of urban inner-city school reform. Then I move to an examination of one locally driven, yet federally supported, building-based approach to improving urban schools: comprehensive school reform. Next, I explain school choice as a distinct, yet still building-based approach, to improving urban schools. I continue to examine a set of factors that stand to challenge the assumptions upon which school choice stands—neighborhood effects. Finally, I move on to analyze approaches to improving urban schools that attempt to respond to neighborhood effects—community schools, community organizing, and place-based reforms.

Across the literature, I identify three prominent gaps that have implications for policy implementation and educational leadership researchers and practitioners. With this chapter, I seek to fill some of those gaps and conclude with a call for more helpful frameworks that can inform researchers and practitioners who seek to understand and work within the field of place-based school reform efforts with interventions that blend building-based and place-based approaches.

URBAN INNER-CITY SCHOOL IMPROVEMENT: THE U.S. POLICY CONTEXT

Fragmentation in governance defines American educational policy and practice: between federal, state, and local governments, between citizens and professional educators, between school boards and superintendents, among other conflicting groups and interests. America's tradition of distrust in centralized national authority translated into a tremendously fragmented system of education where the federal government traditionally held no formal responsibility (Cohen & Spillane, 1992; Marsh & Wohlstetter, 2013). Instead, responsibility for education devolved to the states, but most states passed responsibility down to the "smallest possible unit" of government: the local level (Katz, 1987, p. 33). This federalist system became known for its "fragmented" (Cohen & Spillane, 1992) nature, but it was intentionally created "as a response against executive dominance in the colonial era" which make coordination between different levels of government arduous (Kaufman, 1969, p. 3).

It was not until *Brown v. Board of Education* in 1954 when the federal government became active in the American schooling system. Even at this historical landmark, the federal government's mandate was simply to create "a more equitable system of public schooling" (McGuinn, 2006, p. 27). This event, coupled with the "public 'discovery' of poverty" (Vinovskis, 2009, p. 11), hurled the government into a battle to equalize funding for urban school districts as it attempted to educate all students, especially children of color and those in poverty. With the passage of the Elementary and Secondary Education Act (ESEA) of 1965, the federal role in education reform exponentially grew (McGuinn, 2006; Vinovskis, 2009). ESEA provided the largest financial investment ($1 billion) in the American government's history, mainly focused on redress for mostly urban school districts that served large proportions of low-income students (Thomas & Brady, 2005).

Frustrations with persistently low-performing schools were well-documented, but the frustrations reached a crescendo when the federal government released the *A Nation at Risk* (National Commission on Excellence in Education, 1983) report which suggested that America's public schools were in decline, and, therefore, the country's economic prosperity was at risk, which demanded federal intervention. Before NCLB, the most recent ESEA reauthorization, the federal government's role in education policy was limited, linked mostly to encouraging states to achieve higher standards, experimenting with innovative programs, ensuring access to education for all students regardless of physical (dis)ability, and providing equitable resources to districts with high concentrations of minority students.

These standards-and-accountability reforms, with their roots in the 1980s (President George H. W. Bush's Charlottesville Education Summit) and 1990s (President William J. Clinton's Goals 2000 legislation), addressed the issues of (a) education achievement dissonance between students from different racial and class groups, and (b) fragmented and incoherent policies to hold states and localities accountable for student achievement (McDonnell, 2011; Smith & O'Day, 1991). A broader policy regime formulated around the standards-and-accountability role of the federal government which eventually paved the way for the passage of NCLB under President George W. Bush's leadership. Its passage also meant an expanded federal role in education that linked funding and school governance decisions to performance on state-created standardized tests (McGuinn, 2006). Sanctions would be imposed on schools and districts for failing to meet adequate yearly progress, such as allowing families to choose what schools to attend or school closures. In response to this failure, the federal government switched its approach to that of stimulating reform through competitive grant programs embodied by Race to the Top (McGuinn, 2010, 2012). Based on this overview, it is possible to conclude that this federalist system results in a confusing and conflicting landscape that can interfere with the most well-intentioned school reform efforts (Datnow, 2005; Desimone, 2002; Fuhrman & Elmore, 1990). In the next section, I turn attention to one primary local lever of school reform, comprehensive school reform— one policy response to the "problem" of low-performing schools.

COMPREHENSIVE SCHOOL REFORM: A PRIMARY LOCAL LEVER FOR REFORM

Reform efforts targeting urban inner-city schools changed from strict categorical assistance programs such as Title I to a broader array of reforms which included school-wide or comprehensive school reform programs (Desimone, 2002; Edmonds, 1979; Smith & O'Day, 1991) and other governance reforms such as site-based management and mayoral control of schools (Murphy & Beck, 1995; Hess, 2008). For brevity, I explore only the comprehensive school reform (CSR) literature.[1] I conceptualize CSR as "building-based" or "internal-to-school" reforms because (a) the unit of change is the school building, and (b) they typically ignore neighborhood and community factors that could impact student performance.

Growing out of the assumption that "schools currently operate below the production-possibility frontier" (Brighouse & Schouten, 2010, p. 511), comprehensive school reform (CSR) models attempted to develop a comprehensive approach to improving desired outcomes across an entire school. Comprehensive approaches relied on both site-based management to give schools the flexibility needed to change building-based practices (e.g., instruction and professional development) and top-down centralized bureaucratic guidance to support schools throughout the process of change (e.g., providing curricular materials and technical support). While CSR may include district-sponsored efforts, this section conceptualizes CSR as an individual-building intervention. In this section, I briefly discuss an overview of the CSR concept, present the evidence about CSR to date, and offer CSR's limitations.

CSR Overview

CSR grew out of the effective schools movement, which contended that all students can learn regardless of circumstance (Edmonds, 1979). Framed as a challenge to the Coleman report's (Coleman...et al., 1966) contention that a child's social background was the main determinant of student achievement, an effective school was one that "must eliminate the relationship between successful performance and family background" (Edmonds, 1979, p. 21). Based on these studies, Edmonds concluded that the "repudiation of the social science notion that family background is the principal cause of pupil acquisition of basic school skills is probably prerequisite to successful reform of public schooling for the poor" (p. 23). These individual-building, or internal-to-school, approaches to improving poorly performing urban schools sought to "drive up quality to the point where children's disadvantages would disappear" (Raffo et al., 2006, p. 45). CSR efforts sought to implement strategies within a school building that are "most likely to affect student achievement: curriculum, instruction, assessment, grouping, accommodations for struggling students, parent and community involvement, school organization, and professional development" (Slavin, 2008, p. 256). CSR models have focused almost explicitly on urban schools because of these schools' historical struggles with low performance.

CSR Evidence and Unanswered Questions

Some evidence suggested that CSR approaches could be successful if certain criteria are satisfied. Desimone's (2002) analysis articulated a theory of policy attributes which, taken together, provide a five-prong framework for understanding a CSR's chances of success or failure: (a) specificity, (b) consistency with school, district, and state policy, (c) normative, institutional, and individual authority, (d) power versus authority, and (e) stability. The most recent meta-analysis of CSR reported that overall CSR effects are statistically significant and mildly positive. These effects are greater than previous attempts at reducing the achievement gap[2] and improving outcomes for large numbers of low-SES students, such as Title I (Borman,

Hewes, Overman, & Brown, 2003). From this meta-analysis, and from further work by Borman (2005), CSR efforts were not initially successful (years one through four) yet effect sizes grew over time—on average from .25 in year 5 to .5 in years 8 to 14.

Borman et al.'s (2003) analysis also revealed that whether or not a CSR effort required certain components (e.g., on-going professional development and measurable goals for student outcomes) could not explain the outcomes a school could expect. They concluded that "differences in the effectiveness of CSR are largely due to unmeasured program-specific and school-specific differences in implementation" (p. 166), thus aligning with Honig's (2009) assertion that effective implementation is a product of policy, places, and people. Limited data suggested that turnaround investments can be mildly successful, but they were no panacea (Dee, 2012; Klein, 2013; U.S. Department of Education, 2012).

CSR has its limits. First and foremost, student achievement gains did not always result from implementing CSR efforts. In the federal government's evaluation of the CSRP (Orland...et al., 2008), schools that participated in the program did not experience gains in math and reading within three years of implementation. This finding may be read with caution, given Borman et al.'s (2003) finding that schools may not experience gains associated with the CSR effort until the fifth year. However, Thomas, Peng, and Gray (2007), in their longitudinal analysis of school turnarounds, discovered patterns of "improvement cycles" which rarely lasted four or more years.

Datnow (2005) found evidence to suggest that other competing federal, state, and local demands actually detracted from school officials' abilities to implement CSR efforts. Ironically, reform was placed on the "back burner" as some schools intensely focused on state standardized test scores. Recent research (Marsh, Strunk, & Bush, 2013) suggested that districts implementing school turnarounds for many schools at once have difficulty managing the process. Notably, in this study, they noted that because of "decreasing supply of [public school choice initiative] applications affirms that there may be justifiable concerns about the number of organizations interested, willing, and able to take on the turnaround challenge" (p. 518). On the issue of low-performing, high-poverty schools, research also suggests that socioeconomic conditions and neighborhood factors can negatively impact teacher' expectations and, therefore, student performance, thus working against building-based CSR efforts (Entwisle, Alexander, & Olson, 1997).

CSR Final Thoughts

Duke (2012) noted, "Little consideration has been given to the possibility that schools serving large numbers of disadvantaged and low-achieving students might be better served by developing modes of organization and operating procedures uniquely suited to their circumstances" (p. 23). In Bryk et al.'s (2010) analysis, they studied both schools that flourished and schools that lagged. If schools were not strong on the five essential supports—coherent instructional guidance, professional capacity, parent-community-school links, student-centered learning climate, and building-based collaborative leadership—school improvement was not a likely outcome. Not all failing schools are the same (Elmore, 2007), so neither should be their reform efforts. When schools are failing, however, one market-based policy response placed more power in the choice of "educational consumers" that resulted in competition between schools and the threat of closure: school choice.

SCHOOL CHOICE

Given the significant concerns about public education in urban areas, some policymakers and advocates advanced the idea of school choice. Largely an urban phenomenon (Ryan & Heise, 2002), school choice can be simply defined as market-inspired approaches that offer different options for schooling beyond the neighborhood public school (Merrifield, 2008a). In this section, I analyze the school choice literature and show how school choice undermines neighborhood development.

School Choice Overview

School choice programs operate under the premise that competition between schools will increase the quality of all schools. In this sense, education became one more market that could be analyzed, understood, and improved by economic and market interventions (Hoxby, 2003). At least 12 formal policy interventions and practices fall under the school choice umbrella (Merrifield, 2008b), but these interventions and practices can be truncated into six categories: residential choice, intradistrict choice, interdistrict choice, charter schools, vouchers, and private schools (National Center for Education Statistics, 2010).

School choice, as a policy issue, has been framed in terms of classic neoliberal tenets: privatization, deregulation to promote competition, retrenchment of state bureaucracy, elimination of subsidies, and balancing budgets (Klaf & Kwan, 2010). One prominent neoliberal thinker, Milton Friedman (Harvey, 2005), called for the end of government-run education and suggested a national voucher policy where the government would assume only an accrediting function that would approve schools to operate (Friedman,

1962). Proposals for "pure school choice" (Chubb & Moe, 1990), the free market of schools will be able to match all consumers' (parents) needs. School choice's inextricable connection with neoliberalism is clear.

School Choice Evidence and Tensions

Evaluating the impact of school choice is a complicated task. Ideological controversy makes an academic assessment of school choice difficult (Corwin & Schneider, 2005; Merrifield, 2001; Sugarman & Kemerer, 1999), but I offer a brief overview of the evidence both supporting and refuting school choice as an approach to educational improvement.

In Support of School Choice

Hoxby's (2003) study of Michigan and Arizona charters and Milwaukee's voucher program concluded that school choice could improve the productivity of the school, measured by scores on the National Assessment of Educational Progress (NAEP) per $1,000 in per-pupil spending. Hanushek and Rivkin (2003) suggested that competition can produce some moderate increases in teacher quality. Large-scale assessments of school choice programs also found positive, though modest, impact of school choice in academic achievement. Belfield and Levin (2002), Borland and Howsen (1993), Greene (2001), Teske and Schneider (2001), and Walberg (2007) all documented the modest positive gains experienced by students participating in school choice programs. These scholars all attempted to look across the literature to assess the impact of a variety of school choice programs—intradistrict choice, charter schools, vouchers, and magnet schools. Merrifield (2008b) surveyed the literature and reported on the impacts of school choice programs by category. His analysis ultimately concluded by admitting, "We lack any direct answers to pressing questions about market accountability as a transformation catalyst" (p. 246). More recent research by Stanford's Center for Research on Education Outcomes (CREDO. 2013) reported that some charter schools over time were able to increase student performance.

Challenging School Choice

A growing body of literature on school choice calls into question the previous analyses. Using a random assignment method to study school vouchers, Howell and Peterson (2002) concluded that "no overall private school impact of switching to a private school [through vouchers] in the three cities," but did find moderate impact for African Americans (p. 145). Figlio and Rouse (2006), challenging Greene (2001), noted that positive gains reported from Florida's voucher program were probably attributable to student characteristics—not the voucher program as Greene argued. Archibald and Kaplan (2004) reported slightly lower NAEP scores in districts that report magnet schools. In a study regarding private management companies who stepped in to operate 27 schools in Philadelphia, Byrnes (2009) found that these schools performed below schools operated by the public school district. Ballou (2008) reviewed 14 studies about magnet schools: six documenting positive results, three finding no effect, and five producing mixed results. When examining the Chicago Public School choice program, in which nearly half of all students opt out of their local public school, Cullen, Jacob, and Levitt (2005) concluded that, "with the exception of career academies, we find that systemic choice within a public school district does not seem to benefit those who participate" (p. 755).

In one of the most highly publicized school choice "experiments," New Orleans converted many of its schools to charter schools after Hurricane Katrina, and as of 2010 84% of students are served by charter schools (Cowen Institute, 2013). Gray, Merrifield, and Hoppe (2013) concluded, "It is difficult to conclude that the New Orleans [charter public schools] dominant system is responsible for the recent growth in passage rates and [student performance score] increases" (p. 25). In fact, gains in New Orleans student performance began pre-Katrina. Essentially, advocates and opponents of school choice have evidence at their disposal, making it extremely difficult to gauge its effectiveness as a policy intervention (Ryan & Heise, 2002).

Social Tensions

School choice creates at least three social tensions, though. First, numerous scholars have empirically demonstrated that school choice intensifies racial and SES segregation (Eckes & Rapp, 2005; Garcia, 2008; Greene, 2001; Saporito, 2003). Charter school advocates actually expect this segregation to occur (Merrifield, 2008b). Second, low-income parents face challenges in fully using school choice to their advantage. Empirical evidence suggested that parents having access to perfect information about schools, a key assumption of school choice, was a flawed assumption (Bridge, 1978, Henig, 1999; Rothstein, 2006). Low-income parents participating in school choice may actually be participating in their own disenfranchisement (André-Bechely, 2005; Beal & Hendry, 2012; Jacobs, 2013). Information about school quality was withheld from parents or is simply difficult to decipher. Also, parents of privilege guarded desirable schools through mechanisms of cultural capital accumulation. Further, given de facto housing segregation, a parent's preference for a neighborhood charter school became a way to rationalize that parents simply "want" segregated, or racially homogenous, schools.

Finally, school choice negatively impacts neighborhoods. School choice programs have been known to "cream skim," a term referring to when higher-performing students leave schools under school choice plans. Burdick-Will, Keels, and Schuble (2013) found that most closed schools were neighborhood schools located in distressed neighborhoods with high concentrations of people of color and low SES levels. Jacobson and Szczesek (2013) documented the housing market benefits to a neighborhood located near a high-performing charter school, while Bogin and Nguyen-Hoang (2014) documented the declining property values of properties located near low-performing schools.

School choice programs have a common goal of offering inner-city families a way to escape their failing neighborhood school and instead attend school, maybe a better school but maybe not, somewhere else in the city—either run by the district, by a charter school organization, or by a private provider. Within this paradigm, schools can be the saving grace by trumping other characteristics that impact student performance. Essentially, school choice is predicated on the idea that neighborhood effects can be overcome by a "no excuses" approach to education reform (Thernstrom & Thernstrom, 2004). I now explore the literature that documents the impact that neighborhood effects can have on academic achievement and other indicators that are likely to impact school performance.

NEIGHBORHOOD EFFECTS

Decades of social science research have been investigating an important question that could challenge the assumptions of school choice: Do neighborhood characteristics impact individual level outcomes, such as academic achievement? Put differently, does a "neighborhood effect" an individual's life outcomes? In this section, I will define neighborhood effects and offer the key mechanisms through which they operate. Then, I will provide an overview of evidence to date about the extent to which neighborhoods impact individual outcomes. Finally, I offer concluding thoughts about the limitations of neighborhood effects studies, which result in limited practical understanding of how to mediate the neighborhood risk factors.

Definition and Mechanisms

Defining a neighborhood effect is straightforward. When characteristics of the neighborhood in which an individual lives have an individual-level impact on life outcomes, then a "neighborhood effect" is present. The neighborhood effects literature grew out of the Chicago School of

Sociology researchers' interests in the uneven impacts of urbanization on social groups and their processes of socialization across the city. Thus, these researchers flipped the unit of analysis from the individual to the social group. Accordingly, the associated interventions were at the community level (e.g., the Chicago Area Project, see Schlossman & Sedlak, 1983). William Julius Wilson's book *The Truly Disadvantaged* (1987) catalyzed the most recent scholarship that studied neighborhood effects. One key argument was that economically disadvantaged, typically people of color, in central city neighborhoods experience "concentration effects" (Wilson, 1987, p. 46) that contribute to increased rates of social dislocation which included crime, unemployment, out-of-wedlock births, and welfare dependency for Blacks in particular (p. 48, 59).

Since the publication of Wilson's seminal work, social scientists went to great lengths to explore the associations and causal links between neighborhoods and individual outcomes and can be categorized into at least six groups (Brooks-Gunn, Duncan, & Klebanov, 1993; Jencks & Mayer, 1990; Pebley & Sastry, 2004; Sampson, Morenoff, & Gannon-Rowley, 2002). First, normative or epidemic models (Crane, 1991) examined the ways that peers influence individuals to act in a similar way (e.g., peer effects). Second, neighborhood organization and collective socialization (Wilson, 1987) models emphasized the role of adults from within the neighborhood in advancing social control among children. The third mechanism, institutional models (Aber, Gephart, Brooks-Gunn, & Connell, 1997; Small, Jacobs, & Massengill, 2008), cast light on the role adults from outside of the neighborhood had on neighborhood children.

Another mechanism by which neighborhoods may impact individuals was through labor and marriage markets (Duncan & Hoffman, 1991). Parents experiencing difficulty in finding employment would have a more difficult time making ends meet, thus causing more stress on the family unit. Fifth, were routine activities in the neighborhood, which refer to the land use patterns (e.g., vacant, schools, parks, places of employment, restaurants, residential, industrial) and traffic flow of visitors (e.g., who visits the neighborhood and when do they visit) (Sampson et al., 2002). Sixth, and finally, competition for resources between residents referred to the clashes between "advantaged" and "disadvantaged" neighbors (Jencks & Mayer, 1990, p. 116). With the tremendous amounts of possibilities for confounding variables when studying the link between neighborhood and individual characteristics, Duncan and Raudenbush (2001) concluded, "... The task of securing precise, robust and unbiased estimates of neighborhood effects has proved remarkably difficult" (p. 107). I turn my attention to a discussion about whether or not neighborhoods actually matter for individual outcomes independent of other individual or family characteristics.

Do Neighborhoods Impact Individuals? Focusing on Education

Several extensive reviews of the literature tackled this difficult issue (Brooks-Gunn, Duncan, & Klebanov, 1993; Brooks-Gunn, Duncan, & Aber, 1997a,b; Burdick-Will et al., 2011; Jencks & Mayer, 1990; Mayer & Jencks, 1989; Sampson et al., 2002), and it is beyond the scope of this analysis to cover them all. Sampson and colleagues (2002) surveyed 40 quantitative studies and concluded that crime rates are associated with collective socialization measures, such as connections and interactions between neighbors, informal social control, and institutional resources. More recent evidence from a quasi-experimental study documented the adverse impacts of exposure to a homicide on Black student achievement, even if the crime was not witnessed directly (Sharkey, 2010), aligning with findings of observational studies that found similar adverse effects of violence on academic achievement (Aber et al., 1997). Because the neighborhood effects literature is so vast, I will focus on how neighborhood effects impact education for the remainder of this section.

Recent evidence suggested that neighborhoods did impact educational outcomes, such as dropping out (Crowder & South, 2003; Harding, 2009a, b) and academic performance (Sampson, Sharkey, & Raudenbush, 2008; Sharkey, 2010). Regarding dropping out, Crowder and South (2003) found that the odds of dropping out for a student living in the most disadvantaged neighborhoods (90th percentile) is 20% higher than average. Findings also pronounced the racial disparities of neighborhood effects in that the odds of dropping out are twice as large for Black children as opposed to White children. Harding's (2009a) analysis showed that, for males, neighborhood violence accounted for 44% of the correlation between neighborhood disadvantage and high school graduation. Other findings suggested that Blacks were most vulnerable to neighborhood effects on academic achievement. Sampson et al. (2008) found that Blacks living in a disadvantaged neighborhood suffered a loss of verbal ability equivalent to nearly one year of schooling. Sharkey (2010) found that children's scores on assessments were between .5 and .66 standard deviations lower if they witnessed a homicide. He suggested that children who lived in a neighborhood affected by a homicide could experience similar academic harm. Some qualitative evidence demonstrated that students who moved from disadvantaged neighborhoods to advantaged neighborhoods accrue intangible benefits such as social supports and exposure to different occupational norms (Keels, 2008).

However, a divergent line of scholarship challenged the idea that neighborhoods impact individual outcomes (Rothstein, 2005). For example, Jargowsky and Komi (2009) found that school effects explained more of the variance in student test scores than neighborhood variables.[3] Rendón (2013) found that neighborhood SES was a statistically insignificant predictor for dropping out after accounting for school factors in the models. School factors, such as higher proportions of Blacks and Latinos, were found to have a significant effect on dropping out. Owens (2010) also studied neighborhood and schools within the same models and found significant interaction and additive effects. Neighborhood SES was a better predictor for college graduation than high school graduation. Results also suggested that neighborhood characteristics could serve as "grounds for negative competition within high schools," given her finding that relative deprivation of a student's neighborhood compared to classmates' neighborhood negatively predicted high school graduation (p. 307). Finally, and importantly, neighborhood factors still yield statistically significant associations with academic achievement even when school factors are added into her models.

In an evaluation of the Moving to Opportunity Program where residents were randomly selected to move to lower-poverty census tracts (Sanbonmatsu et al., 2011), researchers found no statistically significant differences between groups in terms of academic achievement. On other outcomes, such as physical health (e.g., diabetes and obesity) and mental health (sleep patterns and mood disorders), the experiment showed improvements. In recent research that reevaluated the MTO findings, researchers discovered that people in different cities experienced different outcomes (Burdick-Will et al., 2011). Other scholars mounted serious methodological critiques of the MTO experiment, which called into question the original null findings (Clampet-Lundquist & Massey, 2008). Sampson (2008) questioned the MTO experiment's conclusions by contending, "If we want to learn about the effects of neighborhood interventions in an experimental design, the best method is to randomly assign interventions at the level of neighborhood" (p. 264), which was not done in MTO. Regarding educational outcomes, the divergent findings make for a rich debate about the nature of interventions: should they be individual- and family-level (Duncan, Morris, & Rodrigues, 2011; Yoshikawa, Aber, & Beardslee, 2012), school-level (Rowan, 2011), or community-level (Brighouse & Schouten, 2011)?

Neighborhood Effects Conclusion

Despite methodological challenges, it seems safe to conclude that neighborhoods have *at least some* impact on a variety of life outcomes, especially for child academic achievement and attainment (Burdick-Will et al., 2011). The above analysis also made clear that neither moving people to an affluent neighborhood (MTO) nor artificially increasing income (Duncan,

Morris, & Rodrigues, 2011; Yoshikawa, Aber, & Beardslee, 2012) by themselves will magically undo the documented negative effects of being Black and poor in the central city (Clampet-Lundquist & Massey, 2008; Massey & Denton, 1993; Sharkey, 2013; Wilson, 1987). It is for this reason that the final section of this chapter examines structural interventions and their potential to improve educational outcomes, neighborhood quality, family-level outcomes, economic outcomes, and other quality-of-life indicators.

PLACE-BASED SCHOOL REFORM INITIATIVES

In this section, I turn my attention to the body of literature that examines the current efforts to address low-performing schools through neighborhood-based interventions. Growing out of a new vision of urban school reform (Warren, 2005), these efforts extend beyond the school walls by seeking to engage parents, community stakeholders, educational policymakers, and youth. Despite the paucity of research in this area, I analyze the existing literature that examines the possibilities that neighborhood-based approaches have to improve schooling.

Community Schools

Given a growing consciousness of the ecological model of child development (Bronfenbrenner, 1979), practitioners could understand how (a) problems experienced by schools required solutions that addressed non-curricular barriers to learning, and (b) these interventions were necessary at different levels if they were to change the trajectories of children, especially children in disadvantaged schools. In the 1960s and 1970s, increasing expectations were placed on schools to have guidance counselors, nurses, and other supportive service personnel on staff in hopes of addressing barriers to learning that did not stem from the school (Dryfoos, 1994; Tyack, 1992). Scholarly and practical attention in education has been directed at schools, who take concrete steps to include intensive and expanded services either linked to (Lawson & Briar-Lawson, 1997) or based at (Dryfoos, 1994; Kronick, 2005) the school. In a pivotal book, Joy Dryfoos (1994) studied "full service schools" that met the non-traditional (and non-curricular) needs of students and their families. These schools were known for providing a web of support for children to address mental and physical health in addition to the needs of the surrounding community, but no certain set of prescribed interventions characterized a full service school. Her concept of "full service schools," while focused solely on meeting health needs of children and families, aligned with a larger national movement related to meeting the needs of families, children, *and* communities which was referred to as "community schools" (Brundy & Butrymowicz, 2013; Children's Aid Society, 2013; Hernandez, 2013; Richardson, 2009).

Community Organizing

Community and full service schools attempted to address the non-curricular barriers to learning *in the context of the school building*[4] that would, as the theory of change went, eventually improve educational outcomes. Another strand of literature—community organizing for school reform—focused on the generation of social capital between parents, inner-city neighborhood residents, and parents. This was one more pathway for improving inner-city education. The importance of social capital and schooling was "discovered" in the scholarly sense through the Coleman's (1988) research on Catholic education and disadvantaged children (Driscoll & Kerchner, 1999). Social capital was conceptualized as trusting relationships, social networks, and norms linked to effective sanctions. Shirley (1997) pioneered the study of how community members could work with schools to generate social capital in neighborhoods and, therefore, work to address social inequities rooted in neighborhoods. Within the community, organizing would lead to one-on-one meetings with residents in the neighborhood, community-wide walks for education, neighborhood safety efforts, improved housing campaigns, and job development training. Shirley's (1997) work stood in stark contrast to the "accommodationist" (p. 72) family engagement literature advanced by Joyce Epstein (1995, 2001). Instead of emphasizing things that parents *should be involved* in order to help the school meet *its* goals, Shirley instead thought of parents as powerful actors that ought to be *engaged* in schools and helping to set the agenda. These parents were therefore conceived as "change agents who can transform urban schools and neighborhoods" (Shirley, 1997, p. 73).

Since Shirley's work, several scholars studied particularistic community organizing projects in different localities (Gold, Simon, & Brown, 2002; Kahne, O'Brien, Brown, & Quinn, 2001; Mediratta, 2007; Shirley, 2002; Warren, 2005). From these studies, it was clear that community organizing's bottom-up orientation to school reform challenged traditional top-down bureaucratic approaches to school reform. Warren (2013) pointed to specific ways that parents act as social capital-building agents. While not many studies have studied the actual impact of community organizing/school reform efforts, one analysis (Mediratta...et al., 2008) found evidence to suggest that organizing efforts sustained over a long period of time could yield statistically significant changes in school climate (e.g., teacher–parent trust, teacher outreach to parents), professional culture (peer collaboration, collective responsibility, joint problem solving), and instructional core (e.g., teacher influence in classroom decision-making, coherent curriculum and instruction). Findings also suggested that modest gains in achievement could be experienced as a result of these organizing arrangements. Interestingly, these studies were not focused on the emergent issues and tensions when community organizing efforts were implemented.

Place-Based School Reform

After the election of Barack Obama in 2008, the nation saw a renewed interest in place-based efforts with the creation of the White House Neighborhood Revitalization Initiative (Taylor, McGlynn, & Luter, 2013a). Given the lukewarm success of previous efforts to transform distressed neighborhoods by housing-only strategies such as the federal HOPE VI program (Popkin, Levy, & Buron, 2009), the White House needed to change and broaden its strategy. The White House launched banner programs that would jointly tackle neighborhood distress and low-performing urban schools: CN and PN (Federal Register, 2012, 2011). Notably, the launching of PN was inspired by the work of the Harlem Children's Zone (HCZ) and its orientation toward school-centered community revitalization (HCZ, 2003; Khadduri, Schwartz, & Turnham, 2008). This framework advanced the idea that closing the so-called achievement gap[5] between children of color and Whites could be tackled by attacking the problems of concentrated disadvantage by a holistic model of service delivery, community development, and school reform mechanisms. The model reflected the reality that school reform simply could not exist in a vacuum (Fusarelli, 2011).

PN and CN represented the most comprehensive approaches to revitalizing distressed neighborhoods since the Model Cities program of the 1960s (James, 1972), yet carried with it an emphasis on public school reform and early childhood education. While these programs started in 2011, they have received virtually no scholarly attention. A scholarly search of 70 databases yielded the following results for these search criteria (searched "all text" feature): PN, 16 articles in peer-reviewed publications; CN 17 articles in peer-reviewed publications (upon investigation, only four were relevant); FSCS: 69 articles in peer-reviewed publications (none were directly relevant to the specific implementation of the DoEd's program). These low numbers of publications are even more surprising when considering the diverse groups of scholars who might study these efforts: political science (policy implementation), education (school reform, student achievement), social work (supportive service systems), psychology (social development), urban affairs and planning (community development). In comparison, a scholarly search of the same 70 databases of "school choice," "United States," and "K–12 education" in "all text" yielded 302 citations in peer-reviewed journals. Removing "United States" from the search criteria increased the number of articles to 907. An entire journal has empirically and theoretically examined school choice: *The Journal of School Choice*, which published four issues (approximately six articles per volume) per year since 2006. Vanderbilt University launched the National Center on School Choice, which sought to empirically study impacts of school choice.[6]

Most of what the scholarly and practitioner community knows about PN and CN comes from think-tanks such as the Urban Institute, the Promise Neighborhoods Institute (PNI), PolicyLink, and the Coalition for Community Schools. After analyzing these reports, they seem to fall into five categories: data and evaluation (e.g., Smith, 2011), finance and sustainability (e.g., Joseph & Connors-Tadros, 2011), community engagement (e.g., PNI, n.d.), capacity-building (e.g., Frontline Solutions & BCT Partners, 2012), and partnership development (e.g., Potapchuk, 2013). Based on the authorship and the open online availability of these documents, it is logical to infer that these tools were created for practitioners who are building PN and CN efforts in their localities. The audience did not seem to be teachers or official school personnel. With only one exception that offers a "brief" look at Choice implementation (Pendall & Hendey, 2013), no studies have critically examined the implementation of FSCS, PN, and CN.

ANALYZING THE GAPS

Across the literature, three prominent gaps emerged: (a) gaps about implementation of place-based comprehensive community initiatives (PBCCI) efforts like PN and CN, (b) gaps about the school system's and individual school's role in PBCCI efforts, and (c) gaps resulting from potentially conflicting policy demands. First, implementation of these efforts is challenging and complex to state it mildly. Reviewing the comprehensive community initiative (CCI) literature reveals that multi-sector collaboratives are rife with challenges that require careful attention to clarity in partners' roles, the efforts' theory of change and goals, benchmarks by which success will be measured, alignment with outside funding sources, the role that community engagement and residents will play in the efforts, and how the effort will respond to changing environments (The Aspen Institute, 2011). When educational systems become a part of the CCIs, another layer of complexity is added. Attunements to external political realities become important. As Honig (2009) noted about education policy implementation, the interaction between policy, people, and place become important to understand success or failure.

The complexities of policy implementation for PN, CN, and Full Service Community Schools (FSCS) have simply not been captured in current scholarship. "Third generation partnerships for P-16 pipelines" are becoming more prominent than ground education reform in larger ecological realities which must be fit for the purposes they desire to achieve, appropriate for the context, and timely (Lawson, 2013). However, no literature explored exactly what those partnerships look like and how they will be implemented. Further, while PN and CN attempted to include community members and organizations in the reform of public schools, it is unclear the extent to which community members have *actually been involved* in the planning and implementation of these joint school reform and neighborhood improvement efforts. As Bryk and colleagues (2010) contend, school reform efforts that do not include community engagement as an essential component of reform are more likely to fail. Shirley's (1997) and Warren's (Warren et al., 2011; 2013) work further highlights the benefits associated with community engagement in school reform.

Researchers interested in analyzing such partnerships with these criteria in mind may engage in comparative partnership analysis (Lawson, 2013). These inquiries would be based on comparisons across qualitative case studies, a sort of meta-analysis of case studies—more traditionally known as comparative case studies that would allow for multiple contexts and units of analysis (Yin, 2014). Researchers attempting to compare across cases should be aware of the problems associated with comparing across sites: parochialism, misclassification, "degreeism," and concept stretching (Sartori, 1991). Given that policy implementation is highly context-dependent (Honig, 2009), researchers in different urban areas may benefit from creating research collectives where they share their findings across sites. Samples could be drawn from localities that are implementing PBCCIs, and advocacy organizations such as the PNI[7] could serve as a connection between sites while translating lessons learned to create stronger urban policy.

Next, no present studies examined how school systems were involved in the planning and implementation of place-based comprehensive community initiatives (PBCCIs). Literature presently is either written from a scholarly or a community-development practitioner's perspective. The few articles that did examine early implementation case studies were published in outlets foreign to the education world. With minimal exceptions (Miller, Wills, & Scanlan, 2013; Taylor et al., 2013b), these publications did not appear in outlets that are frequently read by educational scholars and/or practitioners. Uncharted territory means fertile ground when it comes to new understandings that could result in better policies and practices. Educational leaders are important actors in school-linked CCIs (Kahne et al., 2001), but the field only recently uncovered that successful CSR in urban inner-city schools includes redesigning the school to be more connected to families and surrounding communities (Bryk et al., 2010; Klar & Brewer, 2013; Louis, Leithwood, Wahlstrom, & Anderson, 2010; Miller et al., 2013). Focused qualitative studies should be conducted with school leaders involved with PN, CN, and FSCS efforts and contrast findings with recent school leadership literature.

A serious breakdown revealed itself between the school reform literature and PN and CN efforts underway, an area that my colleagues and I have attempted to address with colleagues in the recent *Peabody Journal of Education* special issue on universities' roles related to school reform and neighborhood improvement (Kronick et al., 2013). Crowson and Boyd (2005) captured tensions between two competing strategies exposed by school involvement in PBCCIs: professional coordinated services and community development and empowerment. These conflicting approaches create bidirectional forces that can work against reform.

In a related gap in the literature, we know nothing about the potential of conflicting policy demands placed on Promise and Choice projects. For example, the metrics for a successful PN/CN grant might be the number of children from a neighborhood receiving supportive services at a school. This metric is quite different from a school's ultimate metric for success: student achievement. Concerns about conflicting policy goals are especially relevant in a standards-and-accountability environment that sometimes seems to ignore larger trends related to distressed neighborhoods declining conditions for those who live in them (Fusarelli, 2011; Weiss & Long, 2013). The policy agenda advanced by the *Broader, Bolder Approach to Education* (BBA)[8] group stands in stark contrast to market-based school reform. What do these conflicting demands mean for the federal-local nexus of interaction?

Through PN and CN, though, the same federal government that provides billions of dollars to advance the standards-and-accountability education reform agenda is supporting efforts to align with BBA's conflicting agenda. Further, in cities that have open enrollment policies, one must question whether it impacts place-based efforts. If students are not going to school in the neighborhoods where they live because of school choice and open enrollment, how effective will a place-based approach to reform be (Silver, Weitzman, Mijanovich, & Holleman, 2012)? Indeed, the assumptions of place-based efforts are challenged in an environment of school choice. CSR and education policy implementation literature suggested that conflicting policy goals could promulgate failure (Desimone, 2002). The reality is that the scholarly community knows virtually nothing about how school systems and individual schools navigate involvement in place-based school reform that attempt to improve neighborhood conditions.

Greater scholarly attention to the conditions necessary for implementing effective interventions across school sites, as evidenced by the Carnegie

Foundation for the Advancement of Teaching's work on networked improvement communities, offers guidance on appropriate methods of inquiry relevant to school district implementation of PBCCIs (Bryk, Gomez, & Grunow, 2011). These approaches integrate A-level activities of on-the-ground work, B-level activities of attempts to improve on-the-ground-work, and C-level activities of inter-institutional learning and transmitting lessons learned across sites. Formulating researcher/practitioner networks across sites implementing PBCCIs could result in more sharply defined models for how to "do" the work necessary to implement such cross-sector and multi-site interventions. Social network analysis could also illuminate how collaborative work between in- and out-of-school partners filters down from school leaders to other building staff (Daly & Finnigan, 2011).

Finally, the literature does not offer a comprehensive conceptualization of place-based school reform. Comprehensive community initiatives may involve school reform, but they may not. Community schools could be linked to a place, but this intervention emphasizes service delivery. School-centered community revitalization does not seek to address underlying inequities and policy-level forces that created distressed neighborhoods. Developing the nascent concept of place-based school would include a fusion of theoretical and empirical scholarship where scholars would compare conceptualizations from the literature to perceptions of practitioners working to implement these projects. It is an essential step if the education community, especially school leaders, is to get a handle on what exactly it takes to jointly improve neighborhoods and urban inner-city schools.

ACKNOWLEDGEMENTS

I would like to thank Dr. Stephen L. Jacobson for his encouragement and helpful comments on the chapter.

NOTES

1. For a complete analysis of school governance reforms, such as mayoral control and democratic localism/community control, see Bryk, Sebring, Kerbow, Rollow, & Easton, 1998; Bryk, Sebring, Allensworth, Luppescu, & Easton, 2010; Fantini, Gittell, & Magat, 1970; Hess, 2008; Katz, 1987; Wong & Shen, 2013.
2. The notion of the achievement gap has been problematized because it is overly simplistic, arguing that differences in student achievement have roots in opportunity structure (Carter & Welner, 2013) and civic empowerment (Levinson, 2013) differentials.
3. In their models, neighborhood variables were still statistically significant, signaling the importance of these non-school factors.

4. For a discussion about school-linked versus school-based community school models, see Lawson & Briar-Lawson, 1997
5. See footnote 2
6. http://www.vanderbilt.edu/schoolchoice/index.php
7. www.promiseneighborhoodsinstitute.org
8. http://www.boldapproach.org/

REFERENCES

Aber, J. L., Gephart, M. A., Brooks-Gunn, J., & Connell, J. P. (1997). Development in context: Implications for studying neighborhood effects. In J. Brooks-Gunn, G. J. Duncan, & J. L. Aber (Eds.), *Neighborhood poverty, volume I* (pp. 44–61). New York: Russell Sage Foundation.

André-Bechely, L. (2005). *Could it be otherwise? Parents and the inequities of public school choice.* New York: Routledge.

Archibald, D. A., & Kaplan, D. (2004). Parent choice versus attendance area assignment to schools: Does magnet-based school choice affect NAEP scores? *International Journal of Educational Policy, Research, & Practice, 5*(1), 3–35.

The Aspen Institute. (2011). *Voices from the field III: Reflections on comprehensive community change.* Washington, DC: Author.

Ballou, D. (2008). Magnet school outcomes. In M. Berends (Ed.), *Handbook of research on school choice* (pp. 409–426). New York: Routledge.

Beal, H. K. O., & Hendry, P. M. (2012). The ironies of school choice: Empowering parents and reconceptualizing public education. *American Journal of Education, 118*(4), 521–550.

Belfield, C. R., & Levin, H. M. (2002). The effects of competition between schools on educational outcomes: A review for the United States. *Review of Educational Research, 72*(2), 279–341.

Bogin, A., & Nguyen-Hoang, P. (2014). Property left behind: An unintended consequence of a No Child Left Behind "failing" school designation. *Journal of Regional Science.* doi: 10.1111/jors.12141

Borland, M. V., & Howsen, R. M. (1993). On the determination of the critical level of market concentration in education. *Economics of Education Review, 12*(2), 165–169.

Borman, G. D. (2005). National efforts to bring reform to scale in high-poverty schools: Outcomes and implications. *Review of Research in Education, 29,* 1–27.

Borman, G. D., Hewes G., Overman, L., & Brown, S. (2003). Comprehensive school reform and achievement: A meta-analysis. *Review of Educational Research, 73*(2), 125–230.

Bridge, G. (1978). Information imperfections: The Achilles' Heel of entitlement plans. *The School Review, 86*(3), 504–529

Brighouse, H., & Schouten, G. (2011). Understanding the context for existing reform and research proposals. In G. J. Duncan & R. J. Murnane (Eds.), *Whither opportunity? Rising inequality, schools, and children's life chances* (pp. 507–522). New York: Russell Sage Foundation.

Bronfenbrenner, U. (1979). *The ecology of human development.* Cambridge, MA: Harvard University Press.

Brooks-Gunn, J., Duncan, G., & Aber, J. L. (Eds.). (1997a). *Neighborhood poverty Vol. 1: Context and consequences for children.* New York: Russell Sage Foundation.

Brooks-Gunn, J., Duncan, G. J., & Aber, J. L. (1997b). *Neighborhood poverty Vol. 2: Policy implications in studying neighborhoods.* New York: Russell Sage Foundation.

Brooks-Gunn, J., Duncan, G. J., Klebanov, P. K., & Sealand, N. (1993). Do neighborhoods influence child and adolescent development? *American Journal of Sociology, 99*(2), 353–395.

Brundy, T., & Butrymowicz, S. (2013, June 17). Linking home and classroom, Oakland bets on community schools. *The Atlantic.* Retrieved from http://www.theatlantic.com/national/archive/2013/06/linking-home-and-classroom-oakland-bets-on-community-schools/276858/

Bryk, A. S., Gomez, L. M., & Grunow, A. (2011). *Getting ideas into action: Building networked improvement communities in education.* Sanford, CA: Carnegie Foundation for the Advancement of Teaching. Retrieved from http://cdn.carnegiefoundation.org/wp-content/uploads/2014/09/bryk-gomez_building-nics-education.pdf

Bryk, A. S., Sebring, P. B., Allensworth, E., Luppescu S., & Easton, J. Q. (2010). *Organizing schools for improvement: Lessons from Chicago.* Chicago, IL: University of Chicago Press.

Bryk, A. S., Sebring, P. B., Kerbow, D., Rollow, S., & Easton, J. Q. (1998). *Charting Chicago school reform: Democratic localism as a lever for change.* Boulder, CO: Westview Press.

Burdick-Will, J., Keels, M., & Schuble, T. (2013). Closing and opening schools: The association between neighborhood characteristics and the location of new educational opportunities in a large urban district. *Journal of Urban Affairs, 35*(1), 59–80.

Burdick-Will, J., Ludwig, J., Raudenbush, S. W., Sampson, R. J., Sanbonmatsu, L., & Sharkey, P. (2011). Converging evidence for neighborhood effects on children's test scores: An experimental, quasi-experimental, and observational comparison. In In G. J. Duncan & R. J. Murnane (Eds.), *Whither opportunity? Rising inequality, schools, and children's life chances* (pp. 255–276). New York: Russell Sage.

Byrnes, V. (2009). Getting a feel for the market: The use of privatized school management in Philadelphia. *American Journal of Education, 115*(3), 437–455.

Carter, P. L., & Welner, K. G. (Eds.). (2013). *Closing the opportunity gap: What America must do to give every child an even chance.* New York, NY: Oxford University Press.

Center for Research on Education Outcomes (2013). *National charter school study executive summary.* Stanford, CA: Author. Retrieved from http://credo.stanford.edu/documents/NCSS%202013%20Executive%20Summary.pdf

Children's Aid Society (2013). *Building community schools: A guide for action.* New York: Author. Retrieved from http://www.childrensaidsociety.org/publications/building-community-schools-guide-action-2013-edition

Chubb, J. E., & Moe, T. M. (1990). *Politics, markets, and America's schools.* Washington, DC: The Brookings Institution.

Clampet-Lundquist, S., & Massey, D. S. (2008). Neighborhood effects on economic self-sufficiency: A reconsideration of the Moving to Opportunity experiment. *American Journal of Sociology, 114*(1), 107–143.

Cohen, D. K., & Spillane, J. (1992). Policy and practice: The relations between governance and instruction. In G. Grant (Ed.), *Review of research in education, 18* (pp. 3–49). Washington, DC: American Educational Research Association.

Coleman, J. S. (1988). Social capital in the creation of human capital. *American Journal of Sociology, 94,* S95–120.

Coleman, J. S., Campbell, E. Q., Hobson, C. J., McPartland, J., Mood, A. M., Weinfield, F. D., & York, R. L. (1966). *Equality of educational opportunity.* Washington, DC: US Department of Health, Education and Welfare. Retrieved from http://files.eric.ed.gov/fulltext/ED012275.pdf

Corwin, R. G., & Schneider, E. J. (2005). *The school choice hoax.* London: Praeger.

Cowen Institute (2013). *The state of public education in New Orleans.* New Orleans, LA: Tulane University. Retrieved from http://www.coweninstitute.com/wp-content/uploads/2013/07/2013_SPENO_Final2.pdf

Crane, J. (1991). The epidemic theory of ghettos and neighborhood effects on dropping out and teenage childbearing. *American Journal of Sociology, 96,* 1226–1259.

Crowder, K., & South, S. J. (2003). Neighborhood distress and school dropout: The variable significance of community context. *Social Science Research, 32*(4), 659–698.

Crowson, R., & W. Boyd (2005). New roles for community services in educational reform. In M. Fullan (Ed.), *Fundamental change.* (pp. 207–222). Netherlands: Springer.

Cullen, J. B., Jacob, B. A., & Levitt, S. D. (2005). The impact of school choice on student outcomes: An analysis of the Chicago public schools. *Journal of Public Economics, 89,* 729–760.

Daly, A. J., & Finnigan, K. S. (2011). The ebb and flow of social network ties between district leaders under high-stakes accountability. *American Educational Research Journal, 48*(1), 39–79.

Datnow, A. (2005). The sustainability of comprehensive school reform models in changing district and state contexts. *Educational Administration Quarterly, 41*(1), 121–153.

Dee, T. (2012). School turnaround: Evidence from the 2009 stimulus. *NBER working paper No. 17990.* Cambridge, MA: National Bureau of Economic Research.

Desimone, L. (2002). How can comprehensive school reform models be successfully implemented? *Review of Educational Research, 72*(3), 433–479.

Driscoll, M. E., & Kerchner, C. (1999). The implications of social capital for schools, communities, and cities. In J. Murphy & K. S. Lewis (Eds.), *Handbook of research on educational administration* (2nd ed., pp. 385–404). San Francisco, CA: Jossey-Bass.

Dryfoos, J. (1994). *Full service schools: A revolution for health and social services for children, youth, and families.* San Francisco, CA: Jossey Bass.

Duke, D. L. (2012). Tinkering and turnarounds: Understanding the contemporary campaign to improve low-performing schools. *Journal of Education for Students Placed at Risk, 17*(1–2), 9–24, DOI: 10.1080/10824669.2012.636696

Duncan, G. J., & Hoffman, S. D. (1991). Teenage underclass behavior and subsequent poverty: Have the rules changed? In C. Jencks & P. E. Peterson (Eds.), *The urban underclass* (pp. 155–174). Washington, DC: The Brookings Institution.

Duncan, G. J., Morris, P. A., & Rodrigues, C. (2011). Does money really matter? Estimating impacts of family income on young children's achievement with data from random-assignment experiments. *Developmental Psychology, 47*(5), 1263–1279.

Duncan, G. J., & Raudenbush, S. W. (2001) Neighborhoods and adolescent development: How can we determine the links? In A. Booth & A. C. Crouter (Eds.), *Does it take a village? Community effects on children, adolescents, and families* (pp. 105–136). Mahwah, NJ: Lawrence Erlbaum Associates.

Eckes, S., & Rapp, K. (2005). Charter schools: Trends and implications. In E. St. John (Ed.), *Readings on education* (Vol. 19, pp. 1–26). New York, NY: AMS Press.

Edmonds, R. R. (1979). Effective schools for the urban poor. *Educational Leadership, 37*(1), 15–24.

Elmore, R. F. (2007). *School reform from the inside out: Policy, practice, and performance.* Cambridge, MA: Harvard Education Press.

Entwisle, D. R., & Alexander, K. L. (1993). Entry into school: The beginning school transition and educational stratification in the United States. *Annual Review of Sociology, 19,* 401–423.

Epstein, J. L. (2001). *School, family, and community partnerships: Preparing educators and improving schools.* Boulder, CO: Westview Press.

Epstein, J. L. (1995). School/family/community partnerships: Caring for the children we share. *Phi Delta Kappan, 76*(9), 701–12.

Fantini, M., Gittell, M., & Magat, R. (1970). *Community control and the urban school.* New York: Praeger Publishers.

Federal Register. (2011, July 6). 76, No. 129. Retrieved from http://www.gpo.gov/fdsys/pkg/FR-2011-07-06/pdf/2011-16759.pdf

Federal Register. (2012, May 10). 77, No. 91. Retrieved from http://www.gpo.gov/fdsys/pkg/FR-2012-05-10/pdf/2012-11305.pdf

Figlio, D. N., & Rouse, C. E. (2006). Do accountability and voucher threats improve low-performing schools? *Journal of Public Economics, 90*(1–2), 239–255.

Friedman, M. (1962). The role of government in education. In M. Friedman (Ed.), *Capitalism and freedom* (pp. 85–107). Chicago, IL: University of Chicago Press.

Frontline Solutions & BCT Partners. (2012). *Capacity-building toolkit manual: Planning back-office supports for growing Promise Neighborhoods.* Oakland, CA: Promise Neighborhoods Institute. Retrieved from http://www.promiseneighborhoodsinstitute.org/content/download/6975/100465/file/PNI%20Capacity-Building%20Toolkit%20Manual.July%2019.2012.pdf

Fuhrman, S. H., & Elmore, R. F. (1990). Understanding local control in the wake of state education reform. *Educational Evaluation and Policy Analysis, 12*(1), 82–96.

Fusarelli, L. D. (2011). School reform in a vacuum: Demographic change, social policy, and the future of children. *Peabody Journal of Education, 86*(3), 215–235.

Garcia, D. (2008). The impact of school choice on racial segregation in charter schools. *Educational Policy, 22*(6), 805–829.

Gold, E., Simon, E., & Brown, C. (2002). *Successful community organizing for school reform.* Chicago: Cross City Campaign for Urban School Reform. Retrieved from http://www.researchforaction.org/wp-content/uploads/publication-photos/103/Gold_E_CCC_Strong_Neighborhoods_Strong_Schools.pdf

Gray, N., Merrifield, J., & Hoppe, E. (2013). An assessment of the post-Katrina, charter-led makeover of New Orleans' school system. *University of Texas at San Antonio Working Paper Series # 0047ECO-091-2013*. San Antonio, TX: University of Texas at San Antonio College of Business. Retrieved from http://business.utsa.edu/wps/eco/0047ECO-091-2013.pdf

Greene, J. P. (2001). *An evaluation of the Florida A-Plus Accountability and School Choice program*. Center for Civic Innovation, Manhattan Institute: New York.

Hanushek, E. A., & Rivkin, S. G. (2003). Does public school competition affect teacher quality? In C. M. Hoxby (Ed.), *The economics of school choice* (pp. 23–48). Chicago, IL: University of Chicago Press.

Harding, D. J. (2009a). Collateral consequences of violence in disadvantaged neighborhoods. *Social Forces, 88*(2), 757–784.

Harding, D. J. (2009b). Violence, older peers, and the socialization of adolescent boys in disadvantaged neighborhoods. *American Sociological Review, 74*(3), 445–464.

Harlem Children's Zone (2003). *Business Plan FY 2001–2009*. New York: Author. Retrieved from: http://wac.adef.edgecastcdn.net/80ADEF/hcz.org/wp-content/uploads/2014/04/HCZ-Business-Plan.pdf

Harvey, D. (2005). *A brief history of neoliberalism*. Oxford University Press.

Henig, J. R. (1999). School choice outcomes. In S. Sugarman & F. Kemerer (Eds.), *School choice and social controversy: Politics, policy and law* (pp. 68–110). Washington, DC: Brookings Institution.

Hernandez, J. C. (2013, August 11). Mayoral candidates see Cincinnati as a model for New York schools. *The New York Times*. Retrieved from http://www.nytimes.com/2013/08/12/nyregion/candidates-see-cincinnati-as-model-for-new-york-schools.html?pagewanted=all&_r=2&pagewanted=print/&

Hess, F. M. (2008). Looking for leadership: Assessing the case for mayoral control of urban school systems. *American Journal of Education, 114*(3), 219–245.

Honig, M. I. (2009). What works in defining "what works" in educational improvement. In G. Sykes, B. Schneider, & D. N. Plank (Eds.)., *Handbook of education policy research* (pp. 333–347). New York: Routledge.

Howell, W. G., & Peterson, P. E. (2002). *The education gap: Vouchers and urban schools*. Washington, DC: Brookings Institution Press.

Hoxby, C. M. (2003). School choice and school productivity (or could school choice be a tide that lifts all boats?). *NBER Working Paper No. 8873*. Cambridge, MA: National Bureau of Economic Research.

Jacobs, N. (2013). Understanding school choice location as a determinant of charter school racial, economic, and linguistic segregation. *Education and Urban Society, 45*(4), 459–482.

Jacobson, S. L., & Szczesek, J. (2013). School improvement and urban renewal: The impact of a turnaround school's performance on real property values in its surrounding community. *Leadership and Policy in Schools, 12*(1), 1–11.

James, J. L. (1972). Federalism and the Model Cities experiment. *Publius, 2*(1), 69–94.

Jargowsky, P. A., & Komi, M. E. (2009). Before or after the bell? School context and neighborhood effects on student achievement. *Working Paper 28*. Washington, DC: The Urban Institute. Retrieved from http://www.caldercenter.com/upload/Working-Paper-28_FINAL.pdf

Jencks, C., & Mayer, S. E. (1990). The social consequences of growing up in a poor neighborhood. In L. E. Lynn, Jr., & M. G. H. McGeary (Eds.), *Inner city poverty in the United States* (pp. 111–186). Washington, DC: National Academy Press.

Jennings, J. (2012). Measuring neighborhood distress: A tool for place-based urban revitalization strategies. *Community Development, 43*(4), 464–475.

Joseph, M. H., & Connors-Tadros, L. (2011). *Sustaining community revitalization: A tool for mapping funds for Promise Neighborhood initiatives.* Oakland, CA: Promise Neighborhoods Institute and the Finance Project. Retrieved from http://www.promiseneighborhoodsinstitute.org/Technical-Assistance/Resource-Library/Finance-Project-Toolkit

Kahne, J., O'Brien, J., Brown, A., & Quinn, T. (2001). Leveraging social capital and school improvement: The case of a school network and a comprehensive community initiative in Chicago. *Educational Administration Quarterly, 37*(4), 429–461.

Katz, M. (1987). *Reconstructing American education.* Cambridge, MA: Harvard University Press.

Kaufman, H. (1969). Administrative decentralization and political power. *Public Administration Review, 29*(1), 3–15.

Keels, M. (2008). Neighborhood effects examined through the lens of residential mobility programs. *American Journal of Community Psychology, 42*(3–4), 235–250.

Khadduri, J., Schwartz, H., & Turnham, J. (2008). *Policy roadmap for expanding school-centered community revitalization.* Columbia, Maryland: Enterprise Community Partners.

Klaf, S., & Kwan, M. P. (2010). The neoliberal straitjacket and public education in the United States: Understanding contemporary education reform and its urban implications. *Urban Geography, 31*(2), 194–210.

Klar, H. W., & Brewer, C. A. (2013). Successful leadership in high-needs schools: An examination of core leadership practices enacted in challenging contexts. *Educational Administration Quarterly, 49*(5), 768–808. doi: 10.1177/0013161X13482577

Klein, A. (2013). School Improvement Grant program gets mixed grades in Ed. Dept. analysis. *Education Week.* Retrieved from http://blogs.edweek.org/edweek/campaign-k-12/2013/11/us_department_of_education_ana.html

Kronick, R. F. (2005). *Full service community schools: Prevention of delinquency in students with mental illness and/or poverty.* Springfield, IL: Charles C. Thomas Publishers.

Kronick, R. F., Lester, J. N., & Luter, D. G. (2013). Conclusion to higher education's role in public school reform and community engagement. *Peabody Journal of Education, 88*(5), 657–664.

Lawson, H. A. (2013). Third-generation partnerships for P-16 pipelines and cradle-through-career education systems. *Peabody Journal of Education, 88*(5), 637–656.

Lawson, H. A., & Briar-Lawson, K. (1997). *Connecting the dots: Progress toward the integration of school reform, school, linked services, parent involvement, and community schools.* Unpublished manuscript. Oxford, OH: Miami University, The Danforth Foundation, and the Institute for Educational Renewal. (ERIC No. ED 409 696).

Levinson, M. (2013). Education as a civic right: Using schools to challenge the civic empowerment gap. *Poverty & Race, 22*(3), 1–2, 10–13.

Louis, K. S., Leithwood, K., Wahlstrom, K. L., & Anderson, S. E. (2010). *Learning from leadership: Investigating the links to improved student learning*. New York, NY: Center for Applied Research and Educational Improvement, University of Minnesota. Retrieved from http://www.wallacefoundation.org/knowledge-center/school-leadership/key-research/Documents/Investigating-the-Links-to-Improved-Student-Learning.pdf

Marsh, J., Strunk, K. O., & Bush, S. (2013). Portfolio district reform meets school turnaround: Early implementation findings from the Los Angeles Public School Choice Initiative. *Journal of Educational Administration, 51*(4), 5–5.

Marsh, J. A., & Wohlstetter, P. (2013). Recent trends in intergovernmental relations: The resurgence of local actors in education policy. *Educational Researcher, 42*(5), 276–283.

Mayer, S., & Jencks, C. (1989). Growing up in poor neighborhoods: How much does it matter? *Science, 243*(4897), 1141–1145.McGuinn, P. J. (2006*). No Child Left Behind and the transformation of federal education policy, 1965–2005*. Lawrence, KS: University Press of Kansas.

McGuinn, P. J. (2010). Creating cover and constructing capacity: Assessing the origins, evolution, and impact of Race to the Top. *Education Stimulus Watch Special Report 6*. Washington, DC: American Enterprise Institute. Retrieved from http://www.aei.org/publication/creating-cover-and-constructing-capacity/

McGuinn, P. J. (2012). Stimulating reform: Race to the Top, competitive grants and the Obama education agenda. *Educational Policy, 26*(1), 136–159.

McDonnell, L. M. (2011). Surprising momentum: Spurring education reform in states and localities. In T. Skocpol & L. R. Jacobs *Reaching for a new deal: Ambitious governance, economic meltdown, and polarized politics in Obama's first two years* (pp. 230–271). New York: Russell Sage Foundation.

Mediratta, K. (2007). Outside in: Communities in action for education reform. *Theory into Practice, 46*(3), 194–204.

Mediratta, K., Shah, S., McAlister, S., Fruchter, N., Mokhtar, C., & Lockwood, D. (2008). *Organized communities, stronger schools*. Providence, RI: Annenberg Institute for School Reform at Brown University.

Merrifield, J. (2008a). Dismal science: The shortcomings of US school choice research and how to address them. *Policy Analysis, 616*. Washington, DC: CATO Institute.

Merrifield, J. (2008b). School choice evidence and its significance. *Journal of School Choice, 2*(3), 223–259. doi: 10.1080/15582150802371408.

Merrifield, J. (2001). *The school choice wars*. Lanham, MD: Scarecrow Education.

Miller, P., Wills, N., & Scanlan, M. (2013). Educational leadership on the social frontier: Developing promise neighborhoods in urban and tribal settings. *Educational Administration Quarterly, 49*(4), 543–575.

Murphy, J., & Beck, L. (1995). *School-based management as school reform: Taking stock*. Newbury Park, CA: Corwin Press.

National Center for Education Statistics (2010). *Trends in the use of school choice: 1993–2007*. Washington, DC: Author. Retrieved from http://nces.ed.gov/pubs2010/2010004.pdf

National Commission on Excellence in Education (1983). *A nation at risk*. Washington, DC: United States Department of Education.

Orland, M., Connolly, B., Fong, T., Sosenko, L. D., Tushnet, N. C., Yin, R. K. . . . & Warner, E. (2008). *Evaluation of the Comprehensive School Reform Program: Implementation and outcomes. Third-Year Report.* Washington, DC: US Department of Education. Retrieved from http://files.eric.ed.gov/fulltext/ED504179.pdf

Owens, A. (2010). Neighborhoods and schools as competing and reinforcing contexts for educational attainment. *Sociology of Education, 83*(4) 287–311.

Pebley, A., & Sastry, N. (2004). Neighborhoods, poverty, and children's well-being. In K. M. Neckerman (Ed.), *Social inequality* (pp. 119–145). New York: Russell Sage Foundation.

Pendall, R., & Hendey, L. (2013). *A brief look at the early implementation of Choice Neighborhoods.* Washington, DC: The Urban Institute. Retrieved from http://www.urban.org/UploadedPDF/412940-A-Brief-Look-at-the-Early-Implementation-of-Choice-Neighborhoods.pdf

Popkin, S. J., Levy, D. K., & Buron, L. (2009). Has HOPE VI transformed residents' lives? New evidence from the HOPE VI Panel Study. *Housing Studies 24*(4), 477–502.

Potapchuk, W. R. (2013). *The role of community schools in place-based initiatives: Collaborating for student success.* Washington, DC: Coalition for Community Schools, PolicyLink, Institute for Educational Leadership, and West Coast Collaborative. Retrieved from http://www.communityschools.org/assets/1/Asset-Manager/The%20Role%20of%20Community%20Schools%20in%20Place-Based%20InitiativesFINAL1.pdf

Promise Neighborhoods Institute. (n.d.). *Beyond lessons in the field: Community engagement in Promise Neighborhoods.* Oakland, CA: Author. Retrieved from http://www.promiseneighborhoodsinstitute.org/content/download/3313/37703/version/2/file/PN+webinar+Community+Engagement+FINAL.pdf

Raffo, C., Dyson, A., Gunter, H, Jones, L. Kalambouka, A, & Hall, D. (2006). *Education and poverty: Mapping the terrain and making the links to educational policy.* Paper presented at the International Seminar on Education and Poverty: Manchester, UK. Retrieved from http://www.seed.manchester.ac.uk/medialibrary/Education/research/ed_in_urban_contexts/research_output/mapping_the_terrain.pdf

Rendón, M. G. (2013). Drop out and "disconnected" young adults: Examining the impact of neighborhood and school contexts. *The Urban Review*, 1–28. doi: 10.1007/s11256-013-0251-8

Richardson, J. W. (2009). *The full-service community school movement: Lessons from the James Adams community school.* New York: Palgrave Macmillan.

Rothstein, J. M. (2005). Does competition among public schools benefit students and taxpayers? A comment on Hoxby (2000). *NBER Working Paper No. 11215.* Cambridge, MA: National Bureau of Economic Research.

Rothstein, J. M. (2006). Good principals or good peers? Parental valuation of school characteristics, Tiebout equilibrium, and the incentive effects of competition among jurisdictions. *The American Economic Review, 96*(4), 1333–1350.

Rowan, B. (2011) Intervening to improve the educational opportunity of students' poverty: Lessons from recent work in high-poverty schools. In G. J. Duncan & R. J. Murnane (Eds.), *Whither opportunity? Rising inequality, schools, and children's life chances* (pp. 523–537). New York: Russell Sage.

Ryan, J., & Heise, M. (2002). The political economy of school choice. *Yale Law Journal, 111*, 2043–2136.
Sampson, R. J. (2008). Moving to inequality: Neighborhood effects and experiments meet social structure. *American Journal of Sociology, 114*(1), 189–231.
Sampson, R. J., & Morenoff, J. D. (1997). Ecological perspectives on the neighborhood context of urban poverty: Past and present. In J. Brooks-Gunn, G. J. Duncan, & J. L. Aber (Eds.), *Neighborhood poverty* (pp. 1–22). New York: Russell Sage.
Sampson, R. J., Morenoff, J. D., & Gannon-Rowley, T. (2002). Assessing "neighborhood effects": Social processes and new directions in research. *Annual Review of Sociology, 28,* 443–478.
Sampson, R. J., Sharkey, P., & Raudenbush, S. W. (2008). Durable effects of concentrated disadvantage on verbal ability among African-American children. *Proceedings of the National Academy of Sciences, 105*(3), 845–852.
Sanbonmatsu, L. Ludwig, J, Katz, L. F., Gennetian, L. A., Duncan, G. J., Kessler, R. C., Adam, E., McDade, T. W., & Lindau, S. T. (2011). *Moving to opportunity for fair housing demonstration program: Final impacts evaluation.* Washington, DC: US Department of Housing and Urban Development Office of Policy Development and Research.
Saporito, S. (2003). Private choices, public consequences: Magnet school choice and segregation by race and poverty. *Social Problems 50*(2), 181–203.
Sartori, G. (1991). Comparing and miscomparing. *Journal of Theoretical Politics, 3*(3), 243–257.
Schlossman, S., & Sedlak, M. (1983). The Chicago Area Project revisited. *Crime & Delinquency, 29*(3), 398–462.
Sharkey, P. (2013). *Stuck in place: Urban neighborhoods and the end of progress toward racial equality.* Chicago, IL: University of Chicago Press.
Sharkey, P. (2010). The acute effect of local homicides on children's cognitive performance. *Proceedings of the National Academy of Sciences, 107*(26), 11733–11738.
Shirley, D. (2002). *Valley Interfaith and school reform: Organizing for power in South Texas.* Austin, TX: University of Texas Press.
Shirley, D. (1997). *Community organizing for urban school reform.* Austin, TX: University of Texas Press.
Silver, S., Weitzman, B. C., Mijanovich, T., & Holleman, M. (2012). How residential mobility and school choice challenge assumptions of neighborhood place-based interventions. *American Journal of Health Promotion, 26*(3), 180–183.
Slavin, R. E. (2008). Comprehensive school reform. In T. L. Good (Ed.), *21st century education: A reference handbook, Volume 2* (pp. 259–266). Thousand Oaks, CA: Sage Publications.
Small, M. L., Jacobs, E. M., & Massengill, R. P. (2008). Why organizational ties matter for neighborhood effects: Resource access through childcare centers. *Social Forces, 87*(1), 387–414.
Smith, M. S. & O'Day, J. (1991). Putting the pieces together: Systemic school reform. *CPRE Policy Briefs.* Consortium for Policy Research in Education. Retrieved from http://www.cpre.org/images/stories/cpre_pdfs/rb06.pdf
Smith, R. E. (2011). How to evaluate Choice and Promise Neighborhoods. *Perspectives Brief 19,* Washington, DC: The Urban Institute. Retrieved from http://www.urban.org/publications/412317.html

Sugarman, S. D., & Kemerer, F. R. (Eds.). (1999). *School choice and social controversy: Politics, policy, and law*. Washington, DC: Brookings Institution Press.

Taylor, H. L., McGlynn, L., & Luter, D. G. (2013a). Back to the future: Public schools as neighborhood anchor institutions: The Choice Neighborhood Initiative in Buffalo, NY. In R. M. Silverman & K. L. Patterson (Eds.), *Schools and urban revitalization: Rethinking institutions and community development* (pp. 109–135). New York: Routledge.

Taylor, H. L., McGlynn, L., & Luter, D. G. (2013b). Neighborhoods matter: The role of universities in the school reform neighborhood development movement. *Peabody Journal of Education, 88*(5), 541–563.

Teske, P., & Schneider, M. (2001). What research can tell policymakers about school choice. *Journal of Policy Analysis and Management, 20*(4), 609–631. doi: 10.1002/pam.1020

Thernstrom, A., & Thernstrom, S. (2004). *No excuses: Closing the racial gap in learning*. New York: Simon and Schuster.

Thomas, J. Y., & Brady, K. P. (2005). The Elementary and Secondary Education Act at 40: Equity, accountability, and the evolving federal role in public education. *Review of Research in Education, 29*, 51–67.

Thomas, S., Peng, W. J., & Gray, J. (2007). Modelling patterns of improvement over time: Value added trends in English secondary school performance across ten cohorts. *Oxford Review of Education, 33*(3), 261–295.

Tyack, D. (1992). Health and social services in public schools: Historical perspectives. *The Future of Children, 2*(1), 19–31.

U.S. Department of Education (2012). *U.S. Department of Education releases early snapshot of School Improvement Grants data*. Washington, DC: Author. Retrieved from http://www.ed.gov/news/press-releases/us-department-education-releases-early-snapshot-school-improvement-grants-data

Vinovskis, M. A. (2009). *From A Nation at Risk to No Child Left behind: National education goals and the creation of federal education policy*. New York: Teachers College Press.

Walberg, H. J. (2007). *School choice: The findings*. Washington, DC: Cato Institute.

Warren, M. R. (2005). Communities and schools: A new view of urban education reform. *Harvard Educational Review, 75*(2), 133–173.

Warren, M. R., Mapp, K. L, & Community Organizing and School Reform Project. (2011). *A match on dry grass: Community organizing as a catalyst for school reform*. New York: Oxford University Press.

Weiss, E., & Long, D. (2013). *Market-oriented education reform rhetoric trumps reality: The impacts of test-based teacher evaluations, school closures, and increased charter school access on student outcomes in Chicago, New York City, and Washington, DC*. Washington, DC: Broader, Bolder Approach to Education. Retrieved from http://www.boldapproach.org/rhetoric-trumps-reality

West, M. R., & Peterson, P. E. (2006). The efficacy of choice threats within school accountability systems: Results from legislatively induced experiments. *The Economic Journal, 116*(510), C46–62.

Wilson, W. J. (1987). *The truly disadvantaged: The inner city, the underclass, and public policy*. Chicago, IL: University of Chicago Press.

Wong, K. K., & Shen, F. X. (2013). *Mayoral governance and student achievement: How mayor-led districts are improving school and student performance*.

Washington, DC: Center for American Progress. Retrieved from https://www.americanprogress.org/issues/education/report/2013/03/22/56934/mayoral-governance-and-student-achievement/

Yin, R. K. (2014). *Case study research: Design and methods* (5th ed.). Thousand Oaks, CA: Sage Publications.

Yoshikawa, H., Aber, J. L., & Beardslee, W. R. (2012). The effects of poverty on the mental, emotional, and behavioral health of children and youth: Implications for prevention. *American Psychologist, 67*(4), 272.

CHAPTER 4

CURRENT RESEARCH ON ARAB FEMALE EDUCATIONAL LEADERS' CAREER AND LEADERSHIP

A Review of Extant Literature
and Future Directions for Research

Khalid Arar
The Center for Academic Studies, Israel

Izhar Oplatka
Tel Aviv University

INTRODUCTION

Most of the research on women in educational administration has been limited to Anglo-American and European countries (e.g., Blackmore, 1999; Coleman, 2011: Grogan & Shakeshaft, 2011; Klenke, 2011), yet women are increasingly entering educational administration in other areas of the world, including Arab countries (Al-Suwaihal, 2010; Omair, 2008; Oplatka, 2006). Arab women's reality has become one of the most rapidly changing elements in Arab societies. Women in Arab societies can no longer be described as scared, inferior, domestic women who hardly leave their houses (Omair, 2008). Recently, Arab women have been even appointed to ministerial and parliamentary positions, they run businesses and sit as presidents in national universities (Al-Lamsky, 2007, Dubai Women Establishment 2009).

In this chapter, we relate to women in the societies of the "Arab world." This term is used as defined by the United Nations, referring to the 22 countries of the Arab League, linked by their geographic proximity (in the Middle East and North Africa) and cultural, religious as well as historical similarities. Some of these countries, for example Saudi Arabia and Kuwait, are among the richest in the world due to oil exports, while others, such as Somalia or the Sudan are among the poorest, yet all of them are vulnerable due to their relatively undiversified economies and limited exports (UNDP, 2004). Additionally, we also relate to women in Arab society in Israel which has many common characteristics with the Arab world.

Arab women's participation in the political, economic, or social domains of the Arab world is hindered by a number of unwritten social mores and codes in male-dominated societies, characterized by a patriarchal hierarchic culture. Thus, the voice of Arab women has seldom been heard in public discussions (Omair, 2008, p. 108).

Although there has been a dramatic increase in research on gender and educational leadership in Western countries during the last three decades (Blackmore, 1999; Coleman, 2011; Grogan & Shakeshaft, 2011), our knowledge about gender and educational leadership in developing societies is relatively limited (Arar et al., 2013; Oplatka, 2006). There is also little data concerning cultural determinants that affect female leadership in Arab societies. This chapter seeks to explore cultural and structural determinants and challenges affecting women's educational leadership in the Arab world. More specifically, the chapter poses the following two questions: (a) what are the barriers blocking Arab women's progress in the field of education and the factors facilitating their progress? and (b) what are the characteristics of Arab women leaders and the current challenges that they face in leadership positions in the studied countries? In order to answer these questions, we conducted a systemic review of extant literature on women leaders in education in the Arab world (Booth et al., 2012). In the attempt to respond to these questions, we pay special attention to the identification of cultural determinants that affect female leadership in traditional societies.

The review is built in two parts: first, a review and critical analysis of the limited literature about Arab women in educational leadership both in English and Arabic language, identifying main themes uncovered by this research. The second part presents illustrations of these themes from empirical studies of Arab female educational leaders' voices in several countries, some of them gleaned from interviews conducted and collected by the first author. The chapter concludes with some suggestions for possible further research about Arab women in educational administration in the Arab world.

WOMEN'S LEADERSHIP IN THE ARAB WORLD

Historically, leadership has primarily been associated with masculinity, and women's access to leadership has been constricted by a system of socially transmitted expectations and goals. It has been theorized that men, by nature, seek prestige and status while women aspire to create successful relationships (Coleman, 2011; Grogan & Shakeshaft, 2011). Yet, as more women play a role in the global economy, they have also begun to seek careers in management and leadership. Kanter (1997) referred to the relatively few women given prominent positions in management as "token" women, who are often held up as symbols or representatives for all women. Yet, globally, at almost every level, women managers face blocks to their social and employment mobility; discrimination; and stereotypes (Klenke, 2011).

In the "Western" world as women increasingly studied higher education and entered professions such as law and politics and education, some became activists, voicing women's difficulties in political campaigns and developing new lines of academic study (Moghadam, 2009). Although these developments were rooted in the "Western" world, feminist research and analysis has found surprising similarities in women's development, orders of preference and discourse in different world states (Coleman, 2011; Metcalfe, 2006; Moghadam, 2009). Pioneer women leaders in the Arab world formed study groups, while more radical thinkers joined left-wing parties or underground movements aiming to promote women's rights to equality (ibid.). Yet, the Arab world remains largely conservative and traditional and the dominant patriarchal society has not easily relinquished its hold on power. Pioneer female social and political leaders have encountered serious opposition, some activists lost their lives, others were imprisoned or exiled, for example, in Sudan, and Algeria (Ismael & Ismael, 2008).

To some extent though, the demands of these women have been heard and dramatic changes have been seen in the last few decades throughout the Arab world; for example, in Bahrein, the Gulf States, and even in Egypt and Yemen, so that women appear more in the public sphere and take more responsibility for work, even gradually attaining senior positions in various organizations. Arab women have been appointed to parliamentary and ministerial positions; they direct companies and a few have become university deacons (Al-Suwaihal, 2010; Dubai Women Establishment, 2009).

In addition to facing political pressure for reform, poverty in many Arab countries, especially in Northern Africa, creates an impetus for women to become more active outside the home when families are forced to depend on the additional income that female family members can provide. For example, the ratio of estimated female to male income (2007) was 0.35 in Bahrein and Kuwait, 0.31 and 0.23 in Egypt (Dubai Women Establishment, 2009). According to the International Labor Organization (2013):

> The status of Arab women is undoubtedly central to addressing the challenges faced by Arab economies. Even though Arab women have achieved high levels of education, these have not been translated into economic outcomes....Labor force participation rates for men average 76% in the Middle East and North Africa (MENA) versus 74% for the rest of the world, but the respective rates for women are 27% in MENA versus 56% for the rest of the world. (International Labor Organization, 2014, p. 15)

This general data reflects the under-representative participation of women in the general labor force in the Arab world, ranging from illiterate menial women workers to women holding academic, professional, and administrative roles. Yet, wealthier Arab countries are finding that educated women have much to offer in the public domain and many Arab men have come to appreciate and often respect this development (Moghadem, 2009) and this has led to dramatic developments in certain wealthier states; for example, in Bahrain women labor participation increased 668%, and in the UAE by 548% (International Labor Organization, 2014). Labor laws in many Arab states now protect working women. Constitutions and labor laws in certain Arab countries (such as Jordan and Egypt), explicitly prohibit gender discrimination in the workplace (CAWTAR, 2009). In Algeria, Slackman (2007) reports that women make up 70% of the country's lawyers and 60% of its judges and also dominate the field of medicine, so that, increasingly, women are contributing more to household income than men.

Politically, the Arab world was relatively late in granting universal suffrage to women. New Zealand first gave women the vote in 1893 and the United States in 1920. In comparison, women have had the right to vote in Lebanon since 1952, and in Egypt since 1956, but Saudi Arabia consistently denied this right though the King's decree in 2011 granted women the right to vote from 2015 (Interparliamentary Union for Democracy, 2013). Arab women citizens of Israel have the right to vote since the establishment of the state in 1948.

Women's participation in parliament recorded its highest regional increase (2.8 points to 16%) in the Arab States in 2009, with participation rates ranging from 10.8% in Morocco's lower house (1.1% of its upper house) to 23% in the United Arab Emirates parliament (Dubai Women Establishment, 2009), In Israel, only two women from the Arab minority (20% of the state's population) have been elected and they faced much resistance in Israel's Parliament. Notably, in 2013, King Abdullah appointed

30 women (20%) to the 150-member National Advisory Council (Interparliamentary Union for Democracy, 2013).

Arab Women as Educational Leaders

There is little specific comparative statistical data available concerning Arab women serving in educational administration positions. Due to restrictions on their integration within the public sphere and presumptions concerning their "unfitness" for "masculine" roles there is a high concentration of women in what are considered "female" roles in health and education. In 2014, women comprised 58% of Saudi Arabia's college students but only 14% of its labor force, much lower than in neighboring countries. 85% of employed Saudi women work in education, 6% in public health, and 9.5% in the public sector including a single symbolic woman Education minister who was appointed in 2009 (Miller, 2011). It seems that although Saudi Arabian women are allowed to study, the majority of those who study are unable to implement the knowledge gained in their studies in a professional career.

According to The Center of Arab Women for Training and Research (CAWTAR, 2009) in Morocco, women represent 48% of health sector employees, 33% in primary and secondary education, and 22% of higher education and scientific research. In Saudi Arabia, women account for 7% of total active population and their presence in the health and education sectors reached 90% of the total female active workforce. In 2008, women constituted 28% of Israel's Arab elementary school principals and 14% of principals in middle to high school education (Arar et al., 2013).

Blocks to Women's Professional Advancement in the Arab World—Cultural Determinants

As noted above, women's increased participation in the realms of politics, economics, and society is neither uniform nor consistent in the Arab world. Their integration is often delayed or hindered, even sometimes using threats or violence due to the persistence of traditional cultural codes by those men and institutions that see women's work as undermining their patriarchal domination and control of power. Moghadam (2009) noted that limitations on women's participation in the economy in the Middle East and North Africa (MENA) stem from two factors: neo-liberal globalization and Islamic family law. In particular, she noted the lack of two basic rights: the limitation of women's mobility and free choice of occupation that hinder women's participation in the workforce and increases their dependence on men and the Arab social norm that prohibits women's presence in the public sphere, requiring strict separation of the sexes in public, in prayer, and even in the home (Guthrie, 2001). Discussing the Islamic view of separation of the sexes, Metcalfe (2006) noted that although the principle of separation is not "officially determined" by the religion it continues to limit women's ability to venture beyond the private sphere and to train for and gain access to opportunities for social advancement. This social norm has only just begun to be eroded in the present century yet it still constitutes one of the main obstacles hindering the promotion of Arab women aspiring to attain managerial roles (Al-Suwaihal, 2010; Omair, 2008).

Arab culture shapes expectations regarding leadership so that it is seen as an exclusively male realm of activity (Arar & Oplatka, 2014) and women are seen as unfit and lacking the necessary skills and abilities to become leaders. These values are used to justify male dominance (Al-Suwaihal, 2010). Although women throughout the world encounter resistance when they attempt to break through the "glass ceiling" to senior leadership and management positions, in the Arab world women must also struggle to overcome assumptions about their inability to manage, and must continually prove their worth at the workplace (Ameen, 2001). For example, Al-Hussein (2011) found that leading women in Jordan's Ministry of Education face various challenges to reach leadership positions, most important were: both males' and females' negative stereotypes of women, the women's limited ambition, lack of self-confidence and lack of a sense of self-efficacy. Similarly, Abu-Khader (2012) noted that Saudi-Arabian women face challenges stemming from organizational, technical, and cultural restrictions, a low self-image and lack of empowerment.

In contrast to studies noted above that attempted to identify obstacles that delay Arab women's professional advancement, a study by The Arab Women Leadership Outlook (Dubai Women Establishment, 2009) surveyed four groups of Arab women (94 women in all) to find enabling factors that had allowed them to advance. The groups were: (a) business leaders, (b) political leaders, (c) civil society leaders, and (d) Arab women thought-leaders in the media, academic or cultural spheres. Although the women came from different Arab states, they were found to share common characteristics. In particular, seven key enablers were identified for their ability to advance to positions of leadership and to influence their environment: legal structure, political environment, socioeconomic environment, culture, religion, education and media (ibid.). Following the presentation of the blocks that hinder women's advancement to management positions in general and in particular in education, we now present the method that we used to review the different studies of women leaders in education in the Arab world.

THE LITERATURE REVIEW METHOD

Literature Search

The current chapter is based on a systematic review that aims at providing an exhaustive summary of the literature relevant for the research questions at hand in a thorough and transparent manner (Booth et al., 2012). To access current literature, we conducted an extensive online search of peer reviewed literature and published dissertations from numerous databases, such as GoogleScholar, EMERALD, Taylor and Francis Online, Elsevier, EBSCOhost, Education Resources information Center (ERIC), J-STOR, Springer-Link, SAGE Journals Online, and ProQuest from January 2000 until July 2014, with the exception of one earlier paper Also, we searched for referenced papers and dissertations written in Arabic (the first author's language) in Google-Scholar. The search was carried out using keywords such as "women principals," "Arab countries," "female leaders" plus the name of the Arab country, "female educational leadership," "Middle-East and education."

We included studies in our final review that: (a) were published in English or Arabic; (b) were published in peer-reviewed journals or dissertations from January 2000 until October, 2014; (c) used common quantitative, qualitative, or mixed methodologies; (d) included female teachers or leaders in their sample of participants; (e) were conducted in K–12 education settings; and (f) focused specifically on the career or role of female education leaders in Arab countries. Peer review research used in Business Administration or Organizational Behavior, studies about the status of women in Arab countries in general, and studies relating solely to female teachers and not to principals were excluded. Papers that were written by the same author(s) including similar findings were scrutinized very carefully to prevent repetitions.

In total, 20 studies formed the data base for our review. One of the main weaknesses we identified is a lack of sufficient studies on the topic addressed in this review, especially the scarcity of quantitative or large-scale studies. There is also limited research published in this area in high-impact journals, for this reason we also decided to include two university dissertations on a relevant topic.

A total of 15 studies were retained based on the above-indicated criteria. In addition, five studies were added to this selection by tracing back references included in the retrieved literature. In total, 20 studies formed the basis for answering our research questions. One of the main weaknesses we identified is a lack of sufficient studies on the topic addressed in this review, let alone the very few quantitative or large-scale studies. There is also limited research published in this area in high-impact journals.

Yet, as far as we can ascertain, the collection of 18 papers and two dissertations upon which this review is based constitutes a large proportion of the English-language and Arabic-language articles published on women in educational administration in Arab societies. Table 4.1 presents the reviewed papers/works.

Analysis

We employed qualitative content analysis to analyze the journal papers and dissertation using consistent comparison to discover patterns, emphases, and themes in the array of documents (Altheide, 1996). Initially, each of the empirical research papers selected was subjected to review by the researchers to extract key information about: country of origin, the size and type of sample, the data collection method, the background and context of the research, the theoretical basis for the research, and the key findings.

The first stage of content analysis included extensive reading, sorting, and searching through the papers/dissertation. This led to the coding of categories (e.g., leadership style, barriers to career advancement, the status of women, gendered values). Consistent with the method of qualitative content analysis depicted above, topic analysis, at the first phase, was based on common categories/themes previously identified in "Western" studies of female leadership (e.g., leadership, policy imperatives, gender discrimination, etc.). We were careful to adhere first to common themes prior to any attempt to devise new categories and topics, lest some of them be new titles for existing themes. When a particular topic did not match any of the common categories it was placed into a temporary, new sub-theme (e.g., the place of women in Bedouin society).

At the second stage, new themes and categories were identified and compared until main themes and sub-categories in each article/thesis abstract were identified. "Extreme" and "key" differences within each category were also compared and contrasted (e.g., males and females' perspectives of educational leadership). In the final stage, the data were contextualized and compared with the purposes of their respective articles and themes were then compared among the reviewed works.

The open coding of the abstracts was followed by a comparison of the abstracts and chapters within every category and among the categories to verify clear boundaries between the categories and also to trace inconsistencies. We are aware, nevertheless, of the potential influence of the analysts' own interpretations and personal histories upon the selection of the topics addressed in the papers. Therefore, a colleague trained in qualitative analysis verified a sample of themes grounded from the data and provided useful comments for the analyst. We now present the themes that emerged from the collected data.

TABLE 4.1 Papers/Thesis About Women in Educational Leadership and Administration Within Arab Societies (N = 20 papers)

Author(s)	Purpose(s)	Subject(s)	Themes Expressed	Sample Size	Methodology	Journal	Country
Al-Jaradat, M. (2014)	Describes challenges facing women academic leaders in secondary schools	Female principals	1	187	Quantitative	International Education Studies	Jordan
Abu-Tineh, A. (2013)	Examines professional, social, community and family aspects of the lives of Arab women in managerial roles	Leadership Effectiveness	1	500 teachers	Quantitative	Educational Management Administration and Leadership	Jordan
Al-Jaber, Z. (1996)	Identifies gender differences in leadership style following the Iraqi invasion of Kuwait	Male and female principals	2	759	Quantitative	Educational Management, Administration and Leadership	Kuwait
Al-Suwaihel, O.E (2010)	Identifies how Kuwaiti female leaders perceive cultural influences on their personal and professional experiences in educational leadership positions.	Educational female leaders in government and non-government organizations	2, 3	5 female educational leaders	Qualitative	Contemporary Issues in Education Research	Kuwait

(continued)

TABLE 4.1 Papers/Thesis About Women in Educational Leadership and Administration Within Arab Societies (N = 20 papers) (continued)

Author(s)	Purpose(s)	Subject(s)	Themes Expressed	Sample Size	Methodology	Journal	Country
Askar, A. & Ahmad, M. (2003)	Identifies factors determining attitudes towards women occupying supervisory roles	Women supervisors in	2	278 participants	Quantitative	*Journal of the Social Sciences* (Arabic)	Kuwait
Akkary, R. (2013)	Explores the role of the school principal and compares gender differences in principalship	Secondary school principals	1, 2, 3	53 principals 8 female 45 male	Qualitative	*Educational Management Administration and Leadership*	Lebanon
Saadat, M., & Taiem, M.H. (2011)	Examines the extent of managerial knowledge of male and female school principals in Jenin	Knowledge management	2	127 male and female school principals	Quantitative	*Journal of The Open University of Jerusalem* (Arabic)	Palestinian Authority Territories
Abdul-Ghaffar, N.A. (2011)	Examines management types and their relationship to the thinking styles of female secondary school principals	Female principals management styles	2	118 Female high school principals	Quantitative	*Journal of Literature and Humanities* (Arabic)	Jeddah Saudi Arabia

(continued)

TABLE 4.1 Papers/Thesis About Women in Educational Leadership and Administration Within Arab Societies (N = 20 papers) (continued)

Author(s)	Purpose(s)	Subject(s)	Themes Expressed	Sample Size	Methodology	Journal	Country
Bent-Hatim, S. (2011).	Identifies the professional competencies to lead school change of female principals	Leading change	2, 3	325 female teachers from all education levels	Quantitative	PhD thesis (Arabic)	Makah, Saudi Arabia
Hamdan, A. (2005)	Explores restraints affecting women and achievements of women in the field of education	Socio-political overview	2	NA	Phenomenological Overview	International Education Journal	Saudi Arabia
Esa, A. (2008)	Compares leadership styles of female and male principals and school outcomes	Leadership styles and pedagogic management	2	331 female and male principals	Quantitative	University of Damascus Journal (Arabic)	Damascus, Syria
Kathija, A. (2003)	Identifies barriers to women's advancement, women's current leadership roles and participation in decision making	Female principals	1, 2, 3	15	Qualitative	PhD (Arabic)	United Arab Emirates

(continued)

TABLE 4.1 Papers/Thesis About Women in Educational Leadership and Administration Within Arab Societies (N = 20 papers) (continued)

Author(s)	Purpose(s)	Subject(s)	Themes Expressed	Sample Size	Methodology	Journal	Country
Abu-Asbah, K; Abu-Nasra, M., & Abu-Baker, K. (2014)	Examines gender perceptions of male and female teachers towards female principals' appointment	Female school principals	3	302 Arab male and female teachers	Quantitative	*Journal of Middle East Women Studies*	Arabs in Israel
Abu-Rabia-Queder, S & Oplatka, I. (2008)	Examines barriers facing school inspectors	Female inspectors	1, 3	4	Qualitative	*JEA*	Arab Bedouin society in Israel
Addi-Raccah, A. (2007)	Examines the intersection of the two variables, female gender and minorities in school leadership positions	Survey of national teaching staff	1, 4	25769	Quantitative	*EAQ*	Arabs in Israel
Arar, K & Abu-Rabia-Queder, S. (2011)	Investigates managerial career development of pioneer female Arab principals	Arab Bedouin women vs. Rural women	1, 2	2	Qualitative	*Gender & Education*	Arab society & Bedouin society in Israel

(continued)

TABLE 4.1 Papers/Thesis About Women in Educational Leadership and Administration Within Arab Societies (N = 20 papers) (continued)

Author(s)	Purpose(s)	Subject(s)	Themes Expressed	Sample Size	Methodology	Journal	Country
Arar, K & Oplatka, I. (2012)	Investigates teachers' perceptions of masculinity vs. femininity and gender differences in leadership styles employed by principals	Arab Muslim teachers in MA program	3	38	Qualitative	*School Leadership & Management*	Arab society in Israel
Arar, K. & Abramovitz, R. (2013)	Examines teachers' attitudes towards appointment of Arab women to leadership positions	Arab teachers	2, 3	405 teachers 127 men 240 women	Quantitative	*Management in Education*	Arab society in Israel
Arar, K. (2014)	Discusses the characteristics of women discipline supervisors	Female supervisors	1, 2, 3	4	Qualitative	*Gender & Education*	Arab society in Israel
Shapira, T & Arar, K (2010)	Examines professional, social, community and family aspects of the lives of Arab women in managerial roles	Arab women principals	1, 2	7	Qualitative	*JEA*	Arab society in Israel

THE STATE OF THE ART: FEMALE ARAB LEADERS

Three major themes emerged from the current review; the first theme points to a wide variety of barriers hindering women who aspire to build a managerial career in the Arab world, that have led to the comparatively late entry of Arab women into educational leadership and also to factors facilitating Arab women's career advancement. The second theme deals with female leadership style and teachers' attitudes towards female leadership, and the last theme discusses some of the challenges and issues faced by contemporary Arab women educational leaders in their work.

Half of the studies that investigated the phenomenon of Arab women in education leadership and administration used quantitative methodology (11 papers) researching male and female teachers' attitudes and perceptions of women's leadership, one of these was based on an analysis of national assessment of schools; and two used surveys completed by teaching staff and principals (Addi-Raccah, 2007; Bent-Hatim, 2011). Eight papers used qualitative narrative methodologies, and one used a phenomenological overview (Hamdan, 2005). Most of the reviewed studies were grounded in feminist viewpoints, focusing specifically on women leaders.

With regard to content, nine papers related to the issue of women's resistance to gender distinctions (Abu-Asbah et al., 2014; Abu-Rabia-Queder & Oplatka, 2008; Akkary, 2013; Al-Jaber, 1996; Al-Jaradat, 2014; Al-Suwaihel, 2010; Arar & Abramovitz, 2013; Arar & Abu-Rabia-Queder, 2008; Kathija, 2003) while two papers described a discourse of rebellion against the inferior status of women and patriarchal suppression of women's career path, phenomena deeply rooted in the Arab society (Abu-Rabia-Queder & Oplatka, 2008; Hamdan, 2005). Both these papers describe cultural hindrances to women's advancement in Arab Bedouin societies. Other papers related to the characteristics of women who had reached leadership positions in education, noting characteristics that led to their success and/or their leadership styles.

All of the reviewed studies were conducted after 2000, probably because very few Arab women were appointed to educational leadership positions in the Arab world before the present millennium. These studies provide an opportunity to look at the lives, careers, and development of Arab women's educational leadership in a very unique cultural context. The qualitative studies especially attempted to listen to the usually unheard voices of these women, describing their difficulties in attaining their posts, the characteristics that allow them to cope with and overcome these difficulties and the changes that they bring to the institutions to which they dedicate their work.

A geographical analysis of the reviewed papers shows that a large proportion of them studied female Arab educational leaders who live in Israel (eight papers), while the rest of the papers investigated female educational leaders from Jordan, United Arab Emirates, Lebanon, and Kuwait, Syria, Saudi Arabia and the Palestinian Authority. Unfortunately, we found no available data in English about women educational leaders from many other Arab countries, especially the poorer countries of North Africa such as Egypt.

Six studies were written in Arabic (including two dissertations), all the other papers were written in English. Half of the papers were written by female authors (nine papers), six were co-authored by male and female authors, one co-authored by two male researchers, and four solely by male researchers. Most of the articles were written by Arab authors, three articles were co-authored with non-Arab authors, mainly Jewish researchers, and one was authored by a single Jewish author. Just one article out of the 20 was a phenomenological theoretical paper, while all the others were based on empirical research.

Barriers to and Facilitators of Women's Career Advancement

Nine of the identified articles (see Table 4.1) dealt with the existence of barriers/obstacles to or factors that facilitated women's career-building, some of these obstacles have also been identified by researchers in "Western" societies (e.g., low self-confidence, embedded cultural, and social gender discrimination, low female participation in secondary education, the need for women to balance work-home duties) (Coleman, 2011; Grogan & Shakeshaft, 2011). However, our review revealed particular obstacles for women in Arab societies (e.g., cultural restrictions, low girls' participation in high school education, majority of men in school principalship and in teaching positions, especially in high schools) (Al-Jaradat, 2014; Al-Suwihel, 2010; Shapira, Arar, & Azaize, 2010). A study by Al-Lamsky (2007) among Omani women managers, indicated that the main obstacles for these women were limited opportunities for higher education, discriminatory appointment and promotion practices within the organization, traditional attitudes of male opposition towards working women and towards women in management, a male dominated domain within the organizations, absence of policies and legislations to ensure participation of women in management positions, a lack of professional networking for women, a lack of female role-models, a lack of professional management developing programs, and a lack of day care-centers.

Low Self-Confidence

Some researchers argue that women's low self-confidence and self-esteem with respect to their management capabilities may deter or stunt women's career advancement in school. Perhaps this is a contributory reason for the fact that in Arab society in Israel women were found to have a far longer career path before reaching leadership positions than men; female Arab leaders, therefore, seem to be older compared to colleague men (Addi-Raccah, 2007). In Israel, Arab women's sense of self-efficacy was found to be much lower than men's, despite their better education and professional experience (Arar & Abramovitz, 2013). A similar finding was found among women from Jordan and Saudi-Arabia whose career advancement path was blocked due to retention of traditional images of the "right" women (Al-Jaradat, 2014; Hamdan, 2005). Also in Jordan, Abu-Tineh (2013) found that female direct reports of female leaders in educational institutions rated the effectiveness of their female leaders less than male direct reports of male leaders. Nevertheless, in the same study Abu-Tineh found there were no significant differences between female and male leaders in rating their own leadership effectiveness or in competencies overall or skills overall that could be attributed to their gender.

Entrenched Socio-Cultural Gender Segregation and Discrimination

Another major obstacle to women's access to leadership positions noted in Arab schools is the socio-cultural structuring that bifurcates the society into male and female arenas (Hamdan, 2005), while power is held by males. In fact, the progress of Arab women has always been restrained so that they mostly remain in submissive roles both at home and in their society, as Arar et al. (2013) explain:

> In Arab society a distinction is drawn between two different spheres—the domestic sphere to which a woman is assigned and from which she derives respect and status in her society, and the public sphere which she 'visits' temporarily from time to time to fulfill specified tasks, this includes the organizational-political sphere that is blocked for her. (p. 19)

Hamdan (2005) described a similar state of affairs in Saudi Arabia:

> Women's issues in Saudi society and the gender inequalities that are obvious in its education system are institutionalized and difficult to dislodge through individual action...the uniqueness of Saudi women's situation is derived from their presence and yet non-presence in the public sphere. (p. 45)

Omair (2008) found that embedded gender perceptions slowed the career advancement of Arab women to top positions in many countries. Saudi Arabian women principals' lack of power is a case in point: education is segregated for boys and girls in Saudi Arabia; in most of the girls' public schools in this country the principals are women, but the powerful governing boards are predominately in the hands of the exclusively male religious authority.

Yet, while in Saudi Arabia there is total separation between the genders in the public sphere, in Lebanon and Tunis many schools have mixed classes. Amani Hamdan (2005) argues that women face more challenging cultural deterrents in Saudi Arabia than in other Arab societies, especially because this country has never been colonialized, but rather has been controlled by strong Islamic groups that have marginalized women from all public spheres.

To a far stricter extent than in Western societies, the entrenched cultural norms of many Arab societies (such as, Jordan, Kuwait, United Arab Emirates and Saudi Arabia) attribute certain tasks and spheres of responsibility to each gender (Al-Jaber, 1996; Al-Jaradat, 2014; Hamdan, 2005). Even in Arab society in Israel, where many Arabs have been influenced by modern values, there is still some gender separation in education institutions in rural areas (Abu-Asbah et al., 2014; Arar et al., 2013). According to Al-Lamsky (2007), in the Gulf societies, recently described as "bastions of patriarchy and male chauvinism" (p. 49), it is widely believed that the women's place is primarily at home. If professionally inclined, their participation is expected to be in areas of education, health (mainly nursing) and other support or clerical jobs primarily at the lower end of organizational hierarchies. Leadership positions are typically reserved for men (Al-Jaber, 1996; Al-Lamsky, 2007; Al-Suwiahel, 2010; Hamdan, 2005).

The findings of Addi-Raccah (2007) indicate that in Arab schools in Israel, the glass ceiling effect is already effective at the lowest rank of the schools' administrative positions (see also: Askar & Ahmad, 2003). Addi-Raccah (2007) examined the intersection of women and minorities in school leadership positions and argued that Arab culture suppresses women's attempts to attain high rank positions. Similarly, the study of Akkary (2013) on the role and context of the Lebanese school principal provides empirical data about the female school principal's work context in Lebanon demonstrating how this socio-cultural context prevents women's equal advancement in line with their male counterparts, and how their role is shaped by this environment. Specific cultural and religious beliefs and values that define the feminine role in terms of marriage, especially early marriage, housekeeping and child-raising constitute an additional barrier deterring women from attempting to build a career outside the home.

Studies by Jaber (2005) and Arar et al. (2013) showed that Palestinian women leaders in Arab educational institutions in Israel face legal, political, familial and administrative challenges. The fact that Arab communities in Israel are often far from the urban work market, and that there are cultural restrictions on women's mobility often isolates Arab women and restricts their working opportunities subjecting them to work in local schools where internal municipal political forces hinder their advancement and male candidates are preferred for the limited number of senior posts (Arar et al., 2013).

Low Participation in Secondary Education

Very low levels of girls' participation in primary and secondary education in many Arab societies make it less possible for women to acquire the skills, training, and competencies necessary for professional and managerial positions in education; this is especially true in North African Arab societies such as Morocco, Tunisia and Libya (Hamdan, 2005). In many Arab communities, parents have insufficient finances to pay for their children's education, a poor physical environment and poor infra-structure. Some Bedouin girls in Israel need to walk long distances in order to reach schools (Abu-Rabia-Queder & Oplatka, 2008). A similar situation is witnessed in tribal societies in Libya, Morocco and Saudi Arabia (Hamdan, 2005), where access to education is limited due to poor infra-structure and/or budgetary shortages.

Work–Life Balance

Arab women are still underrepresented in administrative and leadership positions, and this fact was evidenced in most of the reviewed studies. One factor that deters Arab women from becoming educational leaders is the need to continue to cope with family duties and commitments while simultaneously dealing with the external pressures of the workplace (Akkary, 2013; Arar et al., 2013), attempting to achieve a workable balance between the demands of their family role and their role as leaders and administrators in the educational institution (Al-Jaradat, 2014).

Arab societies seem especially reluctant to abandon their traditional view that women should be primarily committed to the home and their children (Mostafa, 2005; Omair, 2008), and most Arab families invest more to educate their sons rather than their daughters, assuming that boys are a greater economic asset (Hamdan, 2005). In the patriarchal family, girls are socialized from childhood to assume a domestic role that fulfills socially stipulated female tasks (Abu-Rabia-Queder & Oplatka, 2008). Women who go out to work are still expected to continue their domestic functions, and it is unacceptable for men to assist in these roles, or to employ assistance from non-family members (Omair, 2008). Yet, in the collectivist Arab society where extended family members live in close vicinity to the nuclear family and in cases where the family approves of the woman's work outside the house the family may assist. This is especially vital in rural societies with poor municipal services, since it is only with family support that the Arab working woman can work for longer hours, leaving babies' care to their grandmothers (Shapira, Arar, & Azaiza, 2010). Despite the achievements of three feminist waves in "Western" countries, women in these countries also still report a similar difficulty of balancing demands of work and home. In the "Western" individualistic society, the nuclear family often lives far away from the extended family and consequently the working woman has limited assistance from mother and siblings.

Facilitators of Women's Career Advancement

In interviews with 21 top Arab women in educational administration in Israel, Arar et al. (2013) concluded that the empowerment processes of women who have successfully reached senior educational management positions started early in their childhood in a supportive family. Women managers described the support of male relatives: fathers, brothers, and spouses, who promoted and funded their higher education and encouraged their aspirations for a professional career despite the resistance and opposition of the patriarchal society in which they lived. Some of the women noted that from an early age they had exhibited leadership qualities which had been respected and encouraged by their local environment.

Several other studies have found that those Arab women who reached educational leadership positions had the support of their parents and spouse, providing them with coping strategies and tools for participation in the public realm. Other factors identified as promoting Arab women's career success are their self-determination and inner drive for success, opportunities for access to all levels of education and academic achievement, self-confidence, diligence and perseverance, job opportunities and potential for professional growth and development (Al-Jaradat, 2014; Abu-Rabia-Queder & Oplatka, 2008; Arar et al., 2013; Omair, 2008).

Al-Jaradat (2014) found that the highest ranked personal traits identified by respondents as ensuring women academic leaders' success in Jordanian secondary schools were energy, self-confidence, and independence (p. 149). A study from the United Arab Emirates (Kathija, 2003) showed that the crucial resource for women leaders was access to educational opportunities. The second most important factor was family support.

Female Leadership Style and Teachers' Attitudes

Fourteen of the studies related to female leadership style and teachers' attitudes towards female leaders (see Table 4.1). Interestingly, from the few reports on women's leadership styles in Arab societies, it seems that women adopt what is usually identified as a "masculine" authoritative leadership style in their early career in educational management (Al-Jaber, 1996; Arar et al., 2013; Esa, 2008). After establishing their authority and leadership in the schools they shift to an "androgenic" style, that is. a combination of "masculine" and "feminine" leadership styles (Oplatka, 2006, p. 614) derived from a combination of the strong authoritarian style of the Arab man (Esa, 2008; Omair, 2008, p. 114), with women's own feminine tendencies and needs (Arar & Oplatka, 2014). It also seems that these women are more likely than men to express and employ emotions in their leadership style (Abdul-Ghaffar, 2011; Arar & Oplatka, 2014). Additionally, most of the women leaders refrain from making decisions concerning building construction because any physical aspect of school management seems to be considered a male issue.

In contrast, Abdul-Ghaffar (2011) found in his study of the management types and thinking styles of female principals in Saudi Arabia that female principals mainly favored an autocratic leadership style compared to male principals who adopted an analytical leadership style. In Syria, Esa (2008) found that while male principals tended to adopt an authoritative leadership style, female school principals were more enthusiastic about meeting school aims and concentrating on students' achievements. In the Palestinian Authority territories, Saadat and Taiem (2011) noted that female school principals used information technology in their management more than male counterparts. Al-Suwaihel (2010) found that the Kuwaiti culture values masculine qualities such as an authoritative, controlling approach to management and this significantly influences leadership practices. Arar and Oplatka (2014) attained similar findings in Arab society in Israel, detailing masculine and feminine styles of leadership, which are influenced by traditional patriarchal norms and attitudes.

Yet, despite male domination of the Arab world's education systems, there was evidence that women leaders in three Arab countries (United Arab Emirates, Kuwait, Lebanon) and in the Arab society in Israel were able to make a difference by manifesting a "feminine" leadership style in the educational institutions they led, even though as Akkary (2013) noted, this was expressed at a moderate level. A common feminine management style has been identified among women managers in different developing countries (Oplatka, 2006). For example, a caring, participatory attitude is expressed by female supervisors in the Arab society in Israel (Arar, 2014). Rania a female Arab supervisor illustrates this leadership style:

> ...Many teachers call me and say, 'you give us tools, we see the changes everywhere.' I don't have to say, 'I'm the supervisor, I'm the principal... I work quietly together with them and the results lead to even more successes.... (Arar, 2014, p. 418)

Similarly, in Lebanon, Akkary (2013) noted female principals' participatory approach in relations with both staff and students. Female principals felt it was crucial to create harmonious staff relations, in order to realize their vision for the school, and this led most of them to adopt a collaborative style of management, which stressed teamwork above individual effort. Likewise, a study by Al-Jaber (1996) among female principals in Kuwait illuminated their caring attitudes and their work to increase trust and personal security. Like their counterparts in Western countries, Arab female educational leaders tend to have a student-focused approach.

Teacher Attitudes

It seems that die-hard attitudes in the Arab world regarding the difference in abilities of men and women continue to color evaluation of the effectiveness of women's work as leaders: a study by Abu-Tineh (2013) in Jordan found that male direct reports of female leaders rated their effectiveness to be, on average, low moderate; while, female direct reports of male leaders rated them to be, on average, high moderate. Studies in the Arab world have found that Arab teachers generally have negative attitudes toward female leadership (Abu-Asbah et al., 2014; Addi-Raccah, 2007; Al-Jaradat, 2014; Akkary, 2013; Arar & Abramovitz, 2013) and often both male and female teachers prefer working with a male principal rather than a female (Akkary, 2013), so that female principals must often face the reluctance of staff to work with female leaders (Al-Jaradat, 2014). The following citation from a female teacher (Hanan) appears in Arar and Oplatka's (2012) study that investigated Arab teachers' attitudes towards women's leadership: "a leader transmits power, security, control, and strength, not gossip. That's why I have always preferred working with a male principal" (p. 12).

Arar and Abramovitz (2013) studied attitudes toward the gradual feminization of school principalship in Arab society in Israel. Their results revealed a wide gap between the attitudes of men and women, with women expressing more favorable attitudes towards working female principalship. Similarly, Abu-Asbah and colleagues (2014) examined gender perceptions of male and female teachers in Israel toward female principals, and found that the teachers, especially the male teachers expressed resistance to the notion of gender equality. The researchers noted that transition of Arab society from traditional to modern society has not eliminated the patriarchal regime, and that neither women's improved level of education nor the increased numbers of women in management have been able to alter attitudes concerning gender equality. Interestingly, findings of a study by Askar and Ahmad (2003) of factors determining attitudes towards women occupying supervisory positions in various organizations (including education institutions) in Kuwait indicated that in general there were relatively positive attitudes towards women managers, although women were more supportive of women in supervisory positions.

Al-Jaradat (2014) in Jordan, concluded that while Arab women are willing to accept more responsibilities in the political, educational, and social spheres, Arab men are not willing to share this responsibility with them.

Yet, he also noted that the situation might change in favor of women in the nearer future, particularly due to the opening of broader educational and employment opportunities (See also Hamdan, 2005 in Saudi Arabia).

Challenges and Issues Facing Arab Women Leaders in the Schools

Nine studies considered this theme (see Table 4.1) Given the negative attitudes towards the inclusion of women in educational leadership positions in many Arab countries, it is unsurprising that many female Arab leaders reported having difficulties with their staff, who tended to repudiate their authority. Lebanese and Israeli Arab female principals reported they had to face staff's resistance and lack of cooperation (Akkary, 2013; Arar et al., 2013). Even in single sex schools (for girls), such as in Saudi Arabia or the Emirates, where women are naturally promoted to leadership positions, women educational leaders still face resistance and hostility during their initial induction into leadership posts (Al-Jaber, 1996; Kathija, 2003). Yet, research findings from various Arab countries show that many women leaders cope effectively with the challenges and resistance that they encounter in the educational institutions that they lead, mainly because of skills and strategies they learn as they overcome many barriers during their long stay in mid-career (Arar et al., 2013).

One major challenge that Arab women face when leading educational institutions is the need to cope with local tribal and "hamulla" (extended family) interests and politics. These powerful interest groups attempt to influence teacher appraisal or layoff, and women educational leaders find it even more difficult than men to rebut these pressures and implement pedagogical and other professional rational decisions (Al-Jaradat, 2014; Arar & Shapira, 2012). The resistance that Arab women meet when they aspire to attain managerial positions in education shapes their career paths. It was found that Arab women enter education leadership positions in older age than their male counterparts but have more professional experience because they had functioned longer in more mid-level management roles before reaching senior management posts than men (Addi-Raccah, 2007; Al-Jaber, 1996).

Some of the qualitative studies point up the way in which female Arab leaders use their posts in educational institutions to fulfill the role of agents of social change. Bent-Hatim (2011) noted that female principals lacked professional competencies to lead change in Makah city in Saudi Arabia, and recommended that there should be a comprehensive plan to train all school principals for professional competencies, and to give them space to act. Yet, Arab women principals often strive to make their schools empowering places and encourage collaboration and caring (Akkary, 2013; Arar, 2014). They attempt to introduce small and gradual changes in their conservative society and focus on improving student learning. Arar et al. (2013) found that Arab women principals in Israel combined revolutionary and traditional methods of social change: they respected the traditional environment to which they belong and did not challenge existing customs; however, they also insisted on the need for structural and pedagogic change within their schools, understanding that each change would eventually seep into the environment. They balanced an authoritative leadership style with one of collaboration and empathy, in line with the feminist concept of the "ethics of care and concern." Arar et al. (2013) also found that in contrast to the more traditional school management style of Arab men that emphasized a hierarchic system with little staff and student participation, Arab women principals empowered their staff and students, seeing it as part of their mission to inculcate a pedagogy of equality. Along the same lines, studies investigating women education supervisors in Lebanon and Bahrain showed that they aimed to promote social justice and they invested efforts and determination to reduce achievement gaps between students (Akkary, 2013; Kathija, 2003). Again, this reflects what has been identified as a feminine style of leadership expressing an approach of care and concern towards students and altruistic motivation (Arar & Oplatka, 2014).

DISCUSSION AND FUTURE DIRECTIONS FOR RESEARCH

This chapter has documented the common themes and characteristics of female educational leadership in Arab countries during the last two decades that emerged from a survey of 20 different studies on this issue. Three main themes were identified in this survey of the research literature: (a) barriers to and facilitators of women's career advancement, (b) female leadership style, and (c) challenges and issues facing Arab women leaders in the schools. While it is clear that the patriarchal culture of the Arab world has delayed women's entry into the public sphere and into positions of influence and power (Ismael & Ismael, 2008; Moghadam, 2009), it is also clear that more and more women are entering senior posts at least in the education systems of certain Arab states and in the Arab education system in Israel (Arar et al., 2013). Moreover, because they are introducing a more feminine style of management and gradually introducing change into their societies, these pioneer women constitute models for imitation for young Arab women (Akkary, 2013; Al-Jaradat, 2014; Shapira, Arar, & Azaize, 2010).

Despite the very limited scope of the current research on Arab female educational leaders, some evidence indicates difference between various Arab nations in respect to the debated issues. For instance, as the Saudi educational systems is totally separated between the genders, the entry of female leaders into girl schools seems to be "natural" literally because of this separation (Al-Jaradat, 2014). Yet, the entry of women to the general "public" sphere is obstructed by the religious leadership in this country and it remains a male domain (Hamdan, 2005). In contrast, in Tunisia, the public educational system is not segregated by gender but women still face many barriers to career advancement in the educational system (Omair, 2008). In Abu-Dhabi and Kuwait, women have recently entered leadership positions in larger numbers than ever before (Kathija, 2003).

It can be seen that this relatively new branch of research is very limited not only in scope but also in its methodologies and conceptual frameworks; most studies have been descriptive and grounded in feminist points of view (Abu-Rabia-Queder & Oplatka, 2008; Hamdan, 2005). What should the next stage of the evolution of this field of research include? Our review indicates the need for studies that could provide further understanding of the phenomenon of Arab female educational leaders. There is a need for research exploring whether there are certain styles and strategies of female educational leadership in Arab countries that are more suitable for traditional and Islamic societies in general and Arab education systems in particular, which help these women to attain professional and pedagogic goals within the institutions in which they work. More specifically, we would encourage researchers to develop research agendas on the topics described below.

Understanding the Facilitators of Arab Women's Advancement

Many studies have focused thus far on the barriers faced by Arab women aspiring to attain leadership positions (Al-Jaradat, 2014; Al-Suwaihel, 2010; Arar et al., 2013). However, we believe we could learn much more from exploring the coping strategies and skills that have helped the few Arab women educational leaders who have managed to overcome common cultural and organizational barriers to break the "glass ceiling" in their traditional societies. Thus, too, as the family lies at the core of the Arab society, playing a major role in political, economic, social, and religious spheres (Ismael & Ismael, 2008), it would be very interesting to explore the influence of the father, mother, and siblings on Arab women's career advancement (Shapira et al., 2010). Since Arab society attributes much significance to family membership, identities and status (Al-Suwaihel, 2010), it would be pertinent to investigate to what extent family links facilitate access to institutions, jobs, and government services and what other paths to progress are available to women who do not have these links (Hamdan, 2005).

To identify other facilitating factors for women's advancement to leadership, research should investigate empowering factors in childhood, such as strong mothers, the role of spouse support, access to higher education, and facilitating political and legal factors. Also attention should be given in future research to the influence of socio-economic changes in many Arab countries on entrenched gender norms in these societies, including attitudes towards female educational leadership, and women's ability to build a professional career.

Exploring the Lives and Careers of Female Arab Leaders

Most of the reviewed studies focused on the career path of Arab women into educational leadership positions, describing "what" they have achieved but little has been written about "how" they have achieved this or the factors for their success or failure (Bent-Hatim, 2011; Esa, 2008; Shapira et al., 2010). For example, deeper study of the profiles of these women could help to elucidate the personality factors that assist their success, the factors that affect their decision making, and the strategies and principles that they employ, for example, to introduce new pedagogies or to improve team work of principal/supervisor-teacher relations. To what extent can they and do they employ a feminine style of administration and mentoring within the masculine dominated world in which they work?

Investigation of career issues, such as the mapping of the different career stages evident among Arab women working in education systems in the Arab world and career aspirations (i.e., how do Arab women shape managerial aspiration in a strongly gendered society?) or commitment (i.e., to whom are female Arab leaders committed and why?), may provide insight into their unique induction process. Researchers may be curious to explore female Arab leader's narratives, describing the development of their careers and how these female leaders balance the demands of family and work.

Additionally, it is recommended that any research that explores the lived experiences and leadership of Arab women educational leaders should endeavor to underpin the study with a wider variety of perspectives than the purely feminist approach employed until now (e.g., post-structuralism, post-feminism, post-modernism, or standpoint theory). The development of different perspectives is necessary, mainly because these women live and work in cultures that are different from those of Anglo-American nations, where the main streams of feminism developed (Abu-Rabia-Queder & Oplatka, 2008; Hamdan, 2005; Shapira et al., 2010). This may help to identify and clarify issues specific to women leaders whose life experiences and careers develop in an entirely "other" socio-cultural sphere than that which prevails in the Western world (Arar et al., 2011; Coleman, 2011).

The Influence of Female Arab Leaders Upon Their Society

There are many indications that the situation will in the future favor the development and acceptance of female Arab leaders in the Arab world, particularly in the domains of education and employment opportunities (Al-Jaradat, 2014). It, therefore, seems important to examine whether and to what extent female educational leadership can influence the character and progress of Arab society. Evidence that Arab culture is submitting to a process of modernization, including greater willingness to accept women in the public sphere, is substantiated in a number of studies (Abu-Asbah et al., 2014; Akkary, 2013; Al-Lamsky, 2007; Arar et al., 2013; Hamdan, 2005). With the passing of time and equal education, it is likely that traditional culture and institutions will have diminishing weight against the forces of modernization, and the quantitative and qualitative changes that women role holders bring with them (Abu-Asbah et al., 2014; Omair, 2008). In such circumstances, it becomes pertinent to better understand to what extent and in which direction women leaders influence the Arab family's attitudes towards education, female education, male educational leaders' career and work, the school's culture etc. (Al-Jaber, 1996). We know, for example, that Saudi Arabian female educational leaders serve as role models that influence girls' aspirations (Hamdan, 2005).

Changes in the status of Arab women and attitudes towards their attainment of leadership positions are slowly taking root, due to the gradually changing social structure of Arab society throughout the Arab world. This seems to depend on the extent to which there is an enabling environment including level of education available, cultural restrictions, an enabling legal framework, and the perceptions of female leaders in the media. Most often an enabling environment is associated with wealthy societies as in the Gulf States or among wealthier echelons in poorer states as in North Africa (Abu-Asbah et al., 2014; Bent-Hatim, 2011; Dubai Women's Establishment, 2009; Moghadam, 2009).

Despite all that has been said above about identifying unique aspects of the development of female Arab education leaders, we would like to emphasize that it is important not to view the Arab world as a unified society, but rather to understand the array of cultural and social distinctions between different Arab societies before conducting a research on women leaders in these societies. This is a critical investigation that must precede any future study on female Arab leaders especially today when the Arab world is divided into many religious and national groups and its different parts are undergoing contradictory political and social upheavals. Thus, comparative studies about female educational leaders in diverse Arab countries are warranted because they will shed light on the status of women educators across the Arab world in different contexts (e.g., Christians, Kurds), and can illuminate the lives and career experiences of the few female educational leaders in different Arab societies within the Arab world.

REFERENCES

Abdul-Ghaffar, N. A. (2011). Management types and their relationships to the thinking styles of female principals in the secondary schools in Jeddah. *Journal of Literature and Humanities, 24*(1), 105–152. [Arabic].

Abu-Asbah, K., Abu-Nasra, M., & Abu-Baker, K. (2014). Gender perceptions of male and female teachers in the Arab education system in Israel. *Journal of Middle East Women Studies, 10*(3), 109–124.

Abu-Khader, S. (2012). Challenges facing the women's academic leaderships in the higher education institutions in Kingdom of Saudi Arabia. *Saudi Higher Education Journal, 3*(7), 28–51.

Abu-Rabia-Queder, S., & Oplatka, I. (2008). The power of femininity. Exploring the gender and ethnic experiences of Muslim women who accessed supervisory roles in a Bedouin society. *Journal of Educational Administration, 16*(3), 396–415.

Abu-Tineh, A. (2013). Leadership effectiveness in Jordanian educational institutions: A comparison of Jordanian female and male leaders. *Educational Management Administration & Leadership, 41*(1) 79–94.

Addi-Raccah, A. (2007). Gender, ethnicity, and principalship in Israel: Comparing two organizational cultures. *International Journal of Inclusive Education, 9* (3), 217–239.

Akkary, R. (2013). The role and role context of the Lebanese school principal: Toward a culturally grounded understanding of the principalship, *Educational Management, Administration and Leadership, 1*(25), 174–191.

Al-Hussein, E. B. (2011). Traits and skills characterizing the Jordanian woman leader and obstacles facing her. *Damascus University Journal, 27*(3, 4), 13–39.

Al-Jaber, Z. (1996). School management in Kuwait after the Iraqi aggression: Problems for principals. *Educational Management, Administration and Leadership, 24*(4), 411–424.

Al-Jaradat, M. M. K. (2014). Challenges facing women academic leadership in secondary schools of Irbid educational area. *International Education Studies, 7*(5), 147–160.

Al-Lamsky, A. (2007). Feminizing leadership in Arab societies: The perspectives of Omani female leaders. *Women in Management Review, 22*(1), 49–67.

Al-Suwaihal, O. E. (2010). Kuwaiti female leaders' perspectives: The influence of culture on their leadership. *Contemporary Issues in Education Research, 3*(3), 29–39.

Altheide, D. L. (1996). *Qualitative media analysis.* Thousand Oaks, CA: Sage Publications.

Ameen, I. (2001). *Women: Identity, difficulties and challenging future.* Beirut: Daralhadi Publication.
Arar, K. (2014). Female supervisors of Arab school education in Israel. *Gender and Education. 26*(4), 414–431.
Arar, K., & Abramovitz, R. (2013). Teachers' attitudes toward the appointment of women as school leaders: The case of the Arab education in Israel. *Management in Education, 27*(1), 29–35.
Arar, K., & Abu-Rabia-Queder, S. (2011). Turning points in the lives of two pioneer Arab women principals in Israel. *Gender and Education, 27*(1), 1–15.
Arar, K., & Oplatka, I. (2014). Muslim and Jewish teachers' conceptions of the male school principal's masculinity: Insights into cultural and social distinctions in principal-teacher relations. *Men and Masculinity. 17*(1), 22–42.
Arar, K., Shapira, T., Azaiza, F., & Hertz-Lazarowitz, R. (2013). *Arab women into leadership and management.* New York: Palgrave McMillan.
Askar, A., & Ahmad, M. (2003). Attitude toward women occupying supervisory positions at various work organizations in Kuwait society. *Journal of the Social Sciences, 31*(4), 857–879.
Bent-Hatim, S. (2011). *Female professional competencies to lead change in governmental public schools in the city of Makah.* PhD thesis, Om El-Qora University, Saudi-Arabia [Arabic].
Blackmore, J. (1999). *Troubling women: Feminism, leadership and educational change.* Buckingham, England: Open University Press.
Booth, A., Papaioannou, D., & Sutton, A. (2012). *Systematic approaches to a successful literature review.* Los Angeles: Sage.
CAWTAR (2009). Recent trends in Arab countries towards addressing gender in public management: Comparative overview on lessons and challenges. Presentation given at the conference, *Addressing gender in public management.* 18 May 2009, Cairo, Egypt. Retrieved from http://www.oecd.org/mena/governance/43087763.pdf
Coleman, M. (2011). *Women at the top—Challenges, choice and changes.* New York: Palgrave Macmillan.
Dubai Women Establishment (2009). *Arab women: Leadership outlook 2009–2011.* Dubai: Dubai Women Establishment, Research and Analysis Division. Retrieved from: http://www.pwc.com/en_GX/gx/women-at-pwc/assets/Arab-Women-Leadership-Outlook.pdf
Esa, A. (2008). Comparison of leadership style and school outcomes of male and female school principals in Damascus and Hems city in Syria. *University of Damascus Journal, 24*(1), 105–152. [Arabic].
Grogan, M., & Shakeshaft, C. (2011). *Women and educational leadership.* California: Jossey Bass.
Guthrie, S. (2001). *Arab women in the middle ages: Private lives and public roles.* London, England: Saqi Books.
Hamdan, A. (2005). Women and education in Saudi Arabia: Challenges and achievements. *International Education Journal, 6*(1), 42–64.
International Labor Organization (2013). *Women's participation in the Palestinian labour force: 2010–201.1 ILO fact sheet.* Retrieved from: http://www.ilo.org/

wcmsp5/groups/public/—-arabstates/—-ro-beirut/documents/publication/wcms_218024.pdf
Interparliamentary Union for Democracy, for Everyone (2013). Women in parliament: The Year in Review Retrieved from: http://www.ipu.org/pdf/publications/WIP2013-e.pdf
Ismael, J., & Ismael, S. (2008). Social policy in the Arab world: The search for social justice. *Arab Studies Quarterly*, 302, 23–44.
Jaber, D. F. (2005). *Obstacles facing the Palestinian woman working in the public sector in the northern governorates of West Bank* (Unpublished Master thesis, An-Najah National University, Nablus, Palestine).
Kanter, R. M. (1997). *Men and women of the corporation*. New York: Basil Books.
Kathija, A. (2003). Women's empowerment and leadership in education: A Key factor for emiratisation in the United Arab Emirates. PhD dissertation. University of South Africa.
Klenke, K. (2011). *Women in leadership—Contextual dynamics and boundaries*. Bingley: Emerald Publications.
Metcalfe, B. D. (2006). Exploring cultural dimensions of gender and management in the Middle East. *Thunderbird International Business Review*, 18(1), 93–107.
Miller, D. E. (May 17, 2011). Saudi Arabia opens world's largest women's university. *Jerusalem Post*, Israel.
Moghadam, V. M. (2009). *Globalization and social movements: Islamism, feminism, and the global justice movement*. Lanham, MD: Rowman and Littlefield.
Mostafa, M. (2005). Attitudes towards women managers in the United Arab Emirates. The effects of patriarchy, age, and sex differences. *Journal of Managerial Psychology*, 20(6), 540–552.
Omair, K. (2008). Women in management in the Arab context. *Education, Business and Society: Contemporary Middle Eastern Issues*, 1(2), 107–123.
Oplatka, I. (2006). Women in educational administration within developing countries. *Journal of Educational Administration*, 44(6), 604–624.
Saadat, M., & Taiem, M.H. (2011). The degree of knowledge management of school managers: A comparison between male and female school managers in Jenin city in Palestine. *Journal of The Open University of Jerusalem*, 24(2), 163–204. [Arabic]
Slackman, M. (2007, May 26). A quiet revolution in Algeria: Gains by women. *The New York Times*. Retrieved 29 August 2011.
Shapira, T., Arar, K., & Azaiza, F. (2010). Arab women principals' empowerment and leadership in Israel. *Journal of Educational Administration*, 48(6), 704–715.
UNDP (United Nations Development Program). (2004). *Progress of Arab women*. Jordan: Arab States Regional Office, UNIFEM.

SECTION II

METHODOLOGICAL CHALLENGES AND INNOVATIONS IN EDUCATIONAL LEADERSHIP RESEARCH

CHAPTER 5

CHALLENGES AND OPPORTUNITIES FOR EDUCATION LEADERSHIP SCHOLARSHIP

A Methodological Critique

Peter Goff
University of Wisconsin–Madison

Maida Finch
Salisbury University

ABSTRACT

In recent years there has been a proliferation of quantitative studies used to better understand and characterize educational leadership. This chapter examines trends in quantitative leadership studies in education with a particular focus on the alignment between the methodologies applied and inferences drawn. We emphasize the potential benefits to research, policy, and practice that emerge from analyses of longitudinal, rather than cross-sectional data. We illustrate the limitations to cross-sectional analyses through an examination of an empirical data set, contrasting inferences drawn from a cross-sectional analysis to those made using longitudinal data. For researchers with a substantive interest in the relationships between latent variables, we use recent literature to illustrate several fruitful alternatives to cross-sectional analyses, each of which permit deeper and more meaningful inquiry.

Keywords: longitudinal analysis, latent variables, leadership evaluation, feedback, instructional leadership

We open this chapter by reiterating the often cited claim that leadership accounts for approximately a quarter of all school-related effects (Leithwood, Seashore Louis, Anderson, & Wahlstrom, 2004; Sammons, Davis, Day, & Gu, 2014). However, understanding exactly how principals improve instruction and achievement faces many challenges: the complexity of the principal's job, variations across different contexts, and a multitude of considerations regarding study design and data collection, to name only a few. It is these last items that we wish to address here: Specifically, that the increasing rigor of research designs that constitute "best practices" coupled with the growing sophistication of methodologies applied to quantitative data present an opportunity to reflect upon what we have learned from prior studies and suggest new directions for future investigations.

Recent policy innovations and programs (e.g., Race to the Top) have proven to be a watershed moment for the collection of data pertaining to education leadership. States and school districts are collecting information on educator evaluations, student outcomes, and other administrative data and, where possible, linking these data to specific individuals even when there are transfers within the district or state. In concert with these efforts, school data systems are increasingly being designed to track students, teachers, and leaders over time (Bowers, 2010). Partnering with local agencies, a research strategy that has been repeatedly advocated by former IES Director John Easton (2011), makes the collection of data, notably longitudinal data, for the scholarship of school leadership far easier now than any time in history.

In addition to access to longitudinal data and the diminishing barriers to tracking participants over time, methodological advances have enhanced researchers' ability to make the most of such data. When data is collected under the right conditions, quasi-experimental methods, such as regression discontinuity, instrumental variables, difference-in-differences, can better illuminate the causal impact of school leadership without necessitating full-scale randomized control trials. Education leadership research is poised to make use of these expanding data systems and proliferation of sophisticated methods.

Although recent reviews of research on education leadership are not uncommon (e.g., Luyten, Visscher, & Witziers, 2005; Robinson, Lloyd,

& Rowe, 2008), with few exceptions (Hallinger & Heck, 1996; Hallinger, 2010), they focus on the substantive findings from these studies rather than the research design and methodological approach. We contend that empirical findings are dependent upon these research elements and, thus, also merit attention. As Hallinger (2010) explains, such an approach "map[s] methodological progress in educational leadership...and raise[s] standards in empirical research" (2010, p. 2) for the field. Our efforts in this chapter parallel similar endeavors in the field of psychology, which caution against the use of cross-sectional analyses while exploring the merits of longitudinal data when exploring mediated relationships (Cole & Maxwell, 2003; Maxwell & Cole, 2007).

A critique of the prevailing scholarship focused on research design and methodology provides a lens through which subsequent research can be evaluated while concurrently providing direction for new avenues of inquiry. In this chapter, we focus a methodological lens on recent research in education leadership to address two goals. First, we review the methodological designs typically applied to quantitative data in education leadership and discuss the contributions and limitations of these studies. This endeavor complements our second goal, which is to empirically illustrate alternative modes of inquiry that we believe will produce more valid conclusions to guide policy and shape practice.

Ideally, the methodology employed in education leadership research should approximate the level of complexity of the phenomenon being studied (e.g., Heck & Hallinger, 2014). In reality however, the suite of analytic methods available is often inadequate to capture the rich and elaborate interplay of direct, reciprocal, and mediating relationships that intersect with school leadership. At a minimum then, we contend that research methods should strive to approximate the degree of complexity present. We close our chapter with an empirical illustration of how cross-sectional data can differ substantially from similar data collected over time, and the use of sophisticated modeling techniques such as HLM and SEM do little to mitigate these problems.

OVERVIEW OF RESEARCH METHODOLOGY ON EDUCATION LEADERSHIP

Quantitative and mixed-methods studies that focus on school leadership employ a variety of instruments and analytic strategies. Surveys and questionnaires are used most often (Brown & Chai, 2012; Heck & Hallinger, 2014), sometimes in conjunction with administrative data; daily logs recording principals' activities have been an innovative contribution (e.g., Camburn, Spillane, & Sebastian, 2010; Camburn et al., 2010). Scheerens (2012) contends leadership effectiveness is best measured by data collected from teachers because the more commonly found principal self-reports often rely on inferential and judgmental, rather than factual, survey items. Nevertheless, others promote the need to understand principals' perceptions and beliefs because of the influence they likely have on leadership (Leithwood, Patten, & Jantzi, 2010; Urick & Bowers, 2011, 2014). Case studies and interviews, coupled with secondary data, are prevalent as well (e.g., Day et al., 2009; Richardson, Imig, & Ndoye, 2012).

To augment our understanding of school leadership, scholars make use of descriptive statistics, correlations, factor analysis, and ordinary least squares (OLS) regression. More recently, sophisticated methods such as structural equation modeling (SEM) and hierarchical linear modeling (HLM) allow for consideration of indirect paths, rather than direct effects, of leadership. Hallinger and Heck (1996) first emphasized the importance of indirect effects models; yet more recently, others have found significant results with direct effects models (Bowers & White, 2014; Coelli & Green, 2012). Whether examining leadership as a direct or indirect effect, the impact of school leadership is a phenomenon that unfolds over time and is best understood as a process rather than an event. Despite the time-embedded nature of school leadership, cross-sectional designs are far more common than longitudinal studies in the scholarship of educational leadership, a point of concern echoed by many researchers (Epstein, Galindo, & Sheldon, 2011; Heck & Hallinger, 2010, 2014; Hochbein & Cunningham, 2013; Luyten et al., 2005; Scheerens, 2012; Thoonen, Sleegers, Oort, & Peetsma, 2012).

Because much of the research on school leadership relies on cross-sectional data, the extent to which we are able to definitively conclude how principal leadership affects school improvement and student learning is limited (Scheerens, 2012). As Luyten et al. (2005) explain, cross-sectional data are appropriate for descriptions about how schools are "being effective" but not "becoming effective" (p. 264). The "snapshot" (Heck & Hallinger, 2010; Luyten et al., 2005; Thoonen et al., 2012) offered by cross-sectional data suggests a "frozen in time" perspective that does not take into account the dynamic nature of schools.

One central component of empirical, quantitative research is establishing causality—identifying when and under what conditions change in one variable provokes a change in another variable. Because evidence from this research is intended for consequential, and maybe even high stakes purposes (e.g., to inform changes in practices in policy), then the means used to produce the evidence should be rigorous and reflect the highest standards of scientific inquiry. Among the criteria required to make causal claims, the most fundamental pertains to the temporal ordering of events, with causal mechanisms preceding the effects (Murnane & Willett, 2011; Shadish, Cook, & Campbell, 2001). The accurate portrayal of temporal ordering is particularly germane in school leadership research because changes that occur as a result of school leadership are believed to impact various mediating factors which then affect student outcomes (Hallinger & Heck, 2011; Heck & Hallinger, 2010, 2014; Sammons et al., 2014; Thoonen et al., 2012).

LITERATURE REVIEW FRAMEWORK

Although we readily acknowledge the contributions of qualitative research to our knowledge in this field due to their potential for augmenting the paucity of causal studies concerning school leadership, our focus in this chapter is on quantitative data and methodology. We invoke Harwell's (2011) approach of discussing research design in light of two assumptions:

> First, is that the idea being pursued is worth pursuing, that is, an idea that could reasonably lead to, and support, the formation of important educational questions and identification of solutions to important educational problems. Second, is that every phase of the research process linked to studying a promising idea is rigorous. (Harwell, 2011, p. 147)

In this discussion, we take up Harwell's (2011) second point, weighing the rigor of a study by considering the extent to which the research method can effectively mitigate unanswered questions relative to the stated aim of the study.

Our goal of describing the methodological approaches commonly employed in education leadership scholarship led us to conduct a search of studies using the terms "school leadership" and "quantitative" or "mixed methods" from 11 prominent education research journals,[1] many with a specific focus on leadership. This search returned 81 articles published between 2010 and 2014. A similar approach was used to identify the frequency of cross-sectional designs to test mediated relationships in psychology (Maxwell & Cole, 2007). Because we also evaluate the contributions and limitations of these designs, and due to space constraints, the articles selected for inclusion in this chapter are necessarily representative of the literature rather than exhaustive.

In consideration of the need for robust and systematic strategies for synthesizing literature (Dixon-Woods, Agarwal, Jones, Young, & Sutton, 2005), we adapted Miles and Huberman's cross-case analyses approach (as cited in Dixon-Woods et al., 2005, p. 49). This method involves developing meta-matrices for gathering and classifying data. In this case, the articles retrieved from our search were first compiled in an initial list with notes regarding the research design and relevance for this chapter. From there, we identified four broad categories into which the studies could be partitioned: causal inference, change over time, comparisons between groups, and descriptive studies. Further analysis of these groupings led us to establish two tiers for our categories. Our discussion of the studies is organized according to these tiers.

The first section discusses what we classify as Tier I quantitative studies, scholarship that supports causal inference. We see quantitative research that can be classified as Tier I as making an unambiguous contribution to the field. In the next section, we address Tier II studies. Included in this section is research that documents change over time, draws comparisons between groups, and describes behavior and conditions. The quantitative studies we classify as Tier II also make a clear contribution to our knowledge base; however when compared to Tier I studies, Tier II research designs tend to leave more unanswered questions and less certainty regarding the findings of Tier II research designs.

We then go on to review the utility of quantitative data and highlight recent scholarship in education leadership using various approaches, illustrating their ability to contribute to the knowledge base, in part because of their ability to minimize lingering, unanswered questions regarding the stated findings. Due to the large number of studies that employ cross-sectional data to examine leadership, we do pay special attention to the benefits that this approach can offer, while noting cases where conclusions have been inappropriately drawn.

TIER I: QUANTITATIVE DATA TO ESTABLISH CAUSAL INFERENCES

Quantitative data employed to examine causal relationships are highly useful. When conditions are present for establishing causality (empirical association, appropriate time-order, non-spuriousness, etc.), research designs with quantitative data can answer questions such as whether school leadership or leadership intervention impacts school improvement, instructional effectiveness, or student outcomes. Quantitative data can help uncover the processes and moderators for these relationships. Experimental designs offer the strongest method for establishing causality, but including plausible counterfactual through quasi-experimental methods also allows for causal inferences, taking into consideration the potential threats to internal validity.

Experimental Design

In education leadership scholarship, there are very few examples of either experimental or quasi-experimental designs, a fact underscored by the inclusion of just seven exemplars in this section. The four studies that randomized participants all examined the effects of professional development on leadership behaviors through various approaches: coaching, and feedback (Goff, Guthrie, Goldring, & Bickman, 2014); a curriculum focused on improving principal's capacity for instructional leadership (Barnes, Camburn, Sanders, & Sebastian, 2010); training and coaching in distributed leadership for school leadership teams (Supovitz & Tognatta, 2013); and a commercially developed professional development program (Jacob, Goddard, Kim, Miller, & Goddard, 2014).

Principals self-reported their activities through daily logs in the Barnes et al. (2010) experiment, and while this can present problems for making causal inferences, the authors supplemented quantitative data with interviews and observations, thus reducing the potential for confounding variables. In contrast, Goff et al. (2014) use an interrupted time-series design to examine teachers' perceptions about changes in principals' behaviors in response to coaching. An alternative approach for making causal claims comes from Supovitz and Tognatta (2013), who surveyed faculty in schools participating in a study regarding the effects of professional development on collaborative decision-making. Their instrument applied a branching technique that asked respondents to first indicate if they were a member of the school's leadership team and directed them to distinct questions based on this response (Supovitz & Tognatta, 2013). In this way, they captured perspectives of both leaders and those affected by the leadership team. Similarly, a study of rural Michigan schools asked principals and teachers parallel questions about leadership at two points in time (Jacob et al., 2014).

Quasi-Experimental Design

In other research, scholars designed a mixed-methods study focused on the initial preparation of principals, specifically how an international experience influenced participants' attitudes about cultural diversity (Richardson et al., 2012). This quasi-experimental design addressed an understudied area of leadership professional development by drawing comparisons between graduate students who participated in an international practicum to those who completed the traditional program offered at a North Carolina university (Richardson et al., 2012).

Finally, just two studies in this Tier I category included student performance as an outcome variable (Corcoran et al., 2012; Heck & Moriyama, 2010). Noting the value of longitudinal data in measuring student growth as well as the challenges to collecting such data, Heck and Moriyama (2010) use regression discontinuity as a viable alternative for random assignment to treatment. To assess the differences in principals trained through a district program and those who completed a traditional leadership route, Corcoran et al. (2012) employed both propensity matching and difference-in-difference regression. In each of these studies, authors' claims regarding the relationship between their variable of interest and the outcome is strengthened by their choice of data collection (often longitudinal) and the contrast with a comparison group.

Examining the research design and methods of these studies can inform future research. To begin, some scholars rely on triangulation of data through multiple instruments and perspectives to substantiate their results (Barnes et al., 2010; Jacob et al., 2014; Supovitz & Tognatta, 2013). In other studies, researchers make use of advanced statistical techniques to minimize threats to validity presented by endogenous relationships (Goff et al., 2014) and nested data (Jacob et al., 2014; Supovitz & Tognatta, 2013).

When random assignment is not possible, as was the case with the Corcoran et al. (2012) study, a difference-in-difference model coupled with propensity matching can ameliorate bias due to the systematic sorting of principals across schools. Also innovative is the use of regression discontinuity analysis in leadership studies with successive cohort data (Heck & Moriyama, 2010). Although these strategies are applied in other areas of education research, the potential for this approach in augmenting our knowledge about the relationship between school leadership and student growth has not been fully realized.

The impediments to longitudinal designs are likely one reason there are so few of these studies in education leadership. Cost is often a factor. In addition, principals at troubled schools may have short tenures, making a several-year study infeasible. Even among the exemplary studies presented here, we note the length of one was shortened due to leadership turnover (Barnes et al., 2010). Finally, although the longitudinal studies discussed here offer the first steps to making causal claims, we should note that none of these analyses exceed three years, possibly limiting the validity of their results. Most researchers note that studies can be limited by the mismatch between the time needed to gather valid data on changes in leadership processes and the time a principal remains in a post (Fullan & Stiegelbauer, 1991), and experience regression to the mean (Miller, 2013).

TIER II: QUANTITATIVE DATA FOR DESCRIPTIVE STUDIES, EXAMINING CHANGE OVER TIME, AND COMPARING GROUPS

Although randomization and variables amenable to manipulation are hallmarks of studies that support causal inferences, they are not always possible in education research. Limitations arise when the primary characteristics of interest, such as principals' race, gender, certification, locus of control, or prior experience, cannot be randomly assigned. Ethical issues, such as the random assignment of school resources or high-stakes accountability policies, may also preclude randomization. The need to analyze leadership at the school level requires sample sizes several times larger than those examining interventions at the student or classroom level, substantially increasing the cost and complexity of randomized studies of school leadership. In these cases, there are other ways quantitative data can provide useful information. In this section, we discuss appropriate uses of longitudinal and cross-sectional data in education leadership scholarship. We concentrate on studies that offer rich descriptions of leadership practices and behaviors, as well as those that have taken advantage of longitudinal data to examine change over time and others that employed cross-sectional data to draw comparisons between groups. The research included in this section is not as conclusive as that presented in the Tier I section, yet, despite some uncertainty regarding the findings, there are notable lessons that can be gleaned from these research designs.

Descriptive Studies

The first collection of Tier II studies we consider consists of those that are primarily descriptive in nature. Descriptive studies are particularly applicable in education contexts because they allow for the gathering of information in a natural setting, without introducing changes to the environment. They are useful in illuminating patterns, depicting behaviors and attitudes, and distinguishing shared characteristics of a group. If limitations are understood, studies that rely on observation, rather than experimentation, can be useful in furthering empirical inquiries.

Descriptive studies are often motivated by an under-studied phenomenon, as in Hallinger and Lee's (2012) exploration of distributed leadership in International Baccalaureate (IB) schools and Urick and Bowers's (2014) study of principal types. Relatedly, Myung and her colleagues (2011) provide the first systematic evidence of principal "tapping," a process of recruiting teachers thus far observed only anecdotally. These descriptive analyses provide "a provocative first look—not as the final word..." for scholars to "...refine, extend, and challenge," (Hess & Kelly, 2007, p. 269) existing paradigms. Findings from descriptive studies can advance hypotheses for future research as well as provide direction for policymakers and practitioners. The latter is exemplified by a study of principals' responses to external mandates (Seashore Louis & Robinson, 2012) and the aforementioned study on principal "tapping" (Myung et al., 2011).

Longitudinal Studies

The longitudinal studies described here are among the few to explicitly integrate temporal ordering in quantitative studies of education leadership. Not intended to advance causal inferences, they rather function as a bridge, augmenting what cross-sectional studies have suggested and laying a foundation for future research and theoretical development.

Three studies take up the issue of principal change and student achievement (Coelli & Green, 2012; Hochbein & Cunningham, 2013; Miller, 2013). Notably, each study considers the immediate effect of a transition in school leader while also allowing for effects to emerge over time. At the high school level, Coelli and Green (2012) find positive effects on English exam scores when principals are given time to realize their potential. Conversely, no effects are found at the elementary level immediately following a principal change or thereafter (Hochbein & Cunningham, 2013). An analysis of nine years of panel data from North Carolina schools reveals that principal transitions tend to be preceded by a decline in student achievement (Miller, 2013). School performance continues to decline for two years after a new principal is installed and then returns to its previous pre-transition functioning; thus, Miller (2013) concludes that rather than being the result of a principal change, the performance variance reflects reversion to the mean.

Another advantage of longitudinal data designs is their capacity to consider mediating influences of principal effects. Understanding the paths through which school leaders impact student outcomes and school performance has been the focus of much research (Heck & Hallinger, 2014), but claims of indirect effects are only suitable when using data that allow for temporal ordering. To conceptualize mediated effects of leadership, researchers have used structural equation modeling because it allows for multiple pathways and accommodates the nested structure of school data (Day et al., 2009; Hallinger & Heck, 2010; Heck & Hallinger, 2009, 2010; Kythreotis et al., 2010; Sammons et al., 2014). Here we emphasize that studies of mediation carry a higher methodological burden than do studies of direct causality. By definition, the temporal ordering of the mediator lies between the cause and the effect and therefore longitudinal data are required to estimate mediated pathways.

Although longitudinal designs such as those described here offer opportunities for advancing our understanding regarding the ways in which school leadership impacts school improvement and student learning over time, they are not without limitations. As illustrated by Coelli and Green's (2012) study of principal stability and student outcomes, where the authors find that principal effects develop over time, questions remain—namely whether principal stability leads to improved achievement or whether there is an alternative factor that is producing high achievement and is correlated with leadership stability. To mitigate such limitations, quantitative data can be supplemented with interviews, observations, and case studies. One example of this is the integrated "cross-case matrix" used in a study of school leadership in England that identified the most salient leadership strategies common across survey and case study findings (Day et al., 2009; Sammons et al., 2014). Heck and Hallinger (2014) note the difficulties of examining the differential effects that principal leadership can have on individual teachers and subsequent student outcomes, and they propose cross-class modeling as an alternative to cross-lagged and growth curve models.

Nevertheless, "longitudinal research designs enable explicit specification and testing of the 'temporal ordering' of relevant organizational processes, thereby shedding new light on the nature of causal relationships," (Heck & Hallinger, 2014, p. 656). Furthermore, research that employs rich longitudinal datasets offers the potential to explore the multiple paths by which leadership impacts instruction, student outcomes, and school improvement (Hallinger & Heck, 1996; Leithwood et al., 2010, 2004).

Cross-Sectional Designs

When temporal influence is not our concern, cross-sectional data can allow us to test assumptions of variations in education leadership across contexts and offer rich descriptions capturing a moment in time. In some cases, these investigations are suited for advanced statistical models such as HLM or latent class analysis, while in others, bivariate correlations, ANOVA, social network analyses, and discriminate analyses are appropriate. Research that compares school leadership across different contexts offers an opportunity to consider moderating influences on school improvement and student learning.

Some scholars have used cross-sectional data to examine the relationship between principals' behaviors (Goldring, Huff, May, & Camburn, 2008) and perceptions (Urick & Bowers, 2014) on how leaders perform their jobs. Others have taken advantage of the burgeoning school choice movement to study the influence of governance structures (Cravens, Goldring, & Penaloza, 2012) and faculty characteristics (Goff, Mavrogordato, & Goldring, 2012) on school leadership in public versus choice schools. In the area of principal preparation, comparisons among different programs enable the identification of effective practices. For example, Greenlee & Karanxha (2010) contrasted the levels of group dynamics associated with group effectiveness among cohort and non-cohort members of a principal preparation program.

Findings from analyses of cross-sectional data can suggest directions for future research. In an exploration of the differential responses of school leaders to policy stipulations, researchers propose qualitative designs and the inclusion of additional variables to facilitate an expanded understanding of how and why school leaders respond in a particular way when facing a policy threat (Daly, Der-Martirosian, Ong-Dean, Park, & Wishard-Guerra, 2011). Studies of this sort are also useful in evaluating the effects of a policy change, as in Jacob's (2011) examination of Chicago principals' decisions to fire teachers. International measures like the Trends in International Math and Science Study (TIMSS), the Program for International Student Assessment (PISA), and the Organization for Economic Development and Cooperation (OCED) are useful in learning about education leadership across countries. For instance, a recent study comparing the relationship between principals' perceptions of leadership and student achievement in reading found few consistencies across Korea, Mexico, and the United States (Shin, Slater, & Backhoff, 2012).

We conclude our discussion regarding high-leverage use of cross-sectional studies with an examination of research that employs both qualitative and quantitative data. Mixed-methods designs offer many benefits that include bridging the differences in information collected by complementary instruments, triangulating results across multiple data sources, and employing the results of one method to inform the development of more fine-grained interpretation of results collected by other methods. One such design, described by Creswell (2007) as sequential explanatory, applies qualitative data to enhance results from numerical data. This strategy has been used recently in education leadership research focused on teachers' perceptions of desirable leadership qualities (Hauserman, Ivankova, & Stick, 2013) and distributed leadership in international schools (Hallinger & Lee, 2012).

Another benefit of mixed-methods designs pertains to participant selection. For example, a large secondary database allowed access to a very diverse sample, atypical in qualitative research in a study of the influence of policy mandates on principals (Seashore Louis & Robinson, 2012). Effective mixed-methods research can also bolster our knowledge of measurement tools. An analysis of principal professional development using open-ended survey questions along with interviews led Kamler, Dodge, and Walker (2013) to conclude that conversations with participants resulted in richer, more nuanced, data than the questionnaire alone. Similarly, a survey of coaching practices identified as helpful by principals led to the development of an instrument for coaches and principals to use in their work together (Wise & Hammack, 2011).

IN PURSUIT OF BETTER METHODS

Despite the prevalence of appropriate uses of cross-sectional research in education leadership scholarship, not all research employing this design is equally meritorious. Our critique lies with studies examining the relationships between two or more latent variables using cross-sectional data, when causality or mediation between the factors motivates the study. The use of latent constructs is a general characteristic of the social sciences; often the most interesting and important constructs are complex social factors that, themselves, are not directly observable. This is in contrast with manifest variables that can be measured directly, such as school type (e.g., public or private) or years of administrative experience.

Latent variables—factors that inherently cannot be measured directly, such as instructional leadership, student knowledge, or locus of control—are frequently used in quantitative school leadership research. Estimates generated from cross-sectional data and distinguishing between direct and indirect effects—an approach commonly used in educational leadership (Luo, 2008; Ross & Gray, 2006)—are often biased, another limitation of designs that do not allow for temporal ordering (Gollob & Reichardt, 1991; Hill & Rowe, 1996).

For example, when examining the relationship between principals' leadership and teacher motivation through a cross-sectional survey of 122 teachers, Eyal and Roth (2011) claim that they found evidence that "leadership styles among school principals play a significant role in teachers' motivation and well-being." Yet, given the data it may be equally probable that teachers' motivation and well-being play a significant role in shaping leadership styles, as might be expected from a situational leadership perspective (Blanchard, Zigarmi, & Nelson, 1993). It may also be that teachers who are more motivated are also more likely to view their principals in a favorable light.

Omitted variables are also a notable concern as one can readily think of factors that would be correlated with both perceptions of leadership and motivation, such as working conditions or favoritism. Eyal and Roth's (2011) study began under the reasonable assumption that one latent variable (school leadership) may be related to another latent variable (teachers' motivation), however by choosing to pursue this research question through the use of cross-sectional survey methods at the conclusion of the study we are left with no greater confidence regarding the relationship between these factors than is provided by theory alone.

In contrast, cross-sectional studies that examine the relationship between manifest and latent factors are often descriptive in nature and eliminate the threat of reciprocal causality. For example, a study examining leadership behaviors (latent) in magnet and traditional public schools (manifest) such as Hausman (2000), brings some clarity to the question of causality because the latent variable cannot *cause* the manifest variable. Thus, we conclude cross-sectional descriptive studies using manifest and latent variables tend to be illuminating and have potential to make notable contributions to the knowledge base, in part through their ability to mitigate some unanswered questions.

One other area where prudence is strongly encouraged pertains to the application of structural equation models (SEM) to mediation effects. In a field where many of the influences of leadership are believed to manifest through intermediates, such as school culture and instructional climate, studies of mediation abound in educational administration. Although the details are beyond the scope of this chapter (but are well documented elsewhere—see Cole & Maxwell, 2003; Maxwell & Cole, 2007), studies of mediated effects using cross-sectional data are particularly prone to bias.

In sum, we find that there are many valuable uses for cross-sectional research to further our knowledge of school leadership. Still, one of the most limiting forms of cross-sectional research pertains to investigations of two latent variables. Often, the foundations motivating these inquiries are solid and build from strong, preexisting conceptual work. However, the use of a cross-sectional survey to pursue these questions is the least suitable option for inquiry. An alternative option may be to administer the survey over multiple time points creating a longitudinal dataset. Another option may be to modify the research question slightly to examine how the latent construct varies across contexts or other meaningful manifest variables. Yet another method is to use the survey to inform sampling for a mixed-methods study. All of these options will produce a research product that has greater ability to make a meaningful contribution to the knowledge base and, ultimately, improve the student experience through better leadership practice. In our concluding section we provide an example of how differing conclusions can be drawn from cross-sectional as compared to longitudinal data, and how increased analytical sophistication does nothing to address this problem.

CROSS-SECTIONAL VERSUS LONGITUDINAL ANALYSES: EVIDENCE FROM PRACTICE

To illustrate how analyses of cross-sectional data can be misleading or simply uninformative, we use data from a longitudinal study of school leadership, contrasting results from multiple models applied to cross-sectional data with the same models applied to longitudinal data. The sample for this study consists of 254 full-time classroom teachers from 12 elementary schools in a mid-sized Southern district who completed surveys during the fall, winter, and spring of the 2010–11 school year. As part of a larger study investigating the effect of leadership coaching and structured feedback, teachers provided their perceptions of leadership effectiveness and teacher–principal trust; two latent constructs.

The measure of leadership effectiveness is a six-item scale derived from the 72-item Vanderbilt Assessment for Leadership in Education (VALEd). The VALEd survey of learning-centered leadership measures the *core components* of schools that effectively support learning, such as performance accountability and quality instruction. The VALEd is also designed to capture the systems principals use—the *key processes*—to implement the core components (Murphy, Goldring, Cravens, Elliot, & Porter, 2011). Our consolidated six-item scale of effective leadership represents each of the six core components and six key processes (one core component and one key process are represented in each item) purposefully selected from the conceptual framework of the VALEd survey. Our six-item measure has a Cronbach alpha reliability of 0.94, and correlates well to the full 72-item VALEd scale (rho = 0.96). Participants indicated their response to items, such as "During the past few months how effective was your principal at ensuring that the school... advocated a rigorous curriculum that honored the diversity of students and their families." using a 5-point Likert scale (ineffective to extremely effective).

Our measure of teacher–principal trust is a five-item scale (alpha 0.90) adapted from the trust scales of Hoy and Tshannen-Morran (1999) (see also Tschannen-Moran & Hoy, 2000). Responding on a four-point Likert scale (strongly disagree to strongly agree), teachers were asked to indicate their agreement with the following statements: (a) teachers can rely on the principal, (b) teachers trust the principal, (c) the principal doesn't really tell teachers what is going on, (d) teachers in this school have faith in the integrity of the principal, and (e) teachers are suspicious of most of the principal's actions.

Given the central importance of learning-centered leadership (e.g., Robinson et al., 2008) coupled with the seminal role of trust in schools (e.g., Schneider & Bryk, 2002), a reasonable line of inquiry would be to examine the extent to which establishing trust between principals and teachers may be a foundational step to implementing effective learning-centered leadership. This is an illustrative example and, thus, has purposefully oversimplified the rich conceptual frameworks built by scholars from both camps. It is reasonable to conceptualize trust and learning-centered leadership to be in a recursive relationship, with increases in one paving the way for increases in the other. For the purposes of this exemplar, however, we rely on the simple, yet reasonable, hypothesis that trust must be established between principal and teacher before we can expect principals to be able to make substantial strides in their learning-centered leadership—especially with respect to practices that require a modicum of professional vulnerability, such as classroom observations and post-observation discussions.

SEEING IS BELIEVING: AN EMPIRICAL EXEMPLAR

In the following section we have used five analytical models to investigate the relationship between the two latent constructs of leadership and trust. Our first model, labeled in Tables 5.2, 5.3, and 5.4 as "OLS," is an unconditional ordinary least-squares regression model that represents our most naive estimation approach. Our second model, labeled "Clustered," layers on cluster-adjustment for non-independence of observations within schools and several control variables for school, principal, and teacher characteristics. School variables include student enrollment and the percent of students eligible for free or reduced price lunch (FRL), minority students, and students testing at or above proficient in math. Principal control variables include principals' gender, years of teaching experience, years of administrative experience, and years as an administrator in the current school. Teacher variables include total years of teaching experience and years working with the current principal.

Our third model, labeled "Fixed-Effects," uses school fixed effects to control for unobserved school-level heterogeneity. In these models, school and principal control variables were not included, as they are constant within schools; teacher control variables remained in these models. Our fourth model is a two-level hierarchical linear model, labeled "HLM," which nests teachers within schools and every school is allowed a random intercept. Our final model is a Structural Equation Model (SEM), which integrates each item in our Trust and Instructional Leadership scales into the model, estimating both a measurement model and a structural model simultaneously. Our SEM is portrayed in Figure 5.1, with TT 1–TT 5 representing the individual Teacher Trust items, and LCL 1 through LCL 6 representing the six Learning-Centered Leadership items.

We apply these five models—OLS, Clustered, Fixed-Effects, HLM, and SEM—to three different specifications of leadership effectiveness and teacher–principal trust. Our first specification of these measures is simply the scaled items as collected during the third (spring) wave of data collection. Shown in Table 5.2, these results are in keeping with typical analyses of cross-sectional data. Table 5.3 presumes that data were collected at two time points, during the winter and the spring.[2] We take advantage of this additional measurement period to construct two change variables, representing the change in trust and change in leadership between these two time points. The intuition here is that data in this form are a closer approximation to

[Figure: Structural Equation Model diagram showing Teacher Trust of Principal (with indicators TT 1–TT 5) leading to Learning Centered Leadership (with indicators LCL 1–LCL 6), with Control Vars feeding into Learning Centered Leadership]

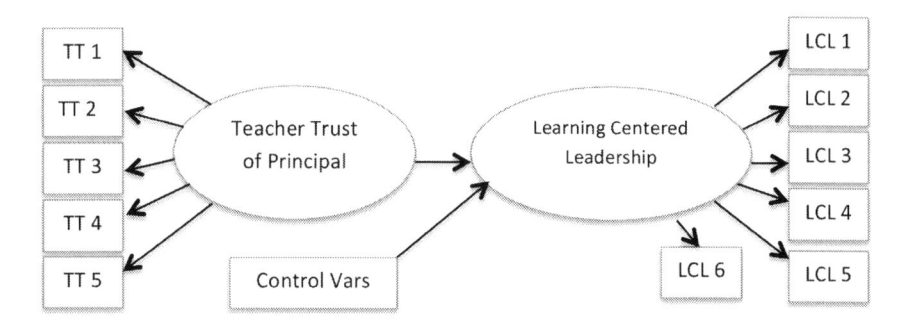

Figure 5.1 Structural Equation Model (error terms not shown).

our underlying theory of action, namely that changes in trust are systematically related to changes in leadership effectiveness.

Lastly, we use all three waves of data to create measures of trust and leadership that most accurately reflect our initial hypothesis that changes in teacher–principal trust will be followed by changes in perceptions of leadership effectiveness. For this final approach, we calculate change in trust using the fall to winter change and calculate change in leadership using the winter to spring measures. This strategy is the best approximation to represent the true temporal ordering of events as supported by the underlying theory of action. Results from this last strategy are presented in Table 5.4.

RESULTS AND DISCUSSION

The descriptive statistics for our sample are presented in Table 5.1. The descriptive statistics are presented at the teacher-level to show the variation across the whole sample, and aggregated to the school-level to provide some intuition for the within/between school variation. As is expected, we note that teachers' perspectives are tempered as they are aggregated across their respective schools; however, substantial between-school variation remains, in both learning-centered leadership and teacher–principal trust. Also worthy of note, is that the changes in leadership and trust are quite small, even at the extremes—a point of central importance that we will return to later.

The results from our first set of analyses using the cross-sectional data collected in the spring are shown in Table 5.2. These results reveal a surprising level of consistency across the five analytical models. In each model we observe a highly significant, positive relationship between teacher–principal trust and effective leadership. Interestingly, this finding is robust across models, diminishing only slightly with the inclusion of school, principal, and teacher covariates. This implies that the trust-leadership relationship is

TABLE 5.1 Descriptive Statistics

	Percentile					
	Teacher-Level			School-Level		
	10th	50th	90th	10th	50th	90th
Learning-Centered Leadership (spring)	2.17	3.67	4.67	2.90	3.59	4.07
Change in Leadership (winter to spring)	–1.00	0.00	0.67	–0.37	–0.08	0.22
Teacher–Principal Trust (spring)	2.00	3.00	4.00	2.53	3.04	3.53
Change in Trust (winter to spring)	–0.80	0.00	0.40	–0.30	–0.12	0.15
Lagged Change in Trust (fall to winter)	–0.60	0.00	0.60	–0.18	–0.07	0.25
Enrollment				179	356	694
Economically disadvantaged (%)				50.1	77.3	91.3

TABLE 5.2 Cross-Sectional Sample to Examine the Effect of Teacher–Principal Trust on Learning-Centered Leadership

	(1) OLS b/se	(2) Clustered b/se	(3) Fixed-Effects b/se	(4) HLM b/se	(5) SEM b/se
Trust	0.963***	0.976***	0.931***	0.935***	0.888***
	(0.05)	(0.06)	(0.06)	(0.06)	(0.060)
Constant	0.586***	0.647	0.696**	0.804	
	(0.16)	(0.49)	(0.21)	(3.08	
School & principal control variables	No	Yes	No	Yes	Yes
Teacher control variables	No	Yes	Yes	Yes	Yes
N	254	254	254	254	254

Note: Table presents the regression coefficients with standard errors in parentheses.
* $p < 0.05$, ** $p < 0.01$, *** $p < 0.001$

consistent across schools in our sample. And while this might be expected in a sample of homogenous schools, Table 5.1 shows that schools in our sample vary substantially across factors such as enrollment and the percent of economically disadvantaged students.

One challenge to analyses that use only cross-sectional data is determining how to meaningfully interpret the results. Looking at the analyses presented in Table 5.2, we can say confidently that when trust is high, leadership effectiveness also appears to be high (and vice versa). However, with only this cross-sectional data, multiple questions remain. Do changes in trust coincide with changes in leadership effectiveness? Do dips in trust coincide with dips in learning-centered leadership? Does trust vary at all over time, or is trust a largely static characteristic of an individual?

It is typical for a study of this type to facilitate interpretation by framing results relative to potential changes in the independent variable. For instance, one may look at Table 5.1 and claim that a one-unit change in teacher–principal trust (which is comparable to moving from the median to the 90th percentile), would be accompanied by a 0.93 unit increase in learning-centered leadership. However, with only cross-sectional data we have no way of knowing if a one-unit change in teacher–principal trust is a reasonable magnitude of change that occurs among teachers. Longitudinal data, even data collected over a fairly short time horizon such as the winter to spring data presented in Table 5.3, are better suited to addressing these lingering questions.

In Table 5.3 we present the results from a simple change model where changes in teachers' perceptions of learning-centered leadership from winter to spring are regressed on teacher–principal trust. And again, we see a strong similarity across models, from the overly simplistic first-order regression (model 6), to the more complex random intercept approach (model 9) and the structural-measurement model as well (model 10). As compared to the cross-sectional analyses shown in Table 5.2, we see that the coefficient is smaller—roughly half the magnitude of prior results. The

TABLE 5.3 The Effect of Changes in Teacher–Principal Trust (Cotemporaneous) on Changes in Learning-Centered Leadership

	(6) OLS b/se	(7) Clustered b/se	(8) Fixed-Effects b/se	(9) HLM b/se	(10) SEM b/se
Change in Trust (winter to spring)	0.537***	0.532***	0.507***	0.512***	0.597***
	(0.07)	(0.06)	(0.07)	(0.07)	(0.09)
Constant	−0.055	1.235*	−0.215	1.123	
	(0.04)	(0.52)	(0.11)	(1.72)	
School & principal control variables	No	Yes	No	Yes	Yes
Teacher control variables	No	Yes	Yes	Yes	Yes
N	254	254	254	254	254

Note: Table presents the regression coefficients with standard errors in parentheses.
* $p < 0.05$, ** $p < 0.01$, *** $p < 0.001$

direct interpretation of these results is that a one-unit increase in trust corresponds with a half-unit increase in changes to teachers' perceptions of learning-centered leadership. However, from the descriptive statistics in Table 5.1 (4th row, teacher level), we can see that one-unit increases do not occur at all in the sample—indeed, the largest change in trust is a –0.80 unit change and the largest increase is 0.40. This provides some perspective that changes in trust do indeed occur, but they tend to be quite modest relative to the implications from Table 5.2.

And while the integration of a change measure has addressed some of the limitations of the cross-sectional analysis, additional questions remain. Notably, with only one prior time point we cannot determine from the analyses shown in Table 5.3 if the changes in trust may be causing the changes in perceived leadership effectiveness or vice versa. Another lingering question might be whether there was one singular factor that was driving changes in both measures. For example, if a teacher was feeling particularly generous during the initial survey administration both trust and leadership ratings may be high; if they were feeling slightly more critical during the subsequent data collection both ratings may be lower.

In survey research this phenomenon is referred to as common method bias (Lindell & Whitney, 2001). It may also be the case that seasonal variation (e.g., lower ratings in the winter as compared to the spring) could be driving the change measures (Goff, Kam, & Kraszewski, 2014). Scenarios of this type would lead to the (artificially) positive correlation in the change measures observed in Table 5.3. Ideally, to provide the most compelling support for the research question motivating this inquiry, we would like to provide some evidence that changes in teachers' perceptions of learning-centered leadership are preceded by changes in teacher–principal trust. To meet this last lingering question we integrate one more round of data to examine if changes in teacher–principal trust (from fall to winter) are statistically and substantively related to subsequent changes in learning-centered leadership (winter to spring), with the results presented in Table 5.4.

The immediate conclusion we can draw from Table 5.4 is that we can no longer make any definitive claims that teacher–principal trust leads to improved learning-centered leadership through any of the four modeling approaches. This suggests that the "common method bias," seasonal variation, or some other unmeasured factor common to both constructs may have been driving the prior correlation.

It is worth pointing out that all these models—one through 15—all have the same sample size of 254, and, thus, have the same power to detect effects (Cohen, 1992; Spybrook, Raudenbush, Liu, Congdon, & Martinez, 2006). However, the cross-sectional analyses (models 1–5) are particularly susceptible to Type I error, creating the illusion of a relationship when none exists. This phenomenon lies contrary to the common wisdom that

TABLE 5.4 The Effect of Changes in Teacher–Principal Trust (Lagged) on Changes in Learning-Centered Leadership

	(11) OLS b/se	(12) Clustered b/se	(13) Fixed-Effects b/se	(14) HLM b/se	(15) SEM b/se
Trust	−0.081	−0.126	−0.095	−0.119	−0.162
	(0.09)	(0.08)	(0.09)	(0.08)	(0.091)
Constant	−0.115**	0.344	−0.308*	0.328	
	(0.04)	(0.79)	(0.12)	(0.90)	
School & principal control variables	No	Yes	No	Yes	Yes
Teacher control variables	No	Yes	Yes	Yes	Yes
N	254	254	254	254	254

Note: Table presents the regression coefficients with standard errors in parentheses.
* $p < 0.05$, ** $p < 0.01$, *** $p < 0.001$

values cross-sectional studies as a way to lay a foundation for future fruitful research.

Importantly, across each of the three samples, the naïve OLS model, the OLS model with covariates and cluster adjustments, the school fixed-effects model, the hierarchical linear model, and the structural equation model were all equally misleading. This serves to underscore the important point that elaborate analytical methods cannot make up for a weak data collection scheme.

CONCLUSIONS

In this chapter we have argued that to advance knowledge on school leadership requires thoughtful research design and selection of analytic strategies. Because numerous topics in education leadership rely on latent constructs and studies frequently utilize cross-sectional data, we find Harwell's (2011) assertion that, the collection of data and choice of methods "limits what can be discovered, emphasizing some possibilities and eliminating others" (p. 180) particularly salient here. To illustrate this point we have outlined the benefits and limitations of various research designs in studies examining education leadership.

Scholarship on school leadership has a long tradition of using cross-sectional analyses to build the research base and inform practice. There are instances when cross-sectional analyses can provide substantive insights to the field, especially through descriptive analyses, when coupled with qualitative research, and when making comparisons between latent and manifest variables. However, the lingering questions that remain from cross-sectional analyses focusing on the relationship between multiple latent constructs tend to be so numerous that they prevent any meaningful scholarly or practical knowledge from being developed, regardless of the sophistication of the analytical methods used. We contend that cross-sectional research involving multiple latent variables often leaves us with more unresolved questions than answers. When researchers are considering research questions that focus on how one latent variable may impact another, we recommend the use of alternative research designs, such as the collection of longitudinal data.

The low cost of administration makes cross-sectional surveys an appealing research option. Indeed, with the creation of reliable online survey portals, such as Qualtrics and Survey Monkey, once a survey is created, the marginal cost of an additional survey administration is close to zero. However, the increasing practice by states and school districts of collecting of longitudinal data for students, teachers, and principals offers new opportunities for researchers. We encourage researchers and practitioners alike to demand more of cross-sectional research, and when cross-sectional research cannot adequately answer the intended question, to consider pursuing alternative options for data collection, many of which we have outlined throughout this chapter.

ACKNOWLEDGEMENTS

The data presented in this paper were collected through a grant (R305A070298) to Leonard Bickman from the U.S. Department of Education's Institute of Education Sciences. All opinions expressed in this paper represent those of the authors and not necessarily the institutions with which they are affiliated or the U.S. Department of Education. Funding for Peter Goff was provided by an IES grant through Vanderbilt's ExpERT program for doctoral training (R305B040110).

NOTES

1. American Educational Research Journal, Economics of Education Review, Education Finance and Policy, Educational Administration Quarterly, Educational Evaluation and Policy Analysis, Educational Researcher, Journal of Educational Administration, Journal of Research on Leadership in Education, Journal of School Leadership, Leadership and Policy in Schools, Leadership Quarterly.
2. Results presented here are congruent with results that determine change using fall to spring measures.

REFERENCES

Barnes, C. A., Camburn, E., Sanders, B. R., & Sebastian, J. (2010). Developing instructional leaders: Using mixed methods to explore the black box of planned change in principals' professional practice. *Educational Administration Quarterly, 46*(2), 241–279. doi:10.1177/1094670510361748

Blanchard, K. H., Zigarmi, D., & Nelson, R. B. (1993). Situational leadership after 25 years: A retrospective. *Journal of Leadership and Organizational Studies, 1*(1), 21–36.

Bowers, A. J. (2010). Analyzing the longitudinal K–12 grading histories of entire cohorts of students: Grades, data driven decision making, dropping out and hierarchical cluster analysis. *Practical Assessment, Research, and Evaluation, 15*(7), 1–18.

Bowers, A. J., & White, B. R. (2014). Do principal preparation and teacher qualifications influence different types of school growth trajectories in Illinois? A growth mixture model analysis. *Journal of Educational Administration, 52*(5), 705–736.

Brown, G. T. L., & Chai, C. (2012). Assessing instructional leadership: A longitudinal study of new principals. *Journal of Educational Administration, 50*(6), 753–772. doi:10.1108/09578231211264676

Camburn, E. M., Huff, J. T., Goldring, E. B., & May, H. (2010). Assessing the validity of an annual survey for measuring principal leadership practice. *The Elementary School Journal, 111*(2), 314–335.

Camburn, E. M., Spillane, J. P., & Sebastian, J. (2010). Assessing the utility of a daily log for measuring principal leadership practice. *Educational Administration Quarterly, 46*(5), 707–737. doi:10.1177/0013161X10377345

Coelli, M., & Green, D. A. (2012). Leadership effects: School principals and student outcomes. *Economics of Education Review, 31*(1), 92–109. doi:10.1016/j.econedurev.2011.09.001

Cohen, J. (1992). Quantitative methods in psychology. *Psychological Bulletin, 112*(1), 155–159.

Cole, D. A, & Maxwell, S. E. (2003). Testing mediational models with longitudinal data: Questions and tips in the use of structural equation modeling. *Journal of Abnormal Psychology, 112*(4), 558–77. doi:10.1037/0021-843X.112.4.558

Corcoran, S. P., Schwartz, A. E., & Weinstein, M. (2012). Training your own: The impact of New York City's aspiring principals program on student achievement. *Educational Evaluation and Policy Analysis, 34*(2), 232–253. doi:10.3102/0162373712437206

Cravens, X. C., Goldring, E., & Penaloza, R. (2012). Leadership practice in the context of U.S. school choice reform. *Leadership and Policy in Schools, 11*(4), 452–476. doi:10.1080/15700763.2012.700989

Creswell, J. (2007). *Designing and conducting mixed methods research*. Thousand Oaks: Sage Publishing.

Daly, A. J., Der-Martirosian, C., Ong-Dean, C., Park, V., & Wishard-Guerra, A. (2011). Leading under sanction: Principals' perceptions of threat rigidity, efficacy, and leadership in underperforming schools. *Leadership and Policy in Schools, 10*(2), 171–206. doi:10.1080/15700763.2011.557517

Day, C., Sammons, P., Hopkins, D., Harris, A., Leithwood, K., Gu, Q., & Kington, A. (2009). *The impact of school leadership on pupil outcomes: Final report.* Nottingham.

Dixon-Woods, M., Agarwal, S., Jones, D., Young, B., & Sutton, A. (2005). Synthesising qualitative and quantitative evidence: A review of possible methods. *Journal of Health Services Research and Policy, 10*(1), 45–53. doi:10.1258/1355819052801804

Easton, J. (2011). Talk to graduating IES fellow at the graduate school of education, University of Pennsylvania. Philadelphia. Retrieved from http://ies.ed.gov/director/pdf/Easton050711.pdf

Epstein, J. L., Galindo, C. L., & Sheldon, S. B. (2011). Levels of leadership: Effects of district and school leaders on the quality of school programs of family and community involvement. *Educational Administration Quarterly, 47*(3), 462–495. doi:10.1177/0013161X10396929

Eyal, O., & Roth, G. (2011). Principals' leadership and teachers' motivation: Self-determination theory analysis. *Journal of Educational Administration, 49*(3), 256–275. doi:10.1108/09578231111129055

Fullan, M. G., & Stiegelbauer, S. (1991). *The new meaning of educational change* (2nd ed.). New York: Teachers College Press.

Goff, P., Kam, J., & Kraszewski, J. (2014). *Timing is everything: Temporal variation in school survey measures.* Paper presented at the annual meeting of the Association for Education Finance and Policy. San Antonio, TX.

Goff, P., Guthrie, E. J., Goldring, E., & Bickman, L. (2014). Changing principals' leadership through feedback and coaching. *Journal Educational Administration, 52*(5).

Goff, P. T., Mavrogordato, M., & Goldring, E. (2012). Instructional leadership in charter schools: Is there an organizational effect or are leadership practices the result of faculty characteristics and preferences? *Leadership and Policy in Schools, 11*(1), 1–25. doi:10.1080/15700763.2011.611923

Goldring, E., Huff, J., May, H., & Camburn, E. (2008). School context and individual characteristics: What influences principal practice? *Journal of Educational Administration, 46*(3), 332–352. doi:10.1108/09578230810869275

Gollob, H. F., & Reichardt, C. S. (1991). Interpreting and estimating indirect effects assuming time lags really matter. In L. M. Collins & L. Horn, John (Eds.), *Best methods for the analysis of change: Recent advances, unanswered questions, future directions.* (pp. 243–259). Washington DC: American Psychological Association.

Greenlee, B. J., & Karanxha, Z. (2010). A study of group dynamics in educational leadership cohort and non-cohort groups. *Journal of Research on Leadership Education, 5*(11), 357–382.

Hallinger, P. (2010). A review of three decades of doctoral studies using the principal instructional management rating scale: A lens on methodological progress in educational leadership. *Educational Administration Quarterly, 47*(2), 271–306. doi:10.1177/0013161X10383412

Hallinger, P., & Heck, R. H. (1996). Reassessing the principal's role in school effectiveness: A review of empirical research, 1980–1995. *Educatational Administration Quarterly, 32*(1), 5–44.

Hallinger, P., & Heck, R. H. (1996). The principal's role in school effectiveness: An assessment of methodological progress, 1980–1995. In K. Leithwood, J. D. Chapman, P. Corson, & P. Hallinger (Eds.), *The international handbook of research on educational leadership and administration* (pp. 723–785). New York: Springer.

Hallinger, P., & Heck, R. H. (2010). Collaborative leadership and school improvement: Understanding the impact on school capacity and student learning. *School Leadership and Management, 30*(2), 95–100.

Hallinger, P., & Heck, R. H. (2011). Conceptual and methodological issues in studying school leadership effects as a reciprocal process. *School Effectiveness and School Improvement, 22*(2), 149–173. doi:10.1080/09243453.2011.565777

Hallinger, P., & Lee, M. (2012). A global study of the practice and impact of distributed instructional leadership in international baccalaureate (IB) schools. *Leadership and Policy in Schools, 11*(4), 477–495. doi:10.1080/15700763.2012.700990

Harwell, M. (2011). Research design in qualitative/quantitative/mixed methods. In C. F. Conrad & R. C. Serlin (Eds.), *The SAGE handbook for research in education: Pursuing ideas as the keystone of exemplary inquiry* (2nd ed., pp. 147–182). Los Angeles: Sage Publishing.

Hauserman, C. P., Ivankova, N. V., & Stick, S. L. (2013, January). Teacher perceptions of principals' leadership qualities: A mixed methods study. *Journal of School Leadership, 23,* 34–64.

Hausman, C. S. (2000). Principal role in magnet schools: Transformed or entrenched? *Journal of Educational Administration, 38*(1), 25–46.

Heck, R. H., & Hallinger, P. (2009). Assessing the contribution of distributed leadership to school improvement and growth in math achievement. *American Educational Research Journal, 46*(3), 659–689. doi:10.3102/0002831209340042

Heck, R. H., & Hallinger, P. (2010). Testing a longitudinal model of distributed leadership effects on school improvement. *The Leadership Quarterly, 21*(5), 867–885. doi:10.1016/j.leaqua.2010.07.013

Heck, R. H., & Hallinger, P. (2014). Modeling the longitudinal effects of school leadership on teaching and learning. *Journal of Educational Administration, 52*(5).

Heck, R. H., & Moriyama, K. (2010). Examining relationships among elementary schools' contexts, leadership, instructional practices, and added-year outcomes: A regression discontinuity approach. *School Effectiveness and School Improvement, 21*(4), 377–408. doi:10.1080/09243453.2010.500097

Hess, F. M., & Kelly, A. P. (2007). Learning to lead: What gets taught in principal-preparation programs. *Teachers College Record, 109*(1), 244–274.

Hill, P. W., & Rowe, K. J. (1996). Multilevel modeling in school effectivenss research. *School Effectiveness and School Improvement, 7*(1), 1–34.

Hochbein, C., & Cunningham, B. C. (2013). An exploratory analysis of the longitudinal impact of principal change on elementary school achievement. *Journal of School Leadership, 23*(1), 64–90.

Hoy, W. K., & Tschannen-Moran, M. (1999). Five faces of trust: An empirical confirmation in urban elementary schools. *Journal of School Leadership, 9,* 184–208.

Jacob, B. A. (2011). Do principals fire the worst teachers? *Educational Evaluation and Policy Analysis, 33*(4), 403–434. doi:10.3102/0162373711414704

Jacob, R., Goddard, R., Kim, M., Miller, R., & Goddard, Y. (2014). Exploring the causal impact of the McREL balanced leadership program on leadership, principal efficacy, instructional climate, educator turnover, and student achievement. *Educational Evaluation and Policy Analysis.* doi:10.3102/0162373714549620

Kamler, E., Dodge, A., & Walker, J. M. T. (2013, January). Growing school leaders : An exploration of perceptions, actions, and support following a formative assessment experience. *Journal of School Leadership, 23*, 4–33.

Kythreotis, A., Pashiardis, P., & Kyriakides, L. (2010). The influence of school leadership styles and culture on students' achievement in Cyprus primary schools. *Journal of Educational Administration, 48*(2), 218–240. doi:10.1108/09578231011027860

Leithwood, K., Patten, S., & Jantzi, D. (2010). Testing a conception of how school leadership influences student learning. *Educational Administration Quarterly, 46*(5), 671–706. doi:10.1177/0013161X10377347

Leithwood, K., Seashore Louis, K., Anderson, S., & Wahlstrom, K. (2004). *How leadership influences student learning: A review of research*. New York. Retrieved from http://conservancy.umn.edu/bitstream/11299/2035/1/CAREI ReviewofResearch How Leadership Influences.pdf

Lindell, M. K., & Whitney, D. J. (2001). Accounting for common method variance in cross-sectional research designs. *Journal of Applied Psychology, 86*(1), 114.

Luo, M. (2008). Structural equation modeling for high school principals' data-driven decision making: An analysis of information use environments. *Educatational Administration Quarterly, 44*(5), 603–634.

Luyten, H., Visscher, A., & Witziers, B. (2005). School effectiveness research: From a review of the criticism to recommendations for further development. *School Effectiveness and School Improvement, 16*(3), 249–279. doi:10.1080/09243450500114884

Maxwell, S. E. & Cole, D. A. (2007). Bias in cross-sectional analyses of longitudinal mediation. *Psychological Methods, 12*(1), 23–44. doi:10.1037/1082-989X.12.1.23

Miller, A. (2013). Principal turnover and student achievement. *Economics of Education Review, 36*, 60–72. doi:10.1016/j.econedurev.2013.05.004

Murnane, R. J., & Willett, J. B. (2011). *Methods matter: Improving causal inference in educational and social science research*. New York: Oxford University Press.

Murphy, J. F., Goldring, E. B., Cravens, X. C., Elliot, S. N., & Porter, A. C. (2011). The Vanderbilt assessment of leadership in education: Measuring learning-centered leadership. *Journal of East China Normal University, 29*(1), 1–10.

Myung, J., Loeb, S., & Horng, E. (2011). Tapping the principal pipeline: Identifying talent for future school leadership in the absence of formal succession management programs. *Educational Administration Quarterly, 47*(5), 695–727. doi:10.1177/0013161X11406112

Richardson, J. W., Imig, S., & Ndoye, A. (2012). Developing culturally aware school leaders: measuring the impact of an international internship using the MGUDS. *Educational Administration Quarterly, 49*(1), 92–123. doi:10.1177/0013161X12455055

Robinson, V. M., Lloyd, C. A., & Rowe, K. J. (2008). The impact of leadership on student outcomes: An analysis of differential effects of leadership types. *Educational Administration Quarterly, 44*(5), 635–674.

Ross, J. A., & Gray, P. (2006). Transformational leadership and teacher commitment to organizational values: The mediating effects of collective teacher efficacy. *School Effectiveness and School Improvement, 17*(2), 179–199.

Sammons, P., Davis, S., Day, C., & Gu, Q. (2014). Using mixed methods to investigate school improvement and the role of leadership: An example of a longitudinal study in England. *Journal of Education Policy, 52*(5).

Scheerens, J. (2012). Summary and conclusions: Instructional leadership in schools as loosely coupled organizations. In J. Scheerens (Ed.), *School leadership effects revisited: Review and meta-analysis of empirical studies* (pp. 131–152). New York: Springer.

Schneider, B., & Bryk, A. S. (2002). *Trust in schools: A core resource for improvement*. New York: Russell Sage Foundation.

Seashore Louis, K. & Robinson, V. M. (2012). External mandates and instructional leadership: School leaders as mediating agents. *Journal of Educational Administration, 50*(5), 629–665. doi:10.1108/09578231211249853

Shadish, W. R., Cook, T. D., & Campbell, D. T. (2001). *Experimental and quasi-experimental designs for generalized causal inference*. Stamford: Cenage Learning.

Shin, S. H., Slater, C. L., & Backhoff, E. (2012). Principal perceptions and student achievement in reading in Korea, Mexico, and the United States: Educational leadership, school autonomy, and use of test tesults. *Educational Administration Quarterly, 49*(3), 489–527. doi:10.1177/0013161X12458796

Spybrook, J., Raudenbush, S. W., Liu, X. I., Congdon, R., & Martinez, A. (2006). *Optimal design for longitudinal and multilevel research: Documentation for the "Optimal Design" software*. Survey Research Center of the Institute of Social Research at University of Michigan.

Supovitz, J. A., & Tognatta, N. (2013). The impact of distributed leadership on collaborative team decision making. *Leadership and Policy in Schools, 12*(2), 101–121. doi:10.1080/15700763.2013.810274

Thoonen, E. E. J., Sleegers, P. J. C., Oort, F. J., & Peetsma, T. T. D. (2012). Building school-wide capacity for improvement: The role of leadership, school organizational conditions, and teacher factors. *School Effectiveness and School Improvement, 23*(4), 441–460. doi:10.1080/09243453.2012.678867

Tschannen-Moran, M., & Hoy, W. K. (2000). A multidisciplinary analysis of the nature, meaning, and measurement of trust. *Review of Educational Research, 70*(4), 547–593.

Urick, A., & Bowers, A. J. (2011). What influences principals' perceptions of academic climate? A nationally representative study of the direct effects of perception on climate. *Leadership and Policy in Schools, 10*(3), 322–348. doi:10.1080/15700763.2011.577925

Urick, A., & Bowers, A. J. (2014, March). The impact of principal perception on student academic climate and achievement in high school: How does it measure up? *Journal of School Leadership, 24*, 386–414.

Urick, A., & Bowers, A. J. (2014). What are the different types of principals across the United States? A latent class analysis of principal perception of leadership. *Educational Administration Quarterly, 50*(1), 96–134. doi:10.1177/0013161X13489019

Wise, D., & Hammack, M. (2011). Leadership coaching: Coaching competencies and best practices. *Journal of School Leadership, 21*(3), 449–477.

CHAPTER 6

ADVANCING EDUCATIONAL LEADERSHIP RESEARCH USING QUALITATIVE COMPARATIVE ANALYSIS (QCA)

Katherine Marie Caves and Johannes Meuer
ETH Zurich

Christian Rupietta
University of Zurich

INTRODUCTION

In 1987, political scientist Charles Ragin developed Qualitative Comparative Analysis (QCA) as an alternative method to statistical techniques that allowed for the use of smaller sample sizes, the inclusion of deep case knowledge, and the analysis of complex relationships among factors. QCA is especially useful when research questions are set theoretic, in situations with complex causality, with data sets of any size, and when a method that bridges qualitative and quantitative approaches is most appropriate. The method has been used in a variety of fields, especially in the social sciences, to find causal pathways, develop typologies, and understand necessity and sufficiency relationships between configurations of causal conditions and

Challenges and Opportunities of Educational Leadership Research and Practice, pages 147–170
Copyright © 2016 by Information Age Publishing
All rights of reproduction in any form reserved.

an outcome. In this chapter, we first introduce QCA as a complement to educational leadership research that can help address two important challenges: the need for practitioner-applicable pathways, and the complex nature of causation in leadership research. After introducing the method, we provide an illustration of QCA in a fictional educational leadership context.

Research in educational leadership investigates how leaders can encourage effective schooling (e.g., Bossert, Dwyer, Rowan, & Lee, 1982; Hallinger, Bickman, & Davis, 1996; Heck, Larsen, & Marcoulides, 1990; Bell, Bolam, & Cubillo, 2003). By clarifying the policies and processes that build the organizational, structural, instructional, and cultural capacity of schools in different contexts, research on educational leadership seeks to determine how school leaders can improve instruction (Neumerski, 2013), thereby indirectly increasing student learning (Fullan, 2007; Ogawa & Bossert, 1995; Hallinger & Heck, 2010, 2011). Currently, research on educational leadership faces at least two key challenges. The first is to understand how research can direct the efforts of school leaders towards effective educational leadership. The second challenge is to understand how these leadership pathways operate across school contexts.

The first challenge—finding reliable pathways for successful school leadership—reflects the shift in focus over time from the characteristics of principals to school-level pathways for improvement. Hallinger & Murphy (1985) start at the principal level but find that school performance differences originate from organizational and environmental factors rather than the personal characteristics of principals. This moved the focus from principals' characteristics to their actions (Duke, 1987) and the general qualities of excellent educational leadership, including administration and teachers (Smith & Andrews, 1989). For example, Dinham (2004) finds that a leadership focus on students and learning is key, rather than the personalities of leaders. Leithwood, Anderson, Mascall, and Strauss (2010) move beyond leadership practices to strategies, and identify four strategic areas—rational, organizational, emotional, and family—through which school leadership indirectly influences learning. However, critiques of educational leadership research point out that it still lacks specifics for *how* leaders should identify and implement effective strategies and practices (Neumerski, 2013). Thus, the first challenge is to help school leaders identify practice pathways that can improve student experiences and, indirectly, learning.

The building blocks of a set of pathways for educational leaders are underway. Models and practices for leadership to affect learning are increasingly clear (Mulford & Silins, 2011; Hallinger & Heck, 2010), as are the specific knowledge and skills leaders need to support teachers (Prestine & Nelson, 2005; Robinson, Lloyd, & Rowe, 2008). However, these elements of leadership are not yet connected into a coherent strategy for on-the-ground leaders, and it remains difficult to integrate individual studies of specific effects into a comprehensive set of strategies. For example, Marzano, Waters, & McNulty (2005) translate research findings into detailed advice for leaders. While scholars increasingly understand effective strategies and practices as well as their underlying mechanisms, prescribing their implementation across different contexts is still a challenge.

The second challenge is to account for school context in the development of leadership strategies. Quite concretely, Hargreaves and Fullan (1998) highlight the role of school context in developing pathways for improvement, stating that "singular recipes oversimplify what it will take to bring about change in your own situation" (p. 106). Similarly, Hallinger (2011), reviews the field and lays out the agenda for future research: "We need to obtain better information not just about 'what works' but 'what works' in different settings" (p. 138). Research on educational leadership needs to integrate general leadership research with real-life tasks and contexts (Opdenakker & van Damme, 2007; Robinson, Lloyd, & Rowe, 2008). There is broad understanding of the importance of context, but it remains difficult to incorporate in actual research designs.

However, the challenge of including context in recommendations to leaders also builds on the first issue of identifying effective leadership pathways. This presents the two-pronged undertaking of identifying strong leadership practices while tailoring their application to a given school's situation (Hallinger & Heck, 2010, 2011; Leithwood et al., 2010; Mulford & Silins, 2011; Leithwood, Patten, & Jantzi, 2010; Marzano, Waters, & McNulty, 2005). The (second) challenge of accounting for school context aggravates the (first) challenge of developing an understanding of effective educational leadership pathways: even if research-based pathways for good leadership are established, they must be embedded in the school's context to be effective. Thus, even the pathways themselves are necessarily complex to avoid losing contextual specificity. Finding leadership that works for diverse schools is certainly no easy task.

One key strategy for addressing both educational leadership challenges is to use a wide variety of research tools. Models need to account for the complex and subtle relationships between school leadership and student achievement. The effects of leadership on student achievement improvement are often indirect, with evidence of reciprocity, mediation, and moderation (Heck, 2012; Hallinger, 2011; Hallinger & Heck, 2010, 2011). Moreover, the collaborative process of educational leadership is distributed across individuals and organizational levels within the school (Leithwood, Patten, & Jantzi, 2010; Heck & Hallinger, 2009). Schools are complex social systems in which causality cannot be easily pinned down. Empirical evidence indicates that interactions among leaders, followers, and contexts form the basis of leadership practice (Neumerski, 2013). Therefore, models and analytical methods need to capture the complex relationships among educational leadership, student achievement, and the factors in between. This view is consistent with current models, which are explicitly designed to account for context and school-level factors (Knapp, Mkhwanazi, & Portin, 2012; Mulford & Silins, 2011; Hallinger & Heck, 2011; Day et al., 2010). However, even though scholars largely agree that educational leadership strategies are context-dependent, the concept is not yet well integrated with the development of leadership pathways—mostly because these processes and levels of complexity are very difficult to model and test.

Overall, research on educational leadership has advanced significantly in the four decades since its inception. For research designs and models to both reflect and incorporate the complexity of schools and schooling, Hallinger & Huber (2012) argue, "no single 'method' is adequate to the task of advancing knowledge in our field" (p. 364). New methods are indispensable for maintaining momentum. As mentioned earlier, QCA is especially useful when causal relationships are highly complex, and for other issues that appear in educational leadership research. The purpose of this chapter is to introduce QCA to the literature on educational leadership, and to demonstrate how researchers may advance our understanding of educational leadership by using QCA.

QCA FOR EDUCATIONAL LEADERSHIP

QCA is a Boolean-algebraic method that has gained in popularity over the last two decades. Originally proposed in the mid-1980s by American sociologist Charles Ragin (1987, 1994, 2000, 2008a), it is now used across disciplines in the social and natural sciences. Rather than examining statistical associations between independent and dependent variables, QCA searches for set relationships. QCA thereby combines the holistic case-based perspective, inductive research approach, and in-depth knowledge used by qualitative researchers with the deductive and trend-seeking standpoint of quantitative work. QCA uses set theory to think about data in terms of sufficiency and necessity, and Boolean algebra to minimize all logically possible configurations of causal conditions to only those important for an outcome.

Instead of isolating individual variables and searching for net effects, QCA searches for combinations of conditions that occur frequently and are consistently associated with an outcome of interest. In the same way that a qualitative researcher would not separate a school from its context and history, QCA explicitly maintains the holistic case as the unit of analysis throughout its process. QCA finds patterns and provides specific measures of their strength and reliability, much as is done in qualitative research. QCA compares entire configurations of interrelated elements, maintaining the integrity of cases rather than splitting them into individual variables (Fritzsche, 2013). This case-level analysis allows researchers to distinguish between irrelevant, contributing, and essential parts of a system.

Conceptualizing and minimizing data in this manner allows QCA to identify four theoretical aspects central to the advancement of research on educational leadership: (a) necessary and sufficient conditions, (b) conjunctural causation where multiple factors together explain an outcome, (c) equifinality where multiple pathways exist to an outcome, and (d) causal asymmetry where configurations for an outcome and its opposite are not necessarily mirror images (Ragin, 2008a).

Necessity and Sufficiency

QCA directly addresses questions of necessity and sufficiency, and the questions of educational leadership are often implicitly about these relations. For example, in their "ten strong claims," Day et al. (2010) talk about essential factors (necessary conditions) for school success and the shared practices (sufficient conditions) of successful leaders. QCA uses set theory to address this kind of relationship between conditions and outcomes. The Venn diagrams in Figure 6.1 illustrate necessity and sufficiency in set-theoretic terms.

In QCA, sufficient conditions are subsets of the outcome of interest. One possible example for sufficiency from research on educational leadership would be student- and learning-focused leadership, which Dinham (2004) identifies as key for school excellence. Sufficiency of that condition for school excellence means that every school with student- and learning-focused leadership will be successful. Some successful schools may not have

Sufficiency *Necessity*

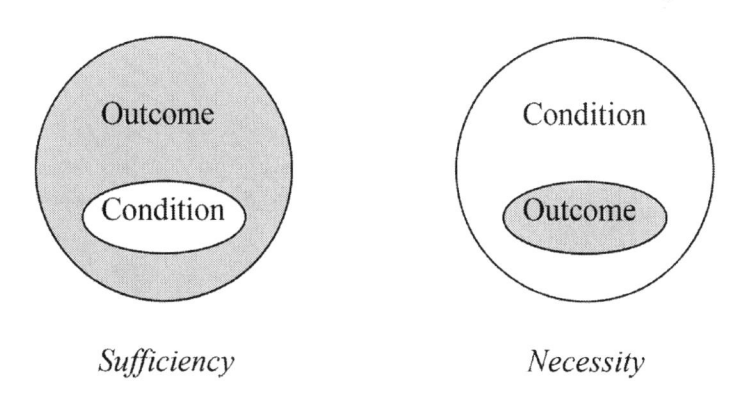

Figure 6.1 Venn diagrams of necessity and sufficiency.

student- and learning-focused leadership, but the schools that do are excellent schools.

In contrast, necessary conditions are supersets of the outcome of interest. For example, if student- and learning-focused leadership is a necessary condition, then every successful school uses this leadership. In this case, the leadership is a basic requirement—or a good starting point—but it is not enough to ensure success on its own. Thus, schools may have this leadership style but low achievement. The question of whether some policy change will improve achievement is often about necessity or sufficiency: do schools need the policy change to improve test scores (necessity), or is the policy enough to improve test scores (sufficiency)? Because QCA is designed to determine the necessity and sufficiency—or the degrees thereof[1]—of conditions of configurations of conditions for an outcome of interest, the technique presents an excellent tool for research in educational leadership.

Conjunctural Causation

QCA looks not only for individually sufficient or necessary conditions, but also for combinations of conditions related to an outcome. It does this by using Boolean logic—combinations of elements like A AND B or A OR B—to define and measure set intersections where the combination of multiple conditions may be necessary or sufficient for the outcome. The analysis of conjunctural causations lends itself to educational leadership by, for example, intersecting context with other conditions.

Leithwood et al. (2010) identify four strategy areas—rational, organizational, emotional, and family—by which school leadership indirectly influences learning by manipulating student-teacher- and school-level characteristics. This model is a useful analogy for concepts of complex causality. Elements of all four areas work in concert and combination with school policies, practices, and the general environment. Different levels of the school organization work together even within strategy areas: in the rational area for example, high-quality teaching at the classroom level is most effective when combined with academic press at the school level. In Boolean terms, good teaching AND academic press are necessary for high achievement rather than either one alone. This keeps policies and practices at different organizational levels connected with one another and the school context. QCA's ability to see conjunctural causation—where conditions influence an outcome in synergistic configurations rather than independently—makes the method well suited for instructional leadership.

Equifinality

Equifinality allows for multiple routes to the same outcome. Equifinality is the argument that "a system can reach the same final state from different initial conditions and by a variety of different paths" (Katz & Kahn, 1978, p. 30). For example, using the four areas again (Leithwood et al., 2010), imagine two recently improved schools: the leadership of school A focused on families, improving parent engagement at home and at school, while school B's leadership used organizational changes to improve by buffering teachers and students from distraction. Both schools improved, but did so using different strategies. In Boolean terms, this solution for improvement in schools A and B is through family OR organizational intervention, where both are equally consistent in their sufficiency for improvement. Schools start at different places, operate in different contexts, and use different resources to boost student achievement, yet perform equally well—there is no single model for a successful school (Day et al., 2010). Thus, in the context of educational leadership, QCA allows to reflect the reality of schools and schooling by allowing for multiple pathways to the same outcome (Fiss, 2011).

Asymmetric Causality

Statistical methods build on the notion of symmetric causality meaning that a variable always has the same effect whether it is low, high, positive, or negative. Instead, QCA allows for asymmetric causality so that the presence and absence of an outcome might have different explanations. QCA separates analysis of configurations leading to the presence of an outcome from those leading to its absence. For research on educational leadership, causal asymmetry questions the implicit assumptions that the effects of a leadership choice and its opposite are equally large, and that the opposite of configurations for success are the configurations for failure and provides insight into the pathways for both successful and unsuccessful educational leadership.

For example, for a school that needs to improve in the emotional area (Leithwood et al., 2010) by increasing support for teacher development, increasing the teacher development budget by 10% might be sufficient for improvement in outcomes. However, it is unlikely that cutting the budget by 10%—the same amount—will result in a drop in outcomes of the exact same magnitude. Similarly, the same intervention might not help a school that already has excellent teacher development in place. In correlational analyses, if increasing one variable generates some increase in the outcome, then the same decrease will have a negative effect of the same size; in the complex world of education, this is not always a valid assumption. Accordingly, the leadership of schools that are successful is not usually the opposite of leadership in schools that are failing. Using the example of the four strategy areas (Leithwood et al., 2010), a successful school might be very strong in all four areas. However, a failing school is not necessarily one that is weak in all four areas—it could be that a failing school is strong in three areas but seriously weak in just one, which could be sufficient for failure.

IMPLEMENTING QCA

The procedure for QCA has three stages: calibration, truth table analysis, and Boolean minimization (Table 6.1). Essentially, the process is one of preparing data, organizing data, and reducing data complexity to key patterns. We briefly discuss the purpose and activities of each stage in the following subsections before demonstrating their use with a fictional empirical illustration.

Calibration

In the first stage, the researcher uses theoretical and substantive knowledge of the cases to determine whether a certain case is more *in* or more *out* of a specified set (Goertz & Mahoney, 2012; Ragin, 2008b). *Crisp sets* are dichotomized to in and out—zero and one. In contrast, *fuzzy sets* range over the entire continuum from zero to one. For capturing variation in support for teacher development rather than strictly presence and absence, a fuzzy set offers increased nuance.

TABLE 6.1 Summary of the QCA Procedure

Stage	Purpose	Activities
1. Calibration	Data preparation	• Specify sets • Define set memberships • Calibrate cases
2. Truth Table Analysis	Data organization	• Create the truth table • Examine configurations • Select cases by setting consistency and frequency cutoffs
3. Boolean Minimization	Data reduction	• Eliminate logical redundancies • Assess the explanatory strength of each configuration • Consider the logic underlying different solutions

To measure a case's membership in a specified set, researchers use calibration, a technique adopted from natural sciences where scales are designed in a way to reflect meaningful floors and ceilings. For example, the Celsius degree scale is calibrated according to the changes in the physical conditions of water: At 0°C (solid to liquid) and 100°C (liquid to gas) the Celsius scale is anchored to meaningful points. Similarly, sets in the social sciences are calibrated to "accurately reflect theoretical concepts and analytical constructs that have precise meaning" (Kvist, 2007, p. 477).

Fuzzy sets can be constructed using direct or indirect methods of calibration.[2] In the direct method, the researcher identifies anchor points that represent where a case is fully out of the set (0), fully in (1), or completely ambiguous (0.5). These anchor points are used to transform the data into set membership scores between 0 and 1. Anchor points are chosen based on external standards or qualitative groupings of cases; when looking at leadership distribution, these might be 0 (fully out) for schools where the principal wields all leadership power, 0.4 (more out than in) where the principal and administrators lead, 0.6 (more in than out) where head teachers are involved, and 1 (fully in) where principals, administrators, and teachers are all involved in school leadership.

If external standards or qualitative boundaries do not exist, the researcher can use indirect calibration. In indirect calibration (also called transformative calibration), regression techniques are used to transform qualitative groupings in the data into set membership scores. The researcher generally groups cases according to their level of membership in the set, and then refines those scores mathematically. Often, the initial groupings can be based on the membership scores of 0.0 for fully out of the set, 0.2 for mostly out, 0.4 for more out than in, 0.6 for more in than out, 0.8 for mostly in, and 1.0 for fully in (for more discussion of both calibration methods, see Ragin, 2008a).

Truth Table Analysis

The second stage, after calibrating the outcome and causal conditions, is truth table analysis. A truth table lists all possible combinations of present and absent conditions, or in other words all theoretically possible configurations of the given conditions. The number of rows in a truth table corresponds to the number of possible configurations, and can be calculated by 2^k, where k is the number of conditions. For example, an analysis of four conditions will yield a truth table with 16 rows. Truth tables allow observation and analysis of cases by grouping cases that share the same configuration of conditions to see if they generate the same outcome. The goal is to identify connections between configurations.

In order to ensure that all cases analyzed for their causal configurations are actually relevant, part of the QCA procedure is to establish cutoffs for consistency and frequency. The consistency cutoff requires that a truth table row's outcomes agree. This ensures that the configurations in the analysis are really associated with the outcome of interest; including inconsistent configurations could distort the determination of conditions that really link to the outcome. Lower consistency indicates that the relationship between the configuration and the outcome is not very strong. The most common consistency cutoffs are 0.7 or 0.8 depending on the sample size and the discretion of the researcher (Ragin, 2008a; Greckhamer, Misangyi, & Fiss, 2013; Schneider & Wagemann, 2012). For example, if all five schools in a truth table row share the same outcome, their consistency score would be 1.0. If four of them agree, the score would be 0.8 and the row would still be included in an analysis of their shared outcome. If, however, three or fewer schools shared the outcome, the consistency would be lower than 0.6 and it would not qualify for the analysis.

The frequency cutoff decides which of the remaining consistent rows to retain in the analysis by requiring each truth table row to represent a certain number of cases. This is simple for smaller samples or those that include a whole population, because then all cases are typically included. Otherwise, the researcher can look for discontinuities in the number of cases per truth table row—if most rows of the table have many cases and some have only a few, those might be best left out of the analysis. Failing that, some external or logical standard can be used to determine the frequency cutoff such that the rows in the analysis represent all common configurations. The frequency cutoff reduces the truth table rows with consistent outcomes to those that can be used to meaningfully explore the occurrence of the outcome. For more on these more complex aspects of QCA, see Schulze-Bentrop (2013) and Marx (2006).

Boolean Minimization

In the third stage, the researcher reduces the complexity of relevant configurations using Boolean minimization. Whereas the truth table provides insights on conditions or configurations sufficient or necessary for the outcome, Boolean minimization highlights only those conditions or configurations that are related to the outcome. With Boolean minimization, row configurations can be reduced to shorter, more parsimonious expressions.

The logic of minimization is based on Mill's method of difference: if two configurations differ in a single condition but share the outcome, that differentiating condition must be irrelevant for explaining the outcome. By eliminating irrelevant conditions, researchers reduce complexity and only the remaining configuration matters for explaining the outcome. Following this logic, QCA systematically minimizes the truth table until only the truly relevant elements of each configuration remain in the solution.[3]

The explanatory strength of a configuration for the outcome is expressed in terms of solution consistency and solution coverage. The solution consistency reflects how often schools that match the configuration have the outcome and is calculated based on the proportion of all matching schools with the outcome. If ten schools have the configuration and nine of them are successful, then the configuration has a solution consistency score of 0.9 for success. Typically, a solution with a consistency score over 0.7 or 0.8 is considered valid (Ragin 2008a; Trujillo & Woulfin, 2014). Instead, coverage describes the number of successful schools that can be accounted for by each configuration. If—in a crisp-set analysis—there are 14 successful schools in total and seven of them have the solution configuration, then the coverage score is 0.5—half of all successful schools match the configuration. Despite some methodological differences, solution coverage functions analogously to the R^2 value of a correlational analysis in that it expresses the degree to which the solution explains the outcome.

The end result is a solution of one or more minimized configurations that are necessary or sufficient for the outcome of interest. In the case of educational leadership, these are pathways that show the combinations of conditions like school policies, structures, and contexts shared by schools with similar outcomes. This allows researchers to examine which conditions are most relevant (or irrelevant) for achievement, how they act and interact configurationally, how schools that succeed differ from those that fail, and which cases might be interesting to explore in more depth.

Through this three-stage procedure, QCA allows researchers to address questions of causal complexity in a wide variety of research settings. QCA is not a mixed-method approach but a distinct tool that can be used for qualitative, quantitative, or meta-analytical investigations (Greckhamer, Misangyi, & Fiss, 2013). Qualitatively, QCA can be used for theory building to find patterns or build typologies (Ragin, 2000). For example, Trujillo and Woulfin (2014) use QCA to identify which configurations of activities by educational intermediaries are linked to instructional change based on interview data. Quantitative researchers can use QCA to analyze necessity and sufficiency in contexts where causality is complex and context is central to meaning. For example, Glaesser and Cooper have critically examined the narrative of educational meritocracy by exposing the necessary and sufficient characteristics of successful students (Cooper, 2005; Cooper & Glaesser, 2008, 2010, 2011; Glaesser & Cooper, 2011, 2014). Finally, in a meta-analysis, QCA can identify leadership features across studies that consistently matter for school achievement, using an approach similar to that of Dunlop, Maggetti, Radaelli, and Russel (2012) for regulatory impact assessment in political science. The method is expanding in educational research (Põder, Kerem, & Lauri, 2013) and in other fields (e.g., Schulze-Bentrop, 2013; Marx, Rihoux, & Ragin, 2014).

In sum, necessity and sufficiency relationships, conjunctural causation, equifinality, and asymmetry are all recognizable in the real world of educational leadership, but difficult to model. QCA conceives of data in set theoretic terms and uses Boolean minimization to search for configurations rather than net effects, allowing it to address these issues directly. QCA is well suited to large, medium, and small sample sizes. Specific reviews address the state of the art and specific methodological technicalities of both larger-n (Cooper, Hammersley, Gomm, & Glaesser, 2012; Schulze-Bentrop, 2013) and smaller-n (Cooper & Glaesser, 2011; Greckhamer, Misangyi, & Fiss, 2013; Schulze-Bentrop, 2013) applications of QCA. In the context of educational leadership, the key benefits of QCA are its application for action-oriented questions formulated in terms of necessity and sufficiency, its ability to provide empirical plans for school improvement, its orientation towards multiple pathways, and its explicit accounting for complex interactions among conditions. In the following section we use fictional data to demonstrate how QCA may be used to contribute to research on educational leadership.

DEMONSTRATING QCA

Suppose that Ms. Baroletti is superintendent of the 15 schools in Circle County School District. Last year the district offered a teacher training program and some schools participated, but there is no strong correlation between participation and achievement of academic benchmarks. From conversations with school leaders and teachers, Ms. Baroletti understands that the success of the program strongly depends on the constellation of participation in the program, school leadership, and the socio-economic background of the school. The training is part of a leadership "recipe" for success that includes the school's leadership and background context. If she can identify the "causal recipes" (Ragin, 2008a, p. 9), she can better recommend which schools should participate in training.

Based on her substantive knowledge of the district and theoretical knowledge of educational leadership, Ms. Baroletti identifies three characteristics that interact to affect achievement: participation in teacher training, principals' communication of curriculum goals to teachers, and the socio-economic context of the school. She uses QCA to identify configurations of high- and low-achieving schools in her district data.

CALIBRATION

Ms. Baroletti's first step is to calibrate her data into sets for each of the three conditions. She chooses calibration methods based on the nature of the data—binary, ordinal, or continuous (Ragin, 2008b). Ms. Baroletti's outcome of interest is whether or not each school met the testing benchmark set by the state. She defines the set of schools that met the target as a crisp set of either success or failure to meet the benchmark. She calls this set "Target."

The first condition is participation in the teacher training program. Ms. Baroletti chooses this policy because teacher and parent feedback indicated that the program was effective, and because ongoing teacher training and professional development is a key lever for improving the learning environment in schools (Hallinger & Heck, 2011; Darling-Hammond, 2008). Ms. Baroletti names this set "Training" and calibrates it as a crisp set where schools that participated in the program are fully in and those that did not are fully out.

For the second condition, Ms. Baroletti uses survey results measuring how well principals communicate curriculum goals to teachers. Substantively, she has observed that communication is a key differentiator among her principals, and theoretical models of effective leadership emphasize the importance of communication for focusing administrative and teaching activities (Hallinger & Heck, 2010). This set is called "Communication," and is based on 1–5 Likert scale data from a survey of teachers—Table 6.2 shows the possible answers. Ms. Baroletti uses the qualitative differences between verbal descriptions to indirectly calibrate the Likert scores onto the interval between zero and one as shown in the "Calibration" column, creating a fuzzy set.

The third condition reflects the socio-economic context (SES) of each school. Beyond the presence of more or fewer resources in schools based on SES, Ms. Baroletti knows that the social and economic context of a school interacts with leadership practices (Day et al., 2010). Ms. Baroletti chooses

TABLE 6.2 Calibrations of Teacher Survey

Scale Score	Survey Prompt	Calibrated Set Membership Scores
1	Strongly Disagree	0.00
2	Disagree	0.25
3	Neutral	0.50
4	Agree	0.75
5	Strongly Agree	1.00

to measure SES using the proportion of students eligible for free or reduced lunch. She examines a plot of her schools' free and reduced lunch statistics and realizes that there is no large discontinuity that would allow her to create natural clusters of schools. Ms. Baroletti also finds no theoretical grounds for any specific cutoff point to be used as a high or low proportion of eligible students. Therefore, she defines the fuzzy "SES" set using direct calibration, setting the set membership cutoffs at the bottom quartile (43% or more free and reduced lunch eligibility) for fully out, the top quartile (28% or lower) for fully in, and the median (37%) for maximally ambiguous (Ragin, 2008a).

Ms. Baroletti chooses these conditions because they differentiate schools in a meaningful way. Conditions that are the same across all schools would be eliminated in minimization since they occur in successful and unsuccessful schools—if both an excellent and a struggling school have distributed leadership structures, that feature cannot be what differentiates the two. If she included different but not meaningful conditions like, for example, whether the school mascots are mammals, they might coincidentally appear in the solution. Moreover, Ms. Baroletti understands that QCA offers opportunities to check at the end of her analysis whether some other condition might explain the outcome.

Ms. Baroletti uses fs/QCA—a free and user-friendly software package for her analysis. She has also heard about an R package that is particularly valuable when analyzing larger datasets, but for her purposes the more user-friendly fs/QCA is more appropriate.[4] In order for the software to process her data, she adds a constant of 0.001 to membership scores that are exactly equal to 0.5. In this case, the scores of School 6 for Communication and School 15 for SES are altered. This change does not affect her result, but ensures that these cases are not dropped from the analysis for being perfectly ambiguous. The raw data becomes calibrated data, in Table 6.3, with each school and its memberships in the causal conditions and outcome.

TRUTH TABLE ANALYSIS

Using the calibrated data, Ms. Baroletti constructs a truth table (Table 6.4), which in this case contains eight rows—one for every possible combination of conditions. For fuzzy sets, the truth table shows simply whether a case is more in or out, and fuzziness is reflected in adjustment of the consistency score. Memberships over 0.5 are listed as one, and those below 0.5 are zeroes; despite the simplified representation of memberships in the truth table, its algorithm considers the fuzziness during the Boolean minimization procedure (for more, see Ragin, 2008a).

The column "Target" indicates whether schools with the combination of causal conditions in each row met their benchmarks more often than not.

TABLE 6.3 Raw and Calibrated Data

School	Raw Data				Calibrated Data			
	Training	Communication	SES	Target	Training	Communication	SES	Target
1	1	5	23%	1	1	1.00	1.00	1
2	0	5	17%	1	0	1.00	1.00	1
3	0	2	38%	0	0	0.25	0.42	0
4	0	4	46%	1	0	0.75	0.00	1
5	1	5	43%	1	1	1.00	0.00	1
6	0	3	43%	0	0	0.50	0.00	0
7	0	4	31%	1	0	0.75	0.83	1
8	1	2	29%	0	1	0.25	0.94	0
9	0	2	44%	0	0	0.25	0.00	0
10	1	4	36%	1	1	0.75	0.56	1
11	0	2	38%	0	0	0.25	0.42	0
12	1	4	27%	1	1	0.75	1.00	1
13	0	1	24%	0	0	0.00	1.00	0
14	0	2	50%	0	0	0.25	0.00	0
15	0	1	37%	0	0	0.00	0.50	0

TABLE 6.4 Truth Table

Row	Training	Communication	SES	Target	n	Consistency	Cases
1	0	0	0	0	4	0.0909	3, 9, 11, 14
2	0	0	1	0	1	0.0789	13
3	0	1	0	0	2	0.4085	4, 6
4	0	1	1	1	2	0.8182	2, 7
5	1	0	0	?	0	0.7826	
6	1	0	1	0	1	0.3333	8
7	1	1	0	1	1	0.9630	5
8	1	1	1	1	3	0.9217	1, 10, 12

Column "n" indicates how many schools are in each row. Finally, "Consistency" shows the proportion of cases in the row that achieved the target, corrected for the strength of their membership in the fuzzy-set conditions.

Ms. Baroletti observes, for example, that four schools (cases 3, 9, 11, and 14) in the first row match the configuration of no training, poor communication, low SES, and not hitting the target. As indicated by the score close to zero in the "Consistency" column, all four schools fail to hit targets. Conversely, row eight—schools that participated in training, scored high on communication of curriculum to teachers, and have fewer students eligible for free or reduced lunch—uniformly achieved their testing targets.

Ms. Baroletti begins analyzing the truth table by making two key decisions: first, the minimum number of empirically observed cases required for a configuration to be considered in the analysis (frequency cutoff); and second, the minimum consistency level (consistency cutoff). Because her dataset is the population of schools in her district, Ms. Baroletti considers every present configuration important for identifying recipes for successful educational leadership. For consistency, she follows recommendations from the literature and uses a consistency cutoff of 0.8, which is analogous to the convention of statistical significance (see Fiss, 2011; Greckhamer, Misangyi, Elms, & Lacey, 2008; Trujillo & Woulfin, 2014).

Applying these cutoffs, Ms. Baroletti identifies truth table rows four, seven, and eight as relevant configurations for her analysis. In Boolean notation, which uses capital letters to denote the presence of a causal condition, lowercase letters to denote its absence, asterisks (*) for logical AND, and plus signs (+) for logical OR, the three configurations in these rows are:

  (4) train*COMMUNICATION*SES
  (7) + TRAIN*COMMUNICATION*ses
  (8) + TRAIN*COMMUNICATION*SES

In other words, the first recipe is a school without training but with excellent communication and high SES. The second recipe is a school with training and excellent communication but low SES. The third recipe is training combined with excellent communication and high SES. These three configurations collectively cover six out of the seven successful schools.

BOOLEAN MINIMIZATION

To eliminate redundancies and determine which configurations are sufficient for schools to achieve their targets, Ms. Baroletti minimizes the truth table using Boolean algebra and Mill's method of difference. For example, both configurations eight and four include effective communication and high SES, yet differ on teacher training participation. Consequently, whether a school participates in the training program is irrelevant for the outcome. Instead, what matters is the combination of excellent communication and high SES (in bold).

(4)   train***COMMUNICATION*SES**
(8) +   **TRAIN*COMMUNICATION*SES**

Ms. Baroletti performs a similar minimization between rows seven and eight. While both configurations are consistent with achieving the outcome, the distinguishing condition between the configurations relates to their context: row seven includes low SES, whereas row eight is high SES. By systematically comparing these two configurations, Ms. Baroletti identifies a second recipe. Table 6.5 summarizes the two reduced recipes consistently sufficient for success.

Matching one of these two profiles is sufficient for achieving test score targets: either good communication of curriculum goals to teachers in a high-SES school, or good communication combined with participation in the teacher training program. A condition that does not appear in a configuration—teacher training in the first and SES in the second—is irrelevant. Thus, schools with excellent communication and high SES will likely

TABLE 6.5   Solution for Achieving Testing Targets

Configuration	Consistency	Raw Coverage	Unique Coverage	Cases
COMMUNICATION*SES	0.874	0.594	0.257	2, 7; 1, 10, 12
TRAINING*COMMUNICATION	0.947	0.514	0.178	5; 1,10,12
Solution	**0.900**	**0.771**		

meet targets regardless of participation in teacher training, and those with training and excellent communication will likely succeed independent of socioeconomic context. So long as the school matches both of the relevant conditions, their configuration is sufficient for success.

It is always important in all types of research to understand how meaningful the results are—how much of the outcome is explained by the solutions, and how fully the analysis represents the problem. In QCA, those questions are answered using the coverage and consistency scores of the solution. If the coverage is high as it is for Ms. Baroletti, the solution's configurations explain most instances of the outcome of interest. In contrast, low coverage would indicate that the outcome often does not match the solution and that some important condition may be missing from the analysis. The consistency score describes how often cases matching the solution configurations exhibit the chosen outcome—if this is low, it is difficult to justify causal claims.

ASYMMETRY: ANALYSIS FOR FAILING SCHOOLS

Ms. Baroletti is understandably excited: these causal recipes provide her with a means of guiding her school leaders. She is eager to rush off and tell her colleagues, but then wonders whether she should first try to develop a better understanding of why some schools are unsuccessful—the principle of asymmetry asserts that the causal recipes for failure are not simply the opposite of those for success.

Ms. Baroletti builds a new truth table in which the outcome set—whether or not schools meet their targets—is negated, or calibrated to schools that do not make the benchmark. She sets the consistency cutoff to 0.8 and again performs minimization, finding solutions for failing to achieve targets—shown in Table 6.6.

The solution again contains two configurations: this time they are either poor communication in schools with high SES or a lack of teacher training in schools with low SES. Ms. Baroletti quickly realizes that it was important to analyze the recipes of unsuccessful schools as well because those recipes are not the counter-image of the recipes of successful schools. Ms. Baroletti

TABLE 6.6 Solution for Failing to Achieve Testing Targets

Configuration	Consistency	Raw Coverage	Unique Coverage	Cases
communication*SES	0.839	0.392	0.225	13; 8
training*ses	0.800	0.583	0.417	3, 9, 11, 14; 4, 6
Solution	**0.802**	**0.808**		

recognizes that the second recipe for failing is especially relevant in her district as it covers six schools, but notices that its cases include school 4, which was successful. She decides to conduct some additional analysis to see where the differences lie between schools 4 and 6, who share a configuration but differ in their outcomes.

POST-HOC ANALYSIS

Schools 4 and 6 share the same structure but have different outcomes—4 is successful while 6 is not, though both have no training, good communication, and low SES. By comparing these two schools, Ms. Baroletti can find some difference that explains why these schools have different outcomes. She goes back into her records and examines the schools in more depth, finding a major difference between the schools in their levels of community involvement. The principal at school 4 has created an environment where parents, families, and community members support the school and volunteer time and effort towards helping the students learn better. In contrast, the principal at school 6 is relatively new and struggles to connect with the community. Ms. Baroletti may want to run the analysis again, this time including a condition based on community involvement.

DISCUSSION AND CONCLUSIONS

In this chapter, we introduce Qualitative Comparative Analysis as a valuable complement to the methodological toolbox of educational leadership research, and highlight how QCA is well suited to address some of the challenges research on educational leadership is facing. To help school leaders improve student achievement, researchers need to understand how leadership acts on student achievement in different contexts at the level of the school, student, or leader. Rather than understanding the impact of individual measures, we follow recent calls (e.g., Neumerski, 2013; Hallinger, 2011) for leadership strategies that are easily implementable, but neither too general to be useful nor too specific to be widely applied.

The methods researchers use to discover and design these pathways must be capable of unraveling the complex causality of schools and schooling. QCA provides one way of addressing those needs. QCA is useful for teasing apart the intricacies of school leadership and student achievement, and can be a valuable complement to other research methodologies. Thus, our goal is to help educational leadership researchers identify, evaluate, and share the means by which school leaders can impact student achievement.

Yet, QCA is not a perfect tool nor is it the only potentially useful tool, and we present QCA as neither the only method for moving the field forward nor the wholesale replacement for the many innovative methods already in use. QCA can be sensitive to the calibration choices made by researchers and their selection of cases, conditions, and outcomes. This can be addressed by applying a version of robustness checking: by slightly modifying the calibrations and the frequency and consistency cutoffs in repeated analyses, one can determine whether they strongly affect the results. One key issue in any analysis is the extent to which it explains the phenomenon in question—how do we know how much we know?

Potentially missing or omitted causes are a problem in all kinds of analytical research, but QCA allows the researcher to identify where new insights might be found and return to the cases for further analysis. This process of QCA of identifying conflicts and returning to the cases is very useful for clarifying areas of confusion and preventing bias from left-out conditions (Schneider & Wagemann, 2012). Post-hoc analysis is a key advantage for QCA in dealing with "unknown unknowns:" it offers researchers the opportunity to go back to the cases and the truth table, searching for explanations in the data that may have been missed.

As in all methods, the responsibility for meaningful and useful results falls to the researcher, and the inclusion of strong substantive, theoretical, and case-based knowledge is critical. Cooper and Glaesser (2011) provide a thoughtful explanation of the "paradoxes and pitfalls" that can arise when using fuzzy-set QCA and how to avoid them. Ragin (2008a) discusses calibration in detail and outlines strategies for creating meaningful set memberships. Finally, it is possible to test the robustness of solutions to calibrations or frequency and consistency cutoffs by varying those cutoffs slightly, especially in larger-n applications of QCA (Fiss, Sharapov, & Cronqvist, 2013; Greckhamer, Misangyi, & Fiss, 2013).

Our demonstration of QCA serves as an introduction to and illustration of the method for its use in educational leadership research, rather than a comprehensive overview of either the method or its possible uses. Typically, QCA is most useful for creating typologies and pathways, or for investigating the complex causes of some outcome. For example, QCA could be used to test the theory of four strategy areas (Leithwood et al., 2010) by measuring schools' membership in sets based on the elements of the all four. One would expect the rational path to combine quality teaching, good classroom management, academic press, and a good disciplinary climate. QCA is an excellent method for testing this theory by examining how well successful and unsuccessful schools match the pathways laid out in the theory (Leithwood et al., 2010). To explain the phenomenon of school turnaround, QCA could generate context-dependent pathways of theoretically important leadership policy and practice conditions. These are of course only illustrations of possible future directions, yet researchers exploring the literature on educational leadership will undoubtedly identify additional questions for relevant research projects.

We hope that our chapter motivates other scholars and researchers to consider the use of QCA for their own research. QCA has potential for both quantitative and qualitative researchers, and can serve as a means of bridging those two types of research in certain situations. The method not only addresses the challenges of educational leadership research—the importance of context and the need for leadership pathways that can be passed on to practitioners—but also creates opportunities for new studies that test existing theories and develop new insights from a novel perspective. The opportunities that QCA offers for both theory-building and theory-testing will allow researchers to build on the valuable contributions of research on educational leadership from the past and to inform new developments.

NOTES

1. Often in the social world, perfect set-subset relations do not exist; for further explanation of quasi-necessity and quasi-sufficiency, see Braumoeller & Goertz (2000).
2. For a comparison between measurement and calibration and a comprehensive discussion of different calibration methods, see Ragin (2008b).
3. The level of parsimony or complexity in the solution is moderated by the inclusion of "logical remainders," or those rows of the truth tables not associated with any outcome either because they do not contain cases (limited diversity) or because they are conflicting. This is further discussed in Ragin (2008a).
4. For more information on software, see compasss.com.

REFERENCES

Bell, L., Bolam, R., & Cubillo, L. (2003). *A systematic review of the impact of school leadership and management on student outcomes*. EPPI-Centre, Social Science Research Unit, Institute of Education, University of London.

Bossert, S. T., Dwyer, D. C., Rowan, B., & Lee, G. V. (1982). The instructional management role of the principal. *Educational Administration Quarterly, 18*(3), 34–64.

Braumoeller, B. F., & Goertz, G. (2000). The methodology of necessary conditions. *American Journal of Political Science*, 844–858.

Cooper, B. (2005). Applying Ragin's crisp and fuzzy set QCA to large datasets: Social class and educational achievement in the National Child Development Study. *Sociological Research Online, 10*(2).

Cooper, B., & Glaesser, J. (2008). How has educational expansion changed the necessary and sufficient conditions for achieving professional, managerial and

technical class positions in Britain? A configurational analysis. *Sociological Research Online, 13*(3), 2.
Cooper, B., & Glaesser, J. (2010). Contrasting variable-analytic and case-based approaches to the analysis of survey datasets: Exploring how achievement varies by ability across configurations of social class and sex. *Methodological innovations online, 5*(1), 4–23.
Cooper, B., & Glaesser, J. (2011). Paradoxes and pitfalls in using fuzzy set QCA: Illustrations from a critical review of a study of educational inequality. *Sociological Research Online, 16*(3), 8.
Cooper, B., Hammersley, M., Gomm, R., & Glaesser, J. (2012). *Challenging the qualitative–quantitative divide: Explorations in case-focused causal analysis.* London, England: Continuum.
Darling-Hammond, L. (2008). Teacher learning that supports student learning. *Teaching for Intelligence, 2,* 91–100.
Day, C., Sammons, P., Leithwood, K., Hopkins, D., Harris, A., Gu, Q., & Brown, E. (2010). *Ten strong claims about successful school leadership.* National College for Leadership of Schools and Children's Services, Nottingham.
Dinham, S. (2004). Principal leadership for outstanding educational outcomes. *Journal of Educational Administration, 43*(4), 338–356.
Duke, D. L. (1987). *School leadership and instructional improvement.* New York: Random House.
Dunlop, C. A., Maggetti, M., Radaelli, C. M., & Russel, D. (2012). The many uses of regulatory impact assessment: A meta-analysis of EU and UK cases. *Regulation & Governance, 6*(1), 23–45.
Fiss, P. C. (2011). Building better causal theories: A fuzzy set approach to typologies in organization research. *Academy of Management Journal, 54*(2), 393–420.
Fiss, P., Sharapov, D., & Cronqvist, L. (2013). Opposites attract? Opportunities and challenges for integrating large-N QCA and econometric analysis. *Political Research Quarterly, 66,* 191–197.
Fritzsche, E. (2013). Making hermeneutics explicit: How QCA supports an insightful dialogue between theory and cases. *International Journal of Social Research Methodology,* (ahead-of-print), 1–24.
Fullan, M. (2007). *The new meaning of educational change.* Routledge: London.
Glaesser, J., & Cooper, B. (2011). Selectivity and flexibility in the German secondary school system: A configurational analysis of recent data from the German Socio-Economic Panel. *European Sociological Review, 27*(5), 570–585.
Glaesser, J., & Cooper, B. (2014). Exploring the consequences of a recalibration of causal conditions when assessing sufficiency with fuzzy set QCA. *International Journal of Social Research Methodology, 17*(4), 387–401.
Goertz, G., & Mahoney, J. (2012). *A tale of two cultures: Qualitative and quantitative research in the social sciences.* Princeton University Press.
Greckhamer, T., Misangyi, V. F., Elms, H., & Lacey, R. (2008). Using qualitative comparative analysis in strategic management research: An examination of combinations of industry, corporate, and business-unit effects. *Organizational Research Methods, 11*(4), 695–726.
Greckhamer, T., Misangyi, V. F., & Fiss, P. C. (2013). The two QCAs: From a small-N to a large-N set theoretic approach. *Research in the Sociology of Organizations, 38,* 49–75.

Hallinger, P. (2011). Leadership for learning: Lessons from 40 years of empirical research. *Journal of Educational Administration, 49*(2), 125–142.
Hallinger, P., Bickman, L., & Davis, K. (1996). School context, principal leadership, and student reading achievement. *The Elementary School Journal,* 527–549.
Hallinger, P., & Heck, R. H. (2010). Collaborative leadership and school improvement: Understanding the impact on school capacity and student learning. *School Leadership and Management, 30*(2), 95–110.
Hallinger, P., & Heck, R. H. (2011). Exploring the journey of school improvement: Classifying and analyzing patterns of change in school improvement processes and learning outcomes. *School Effectiveness and School Improvement, 22*(1), 1–27.
Hallinger, P., & Huber, S. (2012). School leadership that makes a difference: International perspectives. *School Effectiveness and School Improvement, 23*(4), 359–367.
Hallinger, P., & Murphy, J. (1985). Assessing the instructional management behavior of principals. *The Elementary School Journal, 86*(2), 217–247.
Hargreaves, A., & Fullan, M. (1998). *What's worth fighting for out there?* Teachers College Press: New York.
Heck, R. H. (2012). Instructional practice, teacher effectiveness, and growth in student learning in math: Implications for school leadership. In B. G. Barnett, & A. R. Shoho (Eds.), *The changing nature of instructional leadership in the 21st century.* Charlotte, NC: Information Age Publishing.
Heck, R. H., & Hallinger, P. (2009). Assessing the contribution of distributed leadership to school improvement and growth in math achievement. *American Educational Research Journal, 46*(3), 659–689.
Heck, R. H., Larsen, T. J., & Marcoulides, G. A. (1990). Instructional leadership and school achievement: Validation of a causal model. *Educational Administration Quarterly, 26*(2), 94–125.
Katz, D., & Kahn, R. L. (1978). *The social psychology of organizations.* Wiley: London.
Knapp, M. S., Mkhwanazi, S. T., & Portin, B. S. (2012). School-based instructional leadership in demanding environments: New challenges, new practices. In B. G. Barnett & A. R. Shoho (Eds.), *The changing nature of instructional leadership in the 21st century.* Charlotte, NC: Information Age Publishing.
Kvist, J. (2007). Fuzzy set ideal type analysis. *Journal of Business Research, 60*(5), 474–481.
Leithwood, K., Anderson, S. E., Mascall, B., & Strauss, T. (2010). School leaders' influences on student learning: The four paths. *The Principles of Educational Leadership and Management,* 13–30.
Leithwood, K., Patten, S., & Jantzi, D. (2010). Testing a conception of how school leadership influences student learning. *Educational Administration Quarterly, 46*(5), 671–706.
Marx, A. (2006). Towards more robust model specification in QCA: Results from a methodological experiment. *American Sociological Association, Philadelphia, PA.*
Marx, A., Rihoux, B., & Ragin, C. (2014). The origins, development, and application of Qualitative Comparative Analysis: The first 25 years. *European Political Science Review, 6*(1), 115–142.
Marzano, R. J., Waters, T., & McNulty, B. A. (2005). *School leadership that works: From research to results.* Alexandria, VA: Association for Supervision and Curriculum Development.

Mulford, B., & Silins, H. (2011). Revised models and conceptualisation of successful school principalship for improved student outcomes. *International Journal of Educational Management, 25*(1), 61–82.

Neumerski, C. M. (2013). Rethinking instructional leadership, a review: What do we know about principal, teacher, and coach instructional leadership, and where should we go from here? *Educational Administration Quarterly, 49*(2), 310–347.

Ogawa, R. T., & Bossert, S. T. (1995). Leadership as an organizational quality. *Educational Administration Quarterly, 31*(2), 224–243.

Opdenakker, M. C., & van Damme, J. (2007). Do school context, student composition and school leadership affect school practice and outcomes in secondary education? *British Educational Research Journal, 33*(2), 179–206.

Põder, K., Kerem, K., & Lauri, T. (2013). Efficiency and equity within European education systems and school choice policy: Bridging qualitative and quantitative approaches. *Journal of School Choice, 7*(1), 1–36.

Prestine, N. A., & Nelson, B. S. (2005). How can educational leaders support and promote teaching and learning? New conceptions of learning and leading in schools. In *A new agenda for research in educational leadership* (pp. 46–59). New York: Teachers College Press.

Ragin, C.C., (1987). *The comparative method: Moving beyond qualitative and quantitative strategies.* Berkeley, Los Angeles, and London: University of California Press.

Ragin, C. C. (1994). Introduction to qualitative comparative analysis. *The comparative political economy of the welfare state, 299,* 300–309.

Ragin, C. C. (2000). *Fuzzy-set social science.* Chicago: University of Chicago Press.

Ragin, C. C. (2008a). *Redesigning social inquiry: Fuzzy sets and beyond* (pp. 190–212). Chicago: University of Chicago Press.

Ragin, C.C. (2008b). Measurement versus calibration: A set-theoretic approach. In J. M. Box-Steffensmeier, H. E. Brady, & D. Collier (Eds.), *The Oxford handbook of political methodology* (pp. 174–198). Oxford: Oxford University Press.

Robinson, V. M., Lloyd, C. A., & Rowe, K. J. (2008). The impact of leadership on student outcomes: An analysis of the differential effects of leadership types. *Educational Administration Quarterly, 44*(5), 635–674.

Schneider, C. Q., & Wagemann, C. (2012). *Set-theoretic methods for the social sciences: A guide to qualitative comparative analysis.* New York, NY: Cambridge University Press.

Schulze-Bentrop, C. (2013). *Qualitative comparative analysis (QCA) and configurational thinking in management studies.* Pieterlen, Switzerland: Peter Lang.

Smith, W. F., & Andrews, R. L. (1989). *Instructional leadership: How principals make a difference.* Alexandria, VA: Association for Supervision and Curriculum Development.

Trujillo, T. M., & Woulfin, S. L. (2014). Equity-oriented reform amid standards-based accountability: A qualitative comparative analysis of an intermediary's instructional practices. *American Educational Research Journal, 51*(2), 253–293.

SECTION III

RESEARCH ON THE PREPARATION
OF SCHOOL LEADERS

CHAPTER 7

VIABLE AND EFFECTIVE ALTERNATIVES

Preparing Leaders for Non-Traditional Schools

Kristy S. Cooper and Kate Rollert
Michigan State University

In his self-published book chronicling his first two years as principal of a New York City high school for "throwaway teens," Golubtchik (2013) recounts his trial-and-error efforts to provide a humanizing and effective education to 300 students who had been turned away from traditional high schools. Ultimately, Golubtchik reports finding success by drawing upon prior experiences as a special education teacher and elementary school principal and upon the wisdom of dedicated staff members who developed rapport with students. But, such a "sink or swim" approach to learning to run an alternative school should not be the norm, particularly given these schools' uniquely vulnerable students. Yet, as the availability of alternative schools proliferates, the majority of prospective school leaders continue to attend leadership preparation programs that assume

Challenges and Opportunities of Educational Leadership Research and Practice, pages 173–198
Copyright © 2016 by Information Age Publishing
All rights of reproduction in any form reserved.

a traditional school model—emphasizing the oversight of operations, instructional programming, accountability systems, family/community relationships, and data-driven decision-making (National Policy Board for Educational Administration, 2011). While the national standards that guide leadership preparation could certainly be applied to running an alternative school, these standards are rarely applied to such settings during preparation, with the assumption that alternative school principals will not need specialized knowledge and skills.

In this chapter, however, we argue that leadership preparation programs must specifically prepare leaders to effectively lead schools outside the traditional format, and we present a core body of knowledge and skills required for such leaders. To make this case, we demonstrate how alternative education has changed in recent years and how this change has increased the demand for effective leaders who understand the unique challenges and opportunities of alternative schools. We assert that this growing and changing landscape offers leadership preparation programs a timely and critical opportunity to shape the future of alternative education by training high quality leaders for these settings. To this end, we provide an overview of what alternative school leaders need to know, with an emphasis on how these needs differ from those for traditional principals. We conclude by proposing three models for training alternative school leaders. Our goal is to initiate a conversation regarding the extent to which current leadership programs effectively prepare alternative school leaders and how such programs might re-envision their programming for this population. Throughout, we operate under the belief that, through strong and prepared leadership, alternative schools can become viable and effective alternatives for students. Leadership preparation programs can chart this course.

At the foundation of our argument is a distinct, yet broad, definition of alternative schools. While the literature offers a number of definitions, we use the definition from the National Alternative Education Association (NAEA, 2014), which states that an alternative school is one that serves "students who require or thrive in an environment other than a traditional educational setting" (p. 3). This broad definition enables inclusion of an array of schools and students, making it preferable to narrower definitions that focus exclusively on students with behavioral problems or chronic failure (Dunbar, 2001) or that label alternative schools as punitive settings for "bad" students (Leone & Drakeford, 1999). Yet, the NAEA's definition is not without its shortcomings. First, this definition polarizes "alternative" and "traditional" schools, thereby overlooking considerable variation within both types. In reality, schools across the spectrum from traditional to alternative differ considerably in regards to context and student needs—*and* there are many schools that have both traditional and alternative programs. In addition, the NAEA's definition suggests that students who thrive in traditional settings would not also thrive in alternative settings, which is also unlikely to be true. Despite these shortcomings, we adopt the NAEA's loosely worded definition because it forefronts students' needs and is open to the potential for the field of alternative education to expand considerably. This definition also fits with the three main types of alternative schools recognized by most scholars: remedial programs, last-chance programs, and popular innovations (Brown & Beckett, 2007b; Raywid, 1990). Raywid (1994) defines remedial programs as those that focus on rehabilitation and remediation of students with the ultimate goal of placing them back in traditional schools. By contrast, last-chance schools serve students who have been identified as disruptive and/or in need of behavior modifications, making these programs a last stop before expulsion (Raywid, 1994). Finally, popular innovations are schools that incorporate programmatic themes, such as by focusing on a specific subject or a specific mode of instruction such as problem-based learning (Raywid 1994). Across these formats, the NAEA's (2014) definition enables a student-centered examination of "environments other than traditional settings."

THE CHANGING LANDSCAPE OF ALTERNATIVE EDUCATION

The modern alternative education movement began in the early 1960s. Raywid (1981) described the movement as a response to "cold, dehumanizing, irrelevant institutions, largely indifferent to the humanity and 'personhood' of those within them" (p. 551). The new alternative schools were intended to provide extra educational, behavioral, and/or medical services and meet student needs that could not be adequately addressed in traditional settings. Advocates accused traditional schools of conformity and docility and championed schools that would better meet "students' actual needs and desires" (Conley, 2002, p. 7). At the height of the social movements of the 1960s, the public responded well to this student-centered model, and a few schools designed to meet this purpose opened throughout the country (Conley, 2002).

Alternative schools gained more popularity during the 1970s and 1980s, but also developed a secondary purpose to remove incorrigible students from mainstream classrooms (Dunbar, 2001; Noguera, 2003). This tradition of removing disruptive students and placing them in alternative schools shaped these schools as dumping grounds or holding pens, and the student population developed a reputation for being "pervasively disruptive, unhealthy, aggressive, and even violent" (Free, 2008, p. 29). Student behavior became the primary criteria for placing students into alternative education, and many alternative schools became more like correctional facilities where changing inappropriate behavior was prioritized over meeting learning needs (Free, 2008). Students and families quickly recognized that alternative schools were a place for "bad" students who disrupted the learning of "good" students (Noguera, 2003).

In the 1990s and 2000s, alternative schools continued their reputation for warehousing the behaviorally disenfranchised, even as the number of schools grew considerably (Kim, 2011). As shown in Figure 7.1, the number of alternative schools increased from 1,151 schools in 1990 to 6,197 schools in 2010, an increase of 538% in just 20 years (NCES, 2012). Among U.S. secondary schools in 2010, a full 14% were alternative schools, up from only 2% in 1990 (NCES, 2012). The proportion of school districts offering alternative programs has also increased recently. In surveys with nationally representative samples of districts, the percentage of districts reporting alternative programming increased from 39% in 2001 to 64% in 2008 (Carver & Lewis, 2010; Kleiner, Porch, & Farris, 2002). Accordingly, alternative student enrollment has also increased substantially. Figure 7.2 shows that the number of students attending alternative schools grew from 134,161 students in 1990 to 563,449 students in 2010, an increase of 420%. A comparison of Figures 7.1 and 7.2 reveals that, while there was an increase in the number of students attending alternative schools from 2005 to 2010, there was a simultaneous decrease in the number of schools. This drop mirrors a national trend in which the number of U.S. schools has decreased by 70%, while the average school size has increased 500% (Klonsky, 2000). Just the same, the fact that overall enrollment continues to rise demonstrates continued and increasing demand for alternative education. With student enrollment in U.S. schools at 49 million in 2010, the percentage

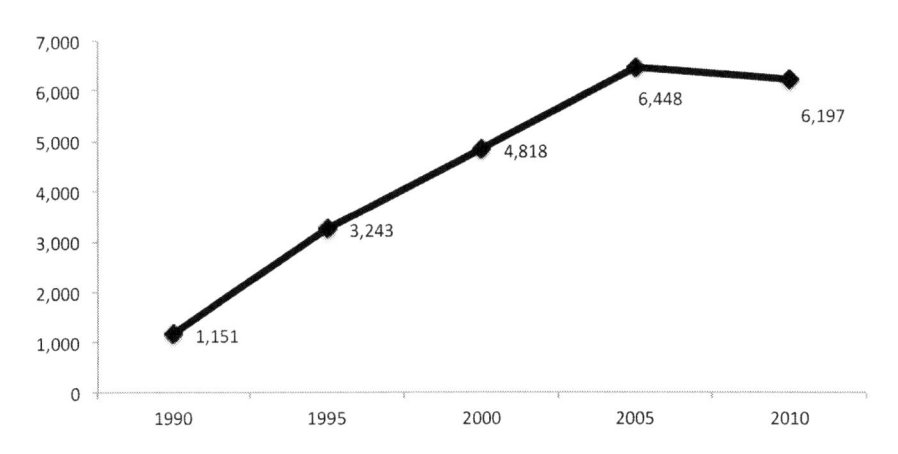

Figure 7.1 Number of alternative schools in the United States from 1990 to 2010. *Source:* NCES (2012).

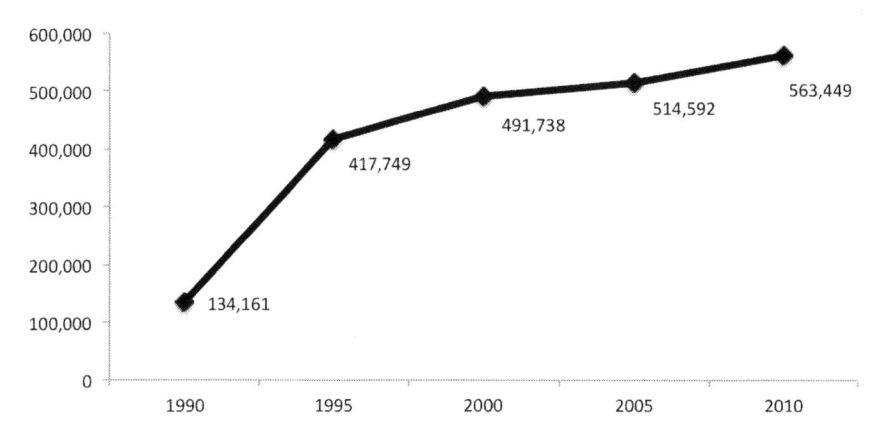

Figure 7.2 Student enrollment in U.S. alternative schools from 1990 to 2010. *Source:* NCES (2012).

of students enrolled in alternative schools was 1.1%, up from just 0.3% in 1990; among secondary school students in grades seven and higher, enrollment quadrupled to 2% from 0.5% in 1990 (NCES, 2012). Of course, in some locations and for some populations, the prevalence and demand for alternative schools are much higher. For example, in a study tracking one cohort of 7,668 third-grade students through the Jefferson County Public Schools from 1997 to 2005, Vanderhaar, Petrosko, and Munoz (2013) found that 10% of the third-graders ultimately enrolled in alternative education by twelfth grade.

Various researchers have posed theories to explain the dramatic increase in alternative schools and programs since 1990. Kim and Taylor (2008) suggest the growth is due to the escalating population of disenfranchised students. Verdugo and Glenn (2006) similarly attribute the change to an increase in minority students and students living in poverty. Tallerico and Burstyn (2004) cite public perceptions of increasing school violence and the role of teachers' unions in influencing the removal of challenging students from mainstream classrooms. Howell (2003) argues that a finding published by Cairns and Cairns in 1994—which stated that approximately one-third of students who dropped out of school entered the criminal justice system—launched concern about the high financial costs of juvenile incarceration and burgeoned the growth of alternative schools to save students before they ended up in prison. Supporting this notion, a U.S. Department of Education study surveyed the 64% of districts with alternative programs to examine the various reasons for which districts allowed schools to transfer students to alternative schools, including physical attacks or fights (allowed by 61% of districts), disruptive verbal behavior (57%), continual academic failure (57%), possession, distribution, or use of alcohol or drugs (excluding tobacco) (57%), chronic truancy (53%), possession or use of a weapon other than a firearm (51%), possession or use of a firearm (42%), arrest or involvement with the criminal justice system (42%), pregnancy or teen parenthood (31%), and mental health needs (27%) (Carver & Lewis, 2010). This data suggest that districts transfer most students to alternative schools for violating behavior policies or school norms. These primarily behavioral—as opposed to academic—reasons for transfer illustrate that alternative schools continue to be considered places for troubled youth. In this era of accountability, policies such as zero tolerance and high-stakes testing have also continued alternative schools' reputations as stopgaps between school and prison (Nolan & Anyon, 2004; Dunning-Lozano, 2014). Lockdown procedures, increased security, routine randomized searches, and the use of metal detectors, security cameras, and chain-linked fences have reinforced this perception (Saltman, 2003).

Despite these circumstances, alternative schools are beginning to position themselves quite differently and are experiencing both successes and challenges (D'Angelo & Zemanick, 2009). This turn aligns with the White House's more optimistic framing of disenfranchised youth (who are not working or in school) as "opportunity youth" (White House Council for Community Solutions, 2012). In an analysis of our nation's 6.7 million opportunity youth (17% of the 16–24 year-old age group), Belfield, Levin, and Rosen (2012) estimated that each opportunity youth costs taxpayers $37,450 per year, with a lifetime burden of $529,030 on society. Aggregated to a full cohort of opportunity youth, the researchers estimate a social burden of $4.75 trillion per cohort. In response, national, state, and local governments are calling for more and higher quality educational and workforce services for this demographic, and initiatives have emerged to meet these needs. At the national level, for example, President Obama convened the White House Council for Community Solutions (2012) to identify ways to educate and support disenfranchised youth. At the state level, Texas awarded over $21 million between 2008 and 2012 to 34 schools and organizations to fund dropout recovery programs that would provide alternative education pathways to students who had left high school without graduating (Texas Education Agency Website, 2013). As a local effort, starting in 2003, New York City began opening hundreds of new small high schools, including 45 schools targeted toward students with particular needs such as evening scheduling or credit recovery or a more emotionally supportive environment (Garland, 2010). These examples of recent public initiatives illustrate the transition from seeing alternative schools as warehouses for storing problematic students to actual centers of learning that could meet students' academic needs.

Given this more positive framing of alternative options, many counties and educational affiliates now offer a "portfolio of schools"—including alternative programs in all three areas of remediation, last chance, and innovation—to optimize resources and meet varying students' needs (Bulkley, Henig, & Levi, 2010). The notion that students and families are consumers seeking the best among multiple options is further reflected in the increasing prevalence of "school choice" and "schools of choice." As part of this expanded programming, the educational community now offers an increasing array of alternative options—including virtual schools, schools for at-risk youth, small alternative schools with flexible scheduling or internship opportunities, schools within juvenile justice centers, and schools following popular models such as "New Tech" or "Big Picture Learning" (Foley & Pang, 2006; Garland, 2010; Martinez & Schilling, 2010). Many districts with alternative programs also serve elementary and middle school students, with increasing availability of alternative options as students age (Tobin & Sprague, 2000; Wetzel et al., 1997). According to the U.S. Department of Education, among the 64% of school districts reporting alternative programs in 2008, the percentages serving students in each grade level increased steadily across the grades, from a low of only 6% of districts serving kindergarteners, to 41% of districts serving sixth-graders, to 63% serving eighth-graders, to 96% serving twelfth-graders (Carver & Lewis, 2010). Research suggests that elementary and middle school programs offer students a proactive chance to address problematic behaviors and habits before serious problems develop (Leone & Drakeford, 1999; Vann, Schubert, & Rogers, 2001), foster the crucial social interactions that lead to school engagement (Best, Price, & McCallum, 2014; de Bilde, et al., 2013), and achieve learning targets (Brown and Beckett, 2007a). Despite the variations in models, contemporary alternative schools have commonalities, including small size, frequent one-on-one interactions between teachers and students, supportive environments, multiple opportunities for success, flexibility in curriculum and structure, and greater emphasis on student decision-making (NAEA, 2014; Tobin & Sprague, 1999). These features differentiate alternative schools from the vast majority of traditional schools and raise questions about whether leadership preparation programs are generating leaders who can most effectively lead alternative schools.

THE DEMAND FOR EFFECTIVE LEADERS IN ALTERNATIVE SCHOOLS

Researchers at the Rennie Center (2014) argue that current alternative school enrollment is far short of the potential demand for such programs, noting, "Alternative education capacity is stretched, with more student demand than schools and programs can accommodate" (p. 12). Data from the U.S. Department of Education support this conclusion. In the 2008 survey of districts, 33% of the districts offering alternative programs reported being unable to enroll new students in such programs because of staffing or space limitations (Carver & Lewis, 2010). This inability to meet demand was even higher in districts with 10,000 or more students (with 46% unable to meet demand) and in cities (46%) (Carver & Lewis, 2010). The emphasis on individualization in alternative settings also keeps enrollment low and limits the number of students in any one program. Whereas a traditional high school can serve 2,000 students with one principal, serving those same 2,000 students in small alternative settings of 250 students would require eight principals. Thus, with their necessarily small size and increasing demand, alternative schools are likely to continue to flourish beyond the current proportion of 14% of U.S. secondary schools (NCES, 2012) and require a number of skillful leaders. Furthermore, the variety of alternative settings—including programs within larger schools, programs in community settings, virtual schools, and self-contained schools—translates into a robust job market for emerging school leaders with relevant knowledge and skills (Hale & Moorman, 2003). In addition to this quantity demand, there is also a quality demand as students within alternative schools are among the most in need of effective education. Students of color, low-income students, and students with disabilities are much more likely to enroll in alternative schools than other students (Vanderhaar, Petrosko, & Munoz, 2013; Verdugo & Glenn, 2006). Given the disproportionate representation of these groups in alternative settings (Golubtchik, 2013; Khalifa, 2012; Rennie Center, 2014), the quality of alternative education also has implications for racial and income equality. In addition, the increasing importance of a high school diploma—with current high school dropouts having fewer job options than previous generations (Rumberger, 2011)—suggests that at-risk and disenfranchised students are in dire need of more effective alternative schools.

Amidst this demand, we know that school leadership matters. Indeed, reports on the qualities of effective alternative schools consistently list strong, knowledgeable leaders as essential (Brown & Beckett, 2007a; Quinn & Poirier, 2006; NAEA, 2014). Leithwood and colleagues (2004) found that leadership is second only to the quality of instruction in impacting student learning and that this impact is particularly strong in schools where student needs are the most extreme. Branch, Hanushek, and Rivkin (2012) found that, in schools with principals more than a standard deviation above the mean on quality measures, students experience annual learning gains 0.05 standard deviations or more above the mean. They also found that the variance in impact between the highest and lowest quality principals is greatest in high-poverty schools, which many alternative schools are, and higher quality principals are more likely to exit high-poverty schools within four years. Research also shows that principal preparation programs matter, with graduates from high quality programs being more likely to engage in effective leadership practices, which in turn are likely to foster school improvement and strong school climates (Darling-Hammond, et al., 2007; Orr & Orphanos, 2011). As such, we assert that leadership preparation programs must fulfill the demand for well-trained leaders in alternative schools by helping aspiring leaders acquire the knowledge and skills relevant to these sites.

KNOWLEDGE & SKILLS FOR EFFECTIVE ALTERNATIVE EDUCATION LEADERS

While we acknowledge a variety of alternative models, the remainder of this chapter focuses on preparing leaders for remedial and last-chance programs, which have relatively common student populations with significant needs and the direst consequences if those needs go unmet. Fundamentally, we argue that overseeing and leading remedial and last-chance schools requires a considerably different set of knowledge and skills than overseeing and leading traditional schools—just as others have argued in regards to training principals for turnaround schools (Duke, 2010) or charter schools (National Alliance for Public Charter Schools, 2008). Although this is likely also the case for popular innovations, such innovations serve a wide array of students—from gifted and talented to students with particular career interests or disabilities—and so share fewer similarities with remedial and last-chance programs. To identify the particular knowledge and skills needed for leaders in remedial and last chance settings, we used three resource guides for developing and running effective alternative schools (Conley, 2002; Kellmayer, 1995; Mottaz, 2002), two research reports on exemplary practices in alternative education (NAEA, 2014; Quinn & Poirier, 2006), and one guide to evaluating alternative schools (National Association of Charter School Authorizers, 2013). We cross-referenced these six sources to create a master list of the skills and knowledge a leader would need to run an effective alternative school. We then grouped related sets of skills and knowledge into a parsimonious list of seven key areas for expertise development among alternative school leaders. In these seven areas, we argue that the knowledge base and skillset for alternative school leaders is different in nature from that needed by traditional principals. The seven areas are: understanding students' social and emotional needs, curriculum and instruction, culture and climate, wraparound services, staffing, professional development, and program evaluation.

Understanding Students' Social and Emotional Needs

Adolescence encapsulates many social, emotional, and hormonal changes that propel rapidly changing behavior and heightened emotions

(Meeus, et al., 1999; Steinberg & Morris, 2001). This is particularly true for youth facing multiple risk factors common to students in alternative schools, such as family instability, homelessness, physical and emotional abuse, poverty, neighborhood crime, and peers who engage in delinquent behaviors (Moore, 2013). These issues can be particularly overwhelming for students facing multiple risk factors without complementary sources of resilience, such as positive relationships with caring adults, effective parenting, problem-solving skills, perceived efficacy, achievement motivation, self-regulation, stress management skills, and effective teachers and schools (Moore, 2013). Indeed, the life circumstances that lead a young person to alternative education can be the same circumstances that make them struggle with adolescence. Given the high levels of risk for alternative students, school leaders must possess particular knowledge on adolescent development, risk, and resilience and the skills to support staff in serving these needs. Leaders will need to plan for the social, emotional, and academic transition from a traditional to alternative school and cultivate a supportive and empowering school culture. Although all principals benefit from understanding child and adolescent development, these insights are fundamental to the work in alternative schools in ways that are not as pressing or central in traditional schools.

In particular, alternative school leaders must have insights into processes of identity formation and peer relationships among students facing the negative stigma of attending an alternative school, which can negatively impact their affect and cognitive development (Kellmayer, 1995). Indeed, the stigma of attending an alternative school can shape identity as adolescents figure out where they fall in socially constructed groups and how peers and society will respond to them based on those memberships (Erikson, 1968; Fraser, Davis, & Singh, 1997; Tatum, 2000). Relationships with peers also begin to carry more weight than those with families, and peers increasingly influence decision-making (Brown, 2004). Students in alternative schools, who are likely to have histories of peer conflict, may struggle with this issue. As such, alternative educators must understand how to facilitate positive identity and relationship formation. Particularly within small alternative settings, principals must model supportive practices and guide other practitioners in implementing social and behavioral programming to nurture and empower students (Brown & Beckett, 2007b; McNulty & Roseboro, 2009).

Curriculum and Instruction

By definition, students in alternative schools were not well served in traditional schools, and so alternative schools that offer instruction mirroring that in traditional settings are likely to be ineffective and not much of an *alternative*. Rather, exemplary practices in curriculum and instruction for alternative schools include high levels of individualization while maintaining rigor and inclusivity for all students (NAEA, 2014). The characteristics and sizes of the student bodies in alternative schools could support individualized instruction if school leaders are adequately prepared for instructional leadership in intensely individualized settings. Yet, the challenges facing remedial and last-chance students make instructional leadership particularly cumbersome. One challenge is the high proportion of students with special needs. In Foley and Pang's (2006) survey with 50 alternative school principals in Illinois, respondents reported that, on average, 50% of their students were identified as having emotional and behavioral disorders, 26% had been classified as having attention deficit disorder (ADD) or attention deficit with hyperactivity (ADHD), and 12% had been diagnosed with learning disabilities. Minimal literacy and numeracy skills also create instructional challenges. In assessments of students in three alternative charter schools in Detroit, Flennaugh, Cooper, and Carter Andrews (2015) found that students were, on average, performing at fourth- or fifth-grade levels in reading, language, and math, with the range of abilities extending from functionally illiterate to well above grade level. Poor student attendance is yet another instructional challenge in alternative settings. For example, New York City's District 79, which houses the district's alternative schools, reported an average daily attendance rate of 64% in 2010–2011, far below the city's overall attendance rate of 90% (NYC Open Data, 2014). With low attendance, alternative instructional models must account for a revolving, inconsistent student population. Amidst this multitude of demands, alternative schools require a great number of experts in different areas, from reading specialists, to special educators and paraprofessionals who can provide one-on-one assistance, to teachers with strong expertise in project-based learning and differentiated instruction (NAEA, 2014).

Despite the need for individualization, alternative schools do not necessarily meet that need, and instructional models vary widely from those that mimic classrooms in traditional schools to those that bear no resemblance. Recently, in efforts to individualize instruction, many alternative schools have purchased online credit recovery programs (e.g., E2020 or Plato) in which students work independently at their own pace through recorded lectures, vocabulary lessons, and quizzes to cover the coursework for high school graduation (Zehr, 2010). Online credit recovery is not unique to alternative schools and is also used in many traditional settings, including large programs in New York City, Chicago, Florida, and Wisconsin (Butrymowicz, 2010; Zehr, 2010). However, numerous alternative schools rely almost exclusively on credit recovery programs. Critics of online credit recovery argue that students do not learn through these programs and can quickly pass courses using shortcuts, while proponents assert that the competency-based approach to assessment is a learner-centered improvement over the standard time-in-seat requirement for passing a course (Butrymowicz, 2010; Watson & Watson, 2011). While research has not yet determined the impact of online credit recovery on student engagement or learning (Zehr, 2010), empirical evidence from studies on mathematics instruction reveal that project-driven instruction, hands-on activities, and other integrative approaches are especially effective with alternative school students (Gagnon & Bottge, 2006). Thus, the effectiveness of credit recovery for learning is likely contingent on its implementation and the types of supplemental learning activities. The school leader plays a significant role in shaping all of these factors. Thus, a strong instructional leader in an alternative setting would be one that can balance the needs for individualization, variable pacing, and simultaneous courses in multiple subject areas for a small population of students with strong need for remediation, a wide variety of ability levels, and low attendance.

Culture and Climate

The quality of the climate in any school is important, but for alternative schools the ability to provide a safe, supportive space in which students feel known and valued is often their strongest draw for attracting and retaining students. Case studies on effective alternative schools consistently cite a strong sense of community and family as one of their defining characteristics (e.g., Brown & Beckett, 2007b; Golubtchik, 2013; Knutson, 1996), and the responsibility for creating and maintaining such a climate rests considerably on the school leader. To this end, alternative school leaders must understand the climatic factors that foster feelings of safety and connection for students in remedial and last-chance settings, and they must know how to lead other adults in eliciting these feelings for students. Research reveals that students in alternative schools achieve greater academic success when they have strong relationships with teachers and peers that facilitate interpersonal respect and acceptance (Brown & Beckett, 2007b; Golubtchik, 2013; Mottaz, 2002; NAEA, 2014; Quinn, et al., 2006; Streeter, et al., 2011). Feelings of respect and acceptance also emerge from equitably enforced rules that students view as fair and through staff members who are open to change and problem solving (Quinn, et al., 2006). As such, youth in alternative settings respond positively to consistent and reliable environments that are flexible and in which adults are sympathetic and understanding of students' lives and challenges (Quinn, et al., 2006). Research also suggests that effective alternative schools focus on reinforcing and rewarding positive behavior choices instead of reprimanding poor decisions with punitive action (Dunbar, 2001; Golubtchik, 2013; NAEA, 2014). Helping students to focus on academic effort, as opposed to making inferences about their intelligence when they struggle, can also be particularly effective for students with a history of school failure and negative self-narratives of their abilities (Dweck, 2000; Oyserman & Markus, 1990). Because of the influence of peer approval on adolescent identity, research also suggests that alternative schools place particular importance on offering opportunities for socialization through after-school activities, clubs, sports teams, and other positive outlets (Barber, 1997; Souza, 1999; Woodland, 2008).

Of course, a supportive culture and climate is not only necessary for students, but also for staff and teachers, whose morale can waver under the persistent challenges of their work and who tend to experience moderate to high levels of stress (Romano & Wahlstrom, 2000). In describing his first day as an alternative school principal, Golubtchik (2013) recalls the assistant principal telling him,

> The kids here are aggressive and have a history of academic failure. This school is like the Wild West, and has been for years. Kids and teachers are constantly getting hurt. This place is truly dangerous and out of control. Every day, we struggle to make it to 3 o'clock. The fact that similar high schools are also failing does not make us feel better. . . . We have some talented teachers in this building, and I believe they can help us improve. Our spirit isn't broken yet, but it's on the brink. (p. 17)

Given such perspectives, alternative school leaders must cultivate positive, motivated, and optimistic working environments for adults. Although leaders can make headway by hiring hopeful and invested staff, they also need to work to keep this mentality alive. To this end, Whitaker, Whitaker, and Lumpa (2013) recommend celebrating victories, both big and small. David (2000) asserts that keeping staff connected through social gatherings to share stories, ideas, laughter, and commiseration can boost morale and keep attitudes positive. Herzberg (1987) also found that effective alternative administrators provide real opportunities for staff to regularly exercise their creative juices and engage in problem solving to develop a sense of ownership for the school. In all these ways, alternative school leaders must understand both student and teacher psychology and create a climate that meets those psychological needs.

Wrap-Around Services

Research also shows that providing extra support and social services can substantially increase student engagement and success in alternative schools when those services are tailored to fit the individual needs of each student (Goldenson, 2011). Such wrap-around services constitute another sizable and critical element of alternative schooling that leaders must staff, implement, manage, and evaluate. Brown and Beckett (2007b) classify wrap-around services as a variety of individually tailored services driven by a team of adult stakeholders in each youth's life. Examples include mental health counseling, family counseling, social work services, healthcare, daycare, tutoring, and employment placement (Goldenson, 2011). Whereas traditional schools commonly offer counseling and career guidance, successful alternative schools customarily help students connect with a broad array of services in the school or community (Kellmayer, 1995). The impacts of wrap-around services are positive. In a 15-year study of 1,539 low-income, mostly Black, children attending alternative schools in Chicago, Reynolds and colleagues (2001) found that those who received services specifically tailored to their needs had better educational and social outcomes by age 20 than their peers without access to alternative services. In research with at-risk youth in Vermont, Yoe and colleagues (1996) found that 94% of youth receiving services showed significant behavioral improvements and that school-based services were more effective than services provided outside the school.

Despite their positive impact, implementing such programs is not a simple endeavor. The fact that services must be tailored to individual students' needs requires school leaders to develop and implement effective procedures for managing and overseeing these systems. Schools must have systematized procedures to assess the needs of each student and identify and provide appropriate services through specialized planning. Research has shown that student support teams work well for designing and implementing such plans (Kellmayer, 1995). Teams typically include the student, family, professional service providers, natural supports from the community, friends, clergy, and anyone else the family may call upon (Dwyer & Osher, 2000). School leaders must ensure these teams work together and with other community agencies to design and deliver the best plan of support. These teams can also help students transition out of alternative settings, as successful reintegration into traditional schools also requires a coordinated process (Valore, Cantrell, & Cantrell, 2006). Unlike traditional schools, in which student support teams assess and plan for a small segment of the school population, the demographics of alternative schools often require wrap-around services for most, if not all, students. As such, wrap-around services constitute a sizable portion of the principal's responsibility (Kellmayer, 1995).

Staffing

As in most schools, principals in alternative schools have the responsibility of hiring, monitoring, and firing their staff. Yet, compared with traditional schools, the staffing needs and considerations in alternative schools are different in a number of ways, particularly in the types of candidates sought and the positions to be staffed. Fundamentally, alternative school leaders must seek job applicants who can take on more flexible roles than they would in traditional schools due to the small school size and the need for each individual to serve in multiple capacities. Kellmayer (1995) argues that alternative school staff should also be prepared to serve in a "continually stressful environment" (p. 72) and be able to serve as unofficial counselors and mentors to help guide students academically, socially, and emotionally, regardless of their official job title. Teachers, in particular, would ideally have experience serving youth from disadvantaged or marginalized backgrounds, and they should be willing to develop the whole child in addition to teaching to rigorous academic standards (Tyler & Lofstrom, 2009). Leaders must also find high-quality candidates for a variety of other critical roles as well. Most alternative schools rely heavily on case managers who provide a direct and reoccurring point of communication between the student's family and school. Case managers constantly check in with students on academic performance, behavioral challenges, and other personal issues (Brown & Beckett, 2007b). Alternative schools also tend to have an array of other roles to be filled, including attendance officers, retention managers, data specialists, student support managers, counselors, and security guards (Flennaugh, et al., 2015). All this said, finding and attracting strong candidates can be challenging for alternative school leaders, particularly considering the academic and behavioral characteristics of many of the students. Indeed, alternative schools face the same staffing challenges of many other high needs schools that fail to attract all the high-quality teachers and support staff they need (Ingersoll, 2004).

Professional Development

Although professional development is fundamental in any school, the considerations are somewhat different for alternative schools, where the necessary skills and knowledge for educators are different from those in traditional schools (Menendez, 2007). In recounting their case study of an alternative school, Brown and Beckett (2007b) conclude that teachers could have better served students had they received professional development on behavior management, socio-emotional issues, specific subject competencies, and how to cultivate trusting relationships with students and parents. Tobin and Sprague (2000) point out that, under the Individuals with Disabilities Education Act of 1997, students with serious discipline problems have the opportunity to attend school in alternative environments rather than being homebound with tutoring or other restrictive placements (U.S. Department of Education, 1994). This option compels administrators to design appropriate professional development for staff to manage serious disciplinary problems through specific strategies and tools, for which staff must be trained (Quinn & Poirier, 2006). As an example, O'Neill and colleagues (1997) advocate for functional behavioral assessments that identify antecedents of problem behavior and inform staff of ways they can manipulate factors under their control (environment, lesson, peer contact) before a serious disciplinary incident occurs. Accurate use of this proactive, as opposed to reactive, tool requires training that must be planned, overseen, and reinforced.

Harro (2000) also asserts that professional development for alternative educators should include discussions of positionality and social class construction. Many students in alternative schools fall into one or more marginalized groups based on social class, race, gender, sexual orientation, and physical and mental capacity. Yet, many staff members will fall into socially constructed classes of privilege. To bridge this divide, leaders must teach staff to understand and address their privilege and positionality (Johnson, 2006). Case managers, in particular, must be skilled in this area because of their frequent and ongoing interactions with teachers and parents (Brown & Beckett, 2007b). Across these focal areas for professional development, alternative school leaders face the unique challenge of blending the pressing need for attention to behavioral interventions without losing sight of the instructional emphasis on individualization, for which most teachers also need considerable training.

Program Evaluation

Finally, as in all schools, alternative educators must be held accountable for the quality of their work. Given these schools' unique circumstances and characteristics, however, crafting appropriate evaluation methods requires leaders to have and implement tools different from those used in other settings. Mandated state standardized exams, for example, may be fairly worthless for evaluating alternative schools where the vast majority of students score extremely low or miss tests due to absenteeism. In considering program evaluation then, alternative school leaders must focus on the purpose of alternative schooling and the outcomes they hope to achieve. In a 2013 report on the challenges to overseeing and evaluating alternative charter schools, the National Association of Charter School Authorizers (NACSA) acknowledges the need to move beyond anecdotes to real measures. They advocate for a mix of quantitative and qualitative data, including academic performance and growth indicators, graduation and dropout rates, attendance data, college and career readiness measures, and grant and scholarship application rates. Qualitatively, they advise considering employment experiences, incarceration and recidivism rates, surveys on students' experiences, reports of personal growth among students, involvement in community programs, and personal characteristics. Scriven (2007), a leading authority on evaluation, suggests using a Key Evaluation Checklist (KEC), which is an organized outline frequently used among alternative educators (e.g., Briere, & Scott, 2012; Davidson, 2005; Patton, 2011; Kellmayer, 1995; Ruhe & Zumbo, 2008). The KEC is considered an efficient tool for alternative school leaders to use in defining, developing, and executing an evaluation that assesses the quality of their program at a given point in time. The KEC can guide improvement by providing information in 14 domains, including the school's context, resources, values, outcomes, and costs. Such alternative approaches to program evaluation provide leaders with multiple options for developing, implementing, and utilizing an evaluation that takes into consideration the unique circumstances of alternative schools. However, school leaders must be prepared for undertaking these evaluations with appropriate data collection and evaluation skills that differ from those required to evaluate a traditional school.

PROPOSED CHANGES TO LEADERSHIP PREPARATION PROGRAMS

Given this unique set of knowledge and skills required for alternative school leaders in remedial and last chance programs, we assert that leadership programs that prepare traditional school leaders are not yet fully prepared to recruit and train leaders who could ultimately reshape the alternative education landscape to fully live up to its potential. As such, we propose three models for training alternative school leaders in leadership programs through coursework, concentrations, and full programs at the Master's and/or Administrator Certification levels.

Coursework

The simplest means by which preparation programs could address the needs presented above is by offering a single course in leading alternative schools. At a minimum, we recommend that all leadership preparation programs include such a course. The content would mirror that described above and focus on contextual considerations particular to alternative settings. For example, one unit in the course could focus on the social and emotional needs of students typically placed in alternative schools, emphasizing research on risk and resilience among vulnerable populations with a history of school failure. Instruction would focus on the psychological benefits to utilizing proactive approaches to managing student behavior and providing wrap-around services to minimize the impact of outside factors on students' academics. The coursework approach would require no special recruiting beyond students already enrolled, and the expected outcome would be to expose students to key issues in alternative education, with the understanding that program graduates could end up leading alternative schools or oversee schools or districts containing alternative programs. Of course, such an approach would not offer specialized certification for students.

Concentrations

In large colleges of education that have multiple departments and that prepare large numbers of school leaders, we recommend offering a concentration in alternative education. Participating students would take regular coursework in leadership preparation alongside a series of courses on alternative education. Students could take relevant courses on adolescent psychology and risk and resilience in other programs such as educational psychology, special education, or child development. Within the department of educational administration, concentration students could take courses focused on leadership issues that would help aspiring leaders understand effective management of alternative settings. Topics could include exemplary practices in implementing wrap-around supports, staffing procedures, and instructional leadership for individualization. This preparation approach would enable future administrators to develop deeper understanding in more areas than in the one-course approach. In internship or practicum experiences required for leadership students, concentration students would have placements in alternative schools to garner relevant experience. The concentration model would be suitable for programs that could not serve full cohorts of alternative educators but that would have a need in the region. Graduates could receive certification or notation on their degrees to certify their expertise in alternative education.

Programs

More intensively, we envision leadership programs in areas with high proportions of alternative schools creating programs to prepare highly qualified leaders for those schools. We advise a cohort model, which research has shown to be ideal for providing peer support and collaborative learning both during and after leadership programs (Hitt, Tucker, & Young, 2012). Through cohorts of 15 to 20, students would build networks among alternative educators in a region that would enable them to share resources, best practices, problem-solving, professional development, and mutual support over the long term. Such support could help with sustainability in the profession and address potential feelings of isolation for alternative school principals. In finding appropriate students, university educators could recruit strong teachers from alternative schools, special educators, juvenile justice educators, and others who have worked with high-need student populations. As with the coursework and concentration models, program curriculum would address skills and knowledge for leading alternative schools, yet could do so through a series of sequenced courses covering discrete skills and knowledge in more depth and through more real-world applications. Ideally, students would learn the fundamentals of school leadership while fully contextualizing that learning in alternative education. For example, in a course on school finance, considerations could include budgeting for and implementing wrap-around services and individualized curriculum; students could examine community partnership models that would alleviate some of these costs or provide additional resources. When studying human resources, program students could consider the full staffing needs of alternative schools, including the specialized experience and training necessary for teachers, academic specialists, case managers, and other support personnel working with alternative students. Throughout the program, course readings would focus on effective practices in alternative education and related issues, such as urban poverty, the school to prison pipeline, and the social constructions of marginalized groups. As with concentrations, programs could utilize cross-enrollment with other departments in colleges of education or universities to provide students with key knowledge and skills in related areas.

Central to a program model would be an internship or residency in an alternative school under the supervision of an experienced alternative administrator who would offer guidance and mentorship, fulfilling critical needs for students to both experience high quality field placements (Orr & Orphanos, 2011) and receive mentoring (Davis & Darling-Hammond, 2012). To facilitate this component, program faculty would need to generate university partnerships with local alternative schools and programs. Such partnerships would not only provide sites for internships, but could also offer a feedback loop to program faculty about current needs and issues facing alternative educators and provide access to a potential pool of future program recruits (Hitt, Tucker, & Young, 2012). In internships, aspiring administrators would ideally engage in building relationships with alternative school staff, students, and families; learn fundamental practices in implementing wraparound services and community partnerships; gain experience in supervising teachers implementing differentiated instruction and remedial programming to meet students' individualized needs; and be exposed to common behaviors exhibited by alternative school students and positive approaches to addressing those behaviors. At the conclusion of a cohort program, graduates would receive certification in alternative education, feel well prepared to lead alternative schools, and have a network of like-minded colleagues for future support.

Potential of Alternative Education

Students in alternative schools share many of the characteristics of other students. They strive to feel valued, connected, autonomous, and competent. They want to be surrounded by adults who know and respect them and who will provide the support and encouragement they need to be successful. The current swing towards viewing these students as "opportunity youth" hinges on this more positive perspective and creates an opportune moment to make alternative schools true and viable alternatives to traditional schools. We envision a landscape of alternative schools that offer a genuine array of high quality options for students with differing needs and interests, such that remedial, last chance, and popular innovation programs all have strong, positive reputations. There is potential for alternative schools to be intentional first choices—not last chances—that proactively set out to educate students who seek small settings and high levels of one-on-one support from teachers, aides, case workers, social workers, and service providers. At the helm of these high functioning alternative schools, we see well prepared leaders who understand and are ready to meet the unique needs of the alternative student population, instructional leaders who understand and are able to navigate the challenges of individualizing instruction for students with widely varying abilities, and cultural leaders who know how to create and maintain climates that support students and teachers. We imagine leaders who are adept at integrating high-quality instructional programs with necessary wrap-around supports and who staff all programs with carefully selected and well trained educators. Finally, we envision leaders who work to continually evaluate and improve those schools through targeted data collection and analysis in areas that accurately reflect the quality of their schools.

At present, however, we are not yet there, in part because there simply are not enough well prepared leaders to fulfill the demand for alternative schools. We argue that colleges of education can play a critical role in fulfilling the potential of alternative schools by recruiting and training effective alternative education leaders. This chapter is a call-to-arms for preparation programs to make alternative education a focal point in leadership preparation. We believe it is both a responsibility of the field, as well as a potentially transformative opportunity, to proactively carve out the types of schools that will be genuine alternatives for our nation's most under-served students.

REFERENCES

Barber, B. K. (1997). Introduction: Adolescent socialization in context—The role of connection, regulation, and autonomy in the family. *Journal of Adolescent Research, 12*(1), 5–11.

Belfield, C. R., Levin, H. M., & Rosen, R. (2012). *The economic value of opportunity youth.* Washington DC: Civic Enterprises.

Best, M., Price, D., & McCallum, F. (2014). 'Go over there and look at the pictures in the book': An investigation of educational marginalisation, social interactions and achievement motivation in an alternative middle school setting. *International Journal of Inclusive Education,* (ahead-of-print), 1–13.

Branch, G. F., Hanushek, E. A., & Rivkin, S. G. (2012). *Estimating the effect of leaders on public sector productivity: The case of school principals* (No. w17803). Cambridge, MA: National Bureau of Economic Research.

Briere, J. N., & Scott, C. (2012). *Principles of trauma therapy: A guide to symptoms, evaluation, and treatment.* Thousand Oaks, CA: Sage.

Brown, B. B. (2004). Adolescents' relationships with peers. In R. M. Lerner & L. Steinberg (Eds.), *Handbook of adolescent psychology* (2nd ed., pp. 363–394). Hoboken, NJ: Wiley & Sons.

Brown, L. H., & Beckett, K. S. (2007a). Parent involvement in an alternative school for students at risk of educational failure. *Education and Urban Society, 39*(4), 498–523.

Brown, L. H., & Beckett, K. S. (2007b). *Building community in an alternative school: The perspective of an African American principal.* New York, NY: Peter Lang.

Bulkley, K. E., Henig, J. R., & Levi, H. M (2010). *Between public and private: Politics, governance and the new portfolio models for urban school reform.* Cambridge, MA: Harvard Education Press.

Butrymowicz, S. (2010, August 2). Students short on educational credits turn to 'recovery' programs. *The Hechinger Report.* Online at http://hechingerreport.org.

Cairns, R. B., & Cairns, B. D. (1994). *Lifelines and risks: Pathways of youth in our time.* Cambridge, UK: Cambridge University Press.

Carver, P. R., & Lewis, L. (2010). *Alternative schools and programs for public school students at risk of educational failure: 2007–08* (NCES 2010-026). U.S. Department of Education, National Center for Education Statistics. Washington, DC: Government Printing Office.

Conley, B. E. (2002). *Alternative schools: A reference handbook.* Santa Barbara, CA: ABC-CLIO.

D'Angelo, F., & Zemanick, R. (2009). The twilight academy: An alternative education program that works. *Preventing School Failure: Alternative Education for Children and Youth, 53*(4), 211–218.

Darling-Hammond, L., LaPointe, M., Meyerson, D., Orr, M. T., & Cohen, C. (2007). *Preparing school leaders for a changing world: Lessons from exemplary leadership development programs.* Stanford, CA: Stanford University, Stanford Educational Leadership Institute.

David, T. (2000). Teacher mentoring—Benefits all around. *Kappa Delta Pi Record, 36*(3), 134–136.

Davidson, E. J. (Ed.). (2005). *Evaluation methodology basics: The nuts and bolts of sound evaluation.* Thousand Oaks, CA: Sage.

Davis, S. H., & Darling-Hammond, L. (2012). Innovative principal preparation programs: What works and how we know. *Planning and Changing, 43*(1/2), 25–45.

de Bilde, J., Van Damme, J., Lamote, C., & De Fraine, B. (2013). Can alternative education increase children's early school engagement? A longitudinal study from kindergarten to third grade. *School Effectiveness and School Improvement, 24*(2), 212–233.

Duke, D., & Salmonowicz, M. (2010). Key decisions of a first-year 'turnaround' principal. *Educational Management Administration & Leadership, 38*(1), 33–58.

Dunbar, C. (2001). *Alternative schooling for African American youth.* New York, NY: Peter Lang.

Dunning-Lozano, J. L. (2014). Race and opportunity in a public alternative school. *Race Ethnicity and Education,* (ahead-of-print), 1–28.

Dweck, C. S. (2000). *Self-theories: Their role in motivation, personality, and development.* Philadelphia, PA: Psychology Press.

Dwyer, K., & Osher, D. (2000). *Safeguarding our children: An action guide. Implementing early warning, timely response.* Washington, DC: American Institutes for Research.

Erikson, E. H. (1968). *Identity: Youth and crisis.* New York, NY: W. W. Norton & Company.

Flennaugh, T. K., Cooper, K. S., & Carter Andrews, D. (2015). *Serving disconnected youth: How educators understand their work in a high-needs context.* Paper presented at the 2015 Annual Meeting of the American Educational Research Association. Chicago, IL.

Foley, R. M., & Pang, L. (2006). Alternative education programs: Program and student characteristics. *The High School Journal, 89*(3), 10–21.

Fraser, J., Davis, P. W., & Singh, R. (1997). Identity work by alternative high school students. *International Journal of Qualitative Studies in Education, 10*(2), 221–236.

Free, J. L. (2008). *First step or last chance: At-risk youth, alternative schooling and juvenile delinquency* (Doctoral dissertation). Boston: Northeastern University.

Gagnon, J. C., & Bottge, B. A. (2006). Mathematics instruction in secondary interim, short-and long-term alternative school placements. *Preventing School Failure: Alternative Education for Children and Youth, 51*(1), 39–47.

Garland, S. (2010). New York City: Big gains in the Big Apple. In *Fighting the dropout crisis: Can the Obama administration get more high schoolers to graduate? A tale of three cities that are trying. A Special Report.* Washington, DC: Washington Monthly.

Goldenson, J. (2011). When there is no blueprint: The provision of mental health services in alternative school programs for suspended and expelled youth. *Child & Youth Services, 32*(2), 108–123.

Golubtchik, H. (2013). *Last chance high school: A principal's crusade to rescue throwaway teens*. CreateSpace Independent Publishing Platform.

Hale, E. L., & Moorman, H. N. (2003). Preparing school principals: A national perspective on policy and program innovations. *Institute for Educational Leadership, Washington, DC and Illinois Education Research Council, Edwardsville, IL, 1*(5), 8.

Harro, B. (2000). The cycle of socialization. In M. Adams, W. J. Blumenfeld, R. Castañeda, H. W. Hackman, M. L. Peters, & X. Zuñiga (Eds.), *Readings for diversity and social justice* (pp.15–21). New York, NY: Routledge.

Herzberg, F. (1987). One more time: How do you motivate employees? Harvard Business Review, *65*(2), 22–29.

Hitt, D. H., Tucker, P. D., & Young, M. D. (2012). *The professional pipeline for educational leadership*. Charlottesville, VA: University Council for Educational Administration.

Howell, J. C. (2003). *Preventing and reducing juvenile delinquency: A comprehensive framework*. Thousand Oaks, CA: Sage.

Ingersoll, R. M. (2004). *Why do high-poverty schools have difficulty staffing their classrooms with qualified teachers?* Washington, DC: Center for American Progress, Institute for America's Future.

Johnson, A. G. (2006). *Privilege, power, and difference* (2nd ed.). New York, NY: McGraw-Hill.

Kellmayer, J. (1995). *How to establish an alternative school*. Thousand Oaks, CA: Corwin.

Khalifa, M. (2012). A re-new-ed paradigm in successful urban school leadership: Principal as community leader. *Educational Administration Quarterly, 48*(3), 424–467.

Kim, J. H. (2011). Narrative inquiry into (re)imagining alternative schools: A case study of Kevin Gonzales. *International Journal of Qualitative Studies in Education, 24*(1), 77–96.

Kim, J. H., & Taylor, K. A. (2008). Rethinking Alternative Education to break the cycle of educational inequality and inequity. *The Journal of Educational Research, 101*(4) 207–219.

Kleiner, B., Porch, R., & Farris, E. (2002). *Public alternative schools and programs for students at risk of education failure: 2000–01* (NCES 2002-004). U.S. Department of Education, Washington, DC: National Center for Education Statistics

Klonsky, M. (2000). Remembering Port Huron. In W. Ayers, M. Klonsky, & G. Lyon (Eds.), *A simple justice: The challenge of small schools*. New York, NY: Teachers College Press.

Knutson, G. G. (1996). Alternative high schools: Models for the future? *The High School Journal, 79*(2), 119–124.

Leithwood, K., Louis, K. S., Anderson, S., & Wahlstrom, K. (2004). *How leadership influences student learning* (Learning from Leadership Project Executive Summary.) New York, NY: The Wallace Foundation.

Leone, P. E., & Drakeford, W. (1999). Alternative education: From a "last chance" to a proactive model. *The Clearing House, 73*(2), 86–88.

Martinez, M., & Schilling, S. (2010). Using technology to engage and educate youth. *New Directions for Youth Development, 2010*(127), 51–61.

McNulty, C. P., & Roseboro, D. L. (2009). "I'm not really that bad": Alternative school students, stigma, and identity politics. *Equity & Excellence in Education, 42*(4), 412–427.

Meeus, W., Iedema, J., Helsen, M., & Vollebergh, W. (1999). Patterns of adolescent identity development: Review of literature and longitudinal analysis. *Developmental Review, 19*(4), 419–461.

Menendez, A. L. (2007). Supports and enhancements designed for alternative school programming. *Preventing School Failure: Alternative Education for Children and Youth, 51*(2), 19–22.

Moore, J. (2013). *Research summary: Resilience and at-risk children and youth.* Washington, DC: National Center for Homeless Education.

Mottaz, C. (2002). *Breaking the cycle of failure: How to build and maintain quality alternative schools.* Lanham, MD: Scarecrow.

National Alliance for Public Charter Schools. (2008). *Charter school executives: Toward a new generation of leadership.* The Working Group of Charter School Leadership, National Alliance for Public Charter Schools. Online at www.publiccharters.org.

National Alternative Education Association. (2014). *Exemplary Practices 2.0: Standards of Quality and Program Evaluation 2014.* Manassas, VA: National Alternative Education Association.

National Association of Charter School Authorizers (2013). *Anecdotes aren't enough: An evidence-based approach to accountability for alternative charter schools.* Chicago, IL: National Association of Charter School Authorizers.

National Center for Education Statistics. (2012). *Digest of Education Statistics, 2012.* Washington, DC: Institute for Education Sciences. Online at nces.ed.gov/programs/digest/d12.

National Policy Board for Educational Administration (NPBEA). (2011). *Educational Leadership Program Standards: 2011 ELCC Building Level.* Washington, DC: National Board for Educational Administration.

Nolan, K., & Anyon, J. (2004). Learning to do time: Willis's model of cultural reproduction in an era of postindustrialism, globalization, and mass incarceration. *Learning to labor in new times* (pp. 129–140). New York, NY: Routledge.

Noguera, P. A. (2003). Schools, prisons, and social implications of punishment: Rethinking disciplinary practices. *Theory into Practice, 42*(4), 341–350.

NYC Open Data. (2014). School Attendance and Enrollment Statistics by District (2010–2011). Online at https://data.cityofnewyork.us/Education/School-Attendance-and-Enrollment-Statistics-by-Dis/7z8d-msnt.

O'Neil, R., Welsh, M., Parke, R. D., Wang, S., & Strand, C. (1997). A longitudinal assessment of the academic correlates of early peer acceptance and rejection. *Journal of Clinical Child Psychology, 26*(3), 290–303.

Orr, M. T., & Orphanos, S. (2011). How graduate-level preparation influences the effectiveness of school leaders: A comparison of the outcomes of exemplary and conventional leadership preparation programs for principals. *Educational Administration Quarterly, 47*(1), 18–70.

Oyserman, D., & Markus, H. R. (1990). Possible selves and delinquency. *Journal of Personality and Social Psychology, 59*(1), 112–125.

Patton, M. Q. (2011). *Essentials of utilization-focused evaluation.* Thousand Oaks: Sage.

Quinn, M. M., & Poirier, J. M. (2006). *Study of effective alternative education programs: Final grant report.* Washington DC: American Institutes for Research.

Quinn, M. M., Poirier, J. M., Faller, S. E., Gable, R. A., & Tonelson, S. W. (2006). An examination of school climate in effective alternative programs. *Preventing School Failure, 51*(1), 11–17.

Raywid, M. A. (1981). The first decade of public school alternatives. *Phi Delta Kappan, 62*(8), 551–553.

Raywid, M. A. (1990). Rethinking school governance. In R. F. Elmore and Associates (Eds.), *Restructuring schools: The next generation of educational reform* (pp. 152–205). San Francisco: Jossey-Bass.

Raywid, M. A. (1994). Alternative schools: The state of the art. *Educational Leadership, 52*(1), 26–31.

Rennie Center for Education Research & Policy (2014, June). *Alternative education: Exploring innovations in learning.* Cambridge, MA: Rennie Center Education Research & Policy.

Reynolds, A. J., Temple, J. A., Robertson, D. L., & Mann, E. A. (2001). Long-term effects of an early childhood intervention on educational achievement and juvenile arrest: A 15-year follow-up of low-income children in public schools. *JAMA: Journal of the American Medical Association, 285*(18), 2339–2346.

Romano, J. L., & Wahlstrom, K. (2000). Professional stress and well-being of K–12 teachers in alternative educational settings: A leadership agenda. *International Journal of Leadership in Education, 3*(2), 121–135.

Ruhe, V., & Zumbo, B. D. (2008). *Evaluation in distance education and e-learning: The unfolding model.* New York, NY: Guilford Press.

Rumberger, R. W. (2011). *Dropping out: Why students drop out of high school and what can be done about it.* Cambridge, MA: Harvard University Press.

Saltman, K. J. (Ed.). (2003). *Education as enforcement: The militarization and corporatization of schools.* New York, NY: Routledge.

Scriven, M. (1991) Key evaluation checklist. In M. Scriven, *Evaluation Thesaurus* (4th ed.). Thousand Oaks, CA: Sage.

Souza, T. J. (1999). Communication and alternative school student socialization. *Communication Education, 48*(2), 91–108.

Steinberg, L., & Morris, A. S. (2001). Adolescent development. *Journal of Cognitive Education and Psychology, 2*(1), 55–87.

Streeter, C. L., Franklin, C., Kim, J. S., & Tripodi, S. J. (2011). Concept mapping: An approach for evaluating a public alternative school program. *Children & Schools, 33*(4), 197–214.

Tallerico, M., & Burstyn, J. N. (2004). Politics and paradox: The case of an urban alternative school. *Planning and Change, 35*(1&2), 33–54.

Tatum, B. D. (2000). The complexity of identity: 'Who am I?' In M. Adams, W. J. Blumenfeld, R. Castañeda, H. W. Hackman, M. L. Peters, & X. Zuñiga (Eds.), *Readings for diversity and social justice* (pp. 9–14). New York, NY: Routledge.

Texas Education Agency Website (Updated 4/16/2013). Dropout Recovery Pilot Program. Accessed on 7/17/14 at http://www.tea.state.tx.us/index3.aspx?id=3686.

Tobin, T., & Sprague, J. (1999). Alternative education programs for at-risk youth: Issues, best practice, and recommendations. *Oregon School Study Council Bulletin, 42*(4).

Tobin, T., & Sprague, J. (2000). Alternative education strategies: Reducing violence in school and the community. *Journal of Emotional and Behavioral Disorders, 8*(3), 177–186.

Tyler, J. H., & Lofstrom, M. (2009). Finishing high school: Alternative pathways and dropout recovery. *The Future of Children, 19*(1), 77–103.

U.S. Department of Education. (1994). To assure the free appropriate public education of all children with disabilities: Sixteenth annual report to Congress on the implementation of the Individuals with Disabilities Education Act. Washington, DC: Westat.

Valore, T. G., Cantrell, M. L., & Cantrell, R. P. (2006). Preparing for passage. *Preventing School Failure: Alternative Education for Children and Youth, 51*(1), 49–54.

Vanderhaar, J. E., Petrosko, J. M., & Munoz, M. (2013). Reconsidering the alternatives: The relationship between suspension, disciplinary alternative school placement, subsequent juvenile detention, and the salience of race. In D. Losen (Ed.), *Closing the school discipline gap: Research for policymakers*. New York, NY: Teachers College Press.

Vann, M., Schubert, S. R., & Rogers, D. (2001). The Big Bayou Association: An alternative education program for middle-school, at-risk juveniles. *Preventing School Failure: Alternative Education for Children and Youth, 45*(1), 31–36.

Verdugo, R., & Glenn, B. (2006). *Race and alternative schools: The new tracking*. Washington, DC: Hamilton Fish Institute on School and Community Violence.

Watson, S. L., & Watson, W. R. (2011). The role of technology and computer-based instruction in a disadvantaged alternative school's culture of learning. *Computers in the Schools, 28*(1), 39–55.

Wetzel, M. C., McNaboe, K. A., Schneidermeyer, S. A., Jones, A. B., & Nash, P. N. (1997). Public and private partnership in an alternative middle school program. *Preventing School Failure: Alternative Education for Children and Youth, 41*(4), 179–184.

Whitaker, T., Whitaker, B., & Lumpa, D. (2013). *Motivating & inspiring teachers: The educational leader's guide for building staff morale*. New York, NY: Routledge.

White House Council for Community Solutions. (2012, June). *Final report: Community solutions for opportunity youth*. Washington DC: Corporation for National & Community Service.

Woodland, M. H. (2008). Whatcha doin' after school? A review of the literature on the influence of after-school programs on young Black males. *Urban Education, 43*(5), 537–560.

Yoe, J. T., Santarcangelo, S., Atkins, M., & Burchard, J. D. (1996). Wraparound care in Vermont: Program development, implementation, and evaluation of a statewide system of individualized services. *Journal of Child and Family Studies, 5*(1), 23–37.

Zehr, M. A. (2010, June 21). Districts embracing online credit-recovery options. *Education Week*. Online at www.edweek.org.

CHAPTER 8

PREPARING LEADERS IN AN ERA OF SCHOOL TURNAROUNDS

The Promise of University/District Partnerships as a Lever for Program Improvement

Chad R. Lochmiller, Colleen E. Chesnut, and Molly S. Stewart
Indiana University

ABSTRACT

School leaders face significant pressure to improve student achievement in low performing schools. This reality poses new challenges for principal preparation programs. In this study, we analyzed 40 participant interviews collected in an external program evaluation to determine how a partnership with school districts impacts university-based programs. Our analysis indicates that the partnership enabled the partners to identify shared strategic interests and that the district used its role in developing the program curriculum to influence the focus of the program. Our analysis also indicates that the partnership enabled the university faculty to cultivate a new understanding of what leadership practice means. We conclude this chapter by noting implications for the field.

School leaders throughout the United States face significant pressure to improve student achievement, particularly in the nation's lowest performing schools. Recent federal policies have called upon principals to serve as "turnaround leaders," who are described as leaders who enter failing schools, quickly determine the underlying causes of poor student achievement, and take specific actions to boost achievement rapidly (Leithwood, Harris, & Strauss, 2010). The need for school principals to act as turnaround leaders poses significant challenges for university-based leadership preparation programs. The expectation that leaders will have the skills to turn around failing schools demands that leaders are prepared with these skills in the first place (Duke, 2014). Much of the existing research, however, suggests that university-based preparation programs likely are not preparing principals with the skills they need. Indeed, these programs have long been the subjects of considerable criticism, with many noting that their curriculum lacks alignment with the realities of school leadership (Briggs, Cheney, Davis, & Moll, 2013; Levine, 2005). Researchers have tried challenging this view by heralding examples of effective preparation programs (Darling-Hammond et al., 2010).

Given the criticisms of preparation programs, the field has long sought new approaches that aim to improve both the rigor of preparation activities and the relevance of preparation activities to school leadership. Partnerships between universities and school districts have increasingly been heralded as a way to achieve both of these aims (Darling-Hammond et al., 2010; Orr, King, & LaPointe, 2010) though the benefits of partnerships have long been known (Barnett, Hall, Berg, & Camarena, 1999; Petersen, 1999; Whitaker & Barnett, 1999). Indeed, in recent years, urban school districts increasingly have engaged universities in seeking to improve preparation program experiences and boost the quality of their applicant pools. As one recent report noted, "To improve education in the nation's troubled urban schools, school districts must make the development of stronger school leadership a top priority" (Mitgang, 2013, p. 7). Indeed, school districts must ensure that they are recruiting and developing leaders "needed to execute their district improvement strategies" (Kimball, 2011, p. 134). While the research is well-developed in regard to the ways that these partnerships develop, the research has not fully considered how these partnerships may impact traditional conceptions of leadership preparation, particularly within the context of the current policy environment which calls upon school leaders to lead school turnarounds.

PURPOSE OF THIS CHAPTER

In this chapter, we focus our discussion on a partnership between a university and urban school district located in the Southeastern region of the

United States. We aim to understand how the presence of school district partners changes the role of the university in a traditional preparation program, particularly when the impetus for the partnership was to prepare principals to work as turnaround leaders. In 2012, the partnership we studied received a multi-million dollar grant from the state education agency to design and implement a preparation program that specifically focused on preparing assistant principals and principals with turnaround leadership skills. The program was designed as a pilot for improving preparation programs statewide. Drawing upon 40 interviews completed with 32 tenure-track faculty, clinical instructors, and district administrators collected as part of an external program evaluation, we explore the ways in which the partnership between the university and district provided an opportunity to reassess roles and renegotiate the relationships in order to prepare principals and assistant principals for turnaround leadership. The chapter proceeds by reviewing the literature related to district/university partnerships for principal preparation. After this, we discuss the methods that we employed in completing our analysis. Then, we present our findings as cross-cutting themes. Finally, we conclude by noting the implications for the field.

LITERATURE REVIEW

Recognizing the weaknesses of existing preparation program activities, particularly their disconnect with leadership practice, partnerships between school districts and universities have been increasingly promoted as important levers to improve the quality of leadership preparation (Darling-Hammond et al., 2010; Orr et al., 2010; Turnbull et al., 2013; Whitaker & Barnett, 1999). For many school districts, the task of improving leaders currently lies beyond the scope of their existing efforts or available resources. Thus, districts historically have deferred to universities for their leadership development needs. In the era of school-based accountability and turnaround leadership, such deference is not seen as sufficient to improve leadership in the schools (Mitgang, 2013). Indeed, researchers have suggested that establishing a robust partnership with a university may be one way to improve the capacity of individuals to lead meaningful changes in classroom instruction that result in improved student achievement outcomes (Darling-Hammond et al., 2010; Kimball, 2011; Orr et al., 2010; Mitgang, 2013). This brief literature review addresses the following three domains of the literature: (a) the advantages to district/university partnerships of leadership preparation, (b) the factors or characteristics that support partnership development, and (c) the impact those partnerships have on aspiring leaders.

Advantages to District/University Partnerships for Principal Preparation

The literature surrounding the value of partnership in leadership preparation is well-developed, with many scholars indicating that such arrangements present districts and universities with significant advantages as they seek to improve principal preparation (Barnett, Hall, Berg, & Camarena, 1999; Whitaker & Barnett, 1999; Petersen, 1999). Whitaker and Barnett's (1999) discussion of the Leadership Development Alliance, which was a forerunner to many current leadership preparation partnerships, highlights the importance of vision, support from top-level leadership at the district and university, clear roles and responsibilities, shared resources, mentor training, and buy-in or commitment from the university faculty. In a similar vein, Scribner and Machell (1999) found that some factors promoted or constrained collaborative leadership development within the context of a statewide doctoral program; these factors included program leadership, logistics, bureaucratic barriers, and cultural differences.

More recent discussions highlight that school district partnerships with universities are seen as particularly valuable tools for the improvement of principal preparation, as these partnerships enable school districts to improve the pool of prospective principals (Darling-Hammond et al., 2010; Kimball, 2011; Mitgang, 2013; Orr et al., 2010). School district-university partnerships also have advantages for leadership preparation programs in that they can be used to address perceived weaknesses in these programs, including preparation experiences that are not well-aligned to practice and program curricula that match poorly with district leadership needs (Levine, 2005; Mitgang, 2013). For universities, these partnerships are beneficial in that they often lead to improved program coherence, long-term sustainability, and increased rigor; all of which have been associated with improved preparation program outcomes (Darling-Hammond et al., 2010). Indeed, these findings were identified in earlier research by Fusarelli and Smith (1999), which noted that partnerships also have the added benefit of affordable cost, improved field experiences, and team teaching.

One of the chief criticisms of many preparation programs is that they lack well-developed curricula with learning experiences tied directly to leadership work (Levine, 2005). Darling-Hammond and colleagues (2010) noted that partnerships between school districts and university-based programs can "create coherence between training and practices as well as pipelines for recruitment, preparation, hiring, and induction" (p. 42). Further, research has highlighted that partnerships may be beneficial in terms of sustaining improvements in programs (Orr & Orphanos, 2011). As researchers have noted, "Pre-service principal training based in universities offers advantages in [terms of] sustainability, compared with the in-district arrangements that may be subject to policy shifts" (Turnbull et al., 2013, p. 15; see also Darling-Hammond et al., 2010; Orr et al., 2010). Indeed, Darling-Hammond and colleagues (2010) suggested that, "universities serve as anchors that sustain programs so that they can successfully evolve" (p. 130). Finally, these partnerships often result in more rigorous and meaningful learning experiences for pre-service principals as they present opportunities for what Ball and Cohen (1999) referred to as learning about practice *in* practice. Within the context of partnerships, districts and universities can create a curriculum that is both "rich in theory and grounded in practice," as well as wraps "highly relevant coursework around field-based experiences" (Darling-Hammond et al., 2010, p. 49). Two related studies found that partnerships facilitated greater program quality and a stronger role for districts in program design and delivery, selection decisions, and the provision of internships (Orr, 2011; Orr & Orphanos, 2011).

Characteristics of Effective Partnerships Between School Districts and Universities

Partnerships between school districts and universities often emerge when a district lacks the capacity to fully meet their leadership development needs or when it becomes clear that leaders who are being prepared lack specific skills that a district needs (Brooks et al., 2010; Mitgang, 2013). Thus, one of the factors associated with an effective partnership is an expressed need on the part of the school district to seek out the resources at a university. Typically, partnerships involve one university and a school district (Hewitt et al., 2012); however, some research indicates that partnerships may come in a variety of configurations in response to external conditions that prompt their development (Barnett, et al., 1999). Research further suggests that individual school districts can wield significant influence on preparation programs by engaging universities (Orr et al., 2010). For example, districts can influence universities by providing scholarships to participate in preferred leadership preparation programs, designating specific programs as preferred providers, or working with universities to co-construct a preparation program that addresses the district's needs (Orr et al., 2010).

Effective partnerships often extend beyond simply identifying in which programs a school leader should participate or providing employees financial assistance. Rather, the literature indicates that the most effective partnerships between districts and universities occur at multiple levels of program development, including recruitment, selection, internship placement, and curriculum development (Darling-Hammond et al., 2010; Kimball, 2011). One of the primary affordances of a partnership between a school district and university is that it allows the district and university to develop a shared understanding about what effective leadership entails and to identify experiences that equip leaders for these behaviors. The result of such collaboration is an expanded pool of potential leaders who understand "specific district and regional contexts" (Darling-Hammond et al., 2010, p. 130).

Impact on Aspiring School Leaders

Evidence concerning the efficacy of district-university partnerships continues to emerge. Direct connections between principal preparation program experience and student achievement outcomes are difficult to make given the indirect impact that principal leadership has on students (Grissom & Loeb, 2012; Hallinger & Heck, 1998; Witziers, Bosker, & Kruger, 2003). Recent discussions of principal preparation program outcomes indicate that the current literature base is limited by an absence of longitudinal data, difficulty attributing student growth to a single principal, and instability in the measures used to attribute achievement growth to principal preparation programs (Fuller & Hollingworth, 2014; Fuller, Young, & Baker, 2011; Grissom, Kalogrides, & Loeb, 2014). However, qualitative evidence suggests that such partnerships are generally perceived by participants as being beneficial to the institutions engaged in them and the students who enroll (Fusarelli & Smith, 1999; Korach, 2011). For example, Darling-Hammond and colleagues (2010) studied eight exemplary preparation programs and noted that those programs that included strong partnerships between the universities and districts were generally perceived by students as being more effective or meaningful. Indeed, such findings align well with other evidence suggesting that participants in district-university partnership programs typically view their programs positively (Borden, Preskill, & DeMoss, 2012; Orr & Barber, 2007).

The primary benefit of partnership programs for participants appears to be the ability for students to make meaningful connections between preparation program experiences and leadership work (Borden et al., 2012). These meaningful connections provide students with greater opportunities to practice leadership skills and thus become more confident engaging in specific leadership behaviors. Several studies highlight the advantages that this approach has for leadership skill development (Orr, 2011; Orr & Barber, 2007; Orr & Orphanos, 2011). Orr and Barber (2007), for example, compared a traditional university-based leadership preparation program with two district-university partnership programs and found that graduates of the partnership programs reported gains in leadership knowledge and skills, leadership career intentions, and actual advancement in leadership positions. Korach (2011) discovered that a district-university partnership resulted in learning not only for the graduates, but also for the district and the university in terms of supporting principals' change oriented behaviors. Clearly research indicates that partnerships are important aspects of improving principal preparation programs. Understanding the factors that influence these partnerships may be an important area for future research.

Research Related to Preparing Turnaround Leaders

Partnerships may be particularly important in regard to preparing aspiring principals for turnaround leadership. Research is relatively consistent in indicating that there are specific leadership actions that are common to turnaround leadership (Duke, 2012; Murphy & Meyers, 2008). In this study, as in the program we evaluated, we conceptualize turnaround leadership as being fundamentally about improving classroom instruction. We thus assume that turnaround leaders must be prepared to enter an organization, quickly diagnose achievement or performance related concerns, implement staff development activities, and monitor changes in professional practice, as these actions have often been used to describe the work of turnaround leaders (Leithwood, Harris, & Strauss, 2010). Recent research on leadership preparation indicates that leaders are best prepared for these activities when they are exposed to: problem-based learning; situated learning; data-based problem-solving; team based assignments; coaching and continuous feedback; sequenced learning activities; and instructors who are role models (Duke, 2014). Given the highly contextualized nature of these activities, it is not surprising that partnerships between school districts and universities are thought to be essential to preparing turnaround leaders (Duke, 2014). The next section presents research regarding organizational partnerships, which we use to frame our analysis of the program we studied.

THEORETICAL FRAMEWORK

Our analysis was framed with research related to organizational partnerships. This research characterizes the ways in which organizations work collaboratively to support specific aims, often by establishing partnerships. Barnett and colleagues (1999) indicated that partnerships are often evolutionary and range from simple collaborative ventures involving two independent organizations to the formal creation of an entirely new organization. Most models describe this evolution in terms of a partnership's "life cycle" (Barnett, et al., 1999, p. 592), through which partnerships emerge, develop, and dissolve.

Our review of the partnership literature (e.g., Schermerhorn, 1979) suggests that the process of forming a partnership often begins by setting goals and expectations. Given partnerships are often created to address complex problems, which we think improving leadership practice is, the importance of setting specific goals and expectations in the early stages is essential for these efforts to flourish (Bullough & Kauchak, 1997; Thomas et al., 2012). Second, researchers highlight the importance of maintaining relationships among stakeholders in partnership programs. The research suggests that relationships affect the broad purposes of partnerships, as well as their effectiveness over the long-term (Domina & Ruzek, 2012). Third, partnerships are resource intensive and thus difficult to sustain. As discussed by Feldman (1993), the amount of time and money needed to fully establish the levels of trust are substantial investments (citing Jackson, 1991, and Johnson, 1990). Stakeholder and participant availability is another serious consideration for the sustainability of partnerships. Staff employed by partnering institutions are often expected to participate in activities that contribute to the partnership goals, but time to participate must be taken away from other activities. There is significant research highlighting the importance of allowing participants to engage in partnership activities (Bullough & Kauchek, 1997; Feldman, 1993). Additionally, some organizations may be more willing than others to use their own resources to support and sustain the work of a partnership, or flexibility may be embedded already.

Finally, the issue of program delivery and sustainability is an important consideration, particularly as past research indicates that it is often after the early developmental stages in partnerships that relationships, operating practices, and norms begin to falter (Barnett, et al., 1999). Taken together, the literature provides a framework within which we can understand how partnerships between universities and school districts emerge. These concepts are consistent with research regarding the evolution of partnerships between universities and districts for the purposes of leadership preparation (Barnett, et al., 1999; Whitaker & Barnett, 1999). The framework sensitizes our understanding of the roles and goals that each of the partners we studied articulated as well as how the partners' behaviors can be represented theoretically. We used these conceptual ideas to develop our coding structure as well as to derive themes from our analysis of the data.

METHODS

The research presented in this chapter draws upon an external program evaluation that focused on the implementation of a research-based principal preparation program funded by Race to the Top. The program evaluation was conducted by the Center for Evaluation and Education Policy (CEEP) at Indiana University. The principal preparation program we evaluated was designed to prepare leaders to turn around low-performing schools in a large, urban school district in the southeast region of the United States. The program was housed at a public university, and was launched in 2012 upon receipt of a multi-million dollar grant from the U.S. Department of Education. The program was described as "innovative" in that it brought together a large, urban school district and the educational leadership program in a public university in a partnership for the sole purpose of preparing principals to turnaround struggling schools. Another innovative aspect of the program is that it has two phases. The first phase of the program prepares teacher leaders to be assistant principals and the second phase of the program prepares assistant principals for the principalship. The grant provided resources to the partnership to develop an accelerated preparation program that combined university-based coursework with an intensive, completely aligned administrative internship/apprenticeship in both phases. The program employed many research-based preparation practices, including rigorous recruitment and selection, job-embedded learning experiences, formative and summative assessment practices, and direct engagement by senior district leadership. Three research questions guided our study of this program: (a) How was the partnership an opportunity to reassess roles and renegotiate the relationships between the university and school district? (b) How did the district attempt to influence the preparation program? (c) What impact, if any, did the district's influence on the program ultimately have?

Data Collection

For this analysis, we focused on 40 interviews conducted with 32 program participants in spring 2014 as part of the evaluation effort. We adopted a purposeful sampling strategy (Patton, 2002) for this study in that we identified faculty, clinical instructors, and district administrators in the program who were actively involved in both planning and delivering the program in the first two formative years of the partnership. The interviews used a semi-structured interview protocol that collected participant responses regarding the program development, the challenges and opportunities presented by the partnership, as well as the ways in which the various partners participated in the development of the program. As illustrated in Table 8.1, the questions presented to each participant were fairly similar. Administrators were generally asked questions about the nature and structure of the partnership while faculty, adjunct faculty, and mentor principals were typically asked to describe the ways in which the partnership was operationalized. The interviews lasted approximately 30–45 minutes and took place face to face and via phone.

TABLE 8.1 Illustrative Interview Questions by Participant Group

University and District Administrators
- What were the primary goals for the partnership between the university and school district?
- How was the partnership between the university and district established?
- What prompted or motivated the university to partner with the district? Likewise, what prompted or motivated the district to partner with the university?
- What opportunities has the partnership afforded the university and/or school district?
- What challenges has the partnership presented?
- How, if at all, have these challenges been resolved?
- What is the district's definition of turnaround leadership?
- From your perspective, how has this definition been implemented in the program?
- In what ways is the district's definition of turnaround leadership informing or influencing the program?

Tenure-Line and Adjunct Faculty
- What were the primary goals for the partnership between the university and school district?
- How was the partnership between the university and district established?
- What has been your role in the partnership?
- How, if at all, has the partnership changed you as a faculty member?
- What challenges or barriers have you faced as a participant in the partnership?
- What is your definition of turnaround leadership?
- In what ways is your definition of turnaround leadership informing or influencing your work in the program?

Mentor Principals
- What were the primary goals for the partnership between the university and school district?
- How was the partnership between the university and district established?
- What was your role in the establishment of the partnership?
- How has the partnership changed your work as a mentor principal (supervisor of principals interning)?
- What challenges has the partnership presented to you as a mentor principal?

PARTICIPANT DESCRIPTION

In this chapter, we draw from a sub-set of the interviews we conducted as part of the larger external evaluation. In total, 32 participants were included in this analysis. This included four district administrators, three university administrators, five tenure line faculty members, 10 adjunct faculty who were also practicing administrators in the school district, and 10 mentor principals who supervised interns and apprentices.

Data Analysis

We completed a thematic analysis of the interviews using ATLAS.ti 7, which is a software package designed to assist the qualitative data analysis process. Prior to beginning our analysis, the interviews were professionally transcribed and then uploaded into an ATLAS.ti project file. An a priori coding scheme was developed (see Table 8.2), which aligned with the literature about principal preparation programs (Darling-Hammond et al., 2010), as well as the opportunities and challenges associated with sustaining inter-organizational partnerships in both education and non-education settings (Barnett et al., 1999; Petersen, 1999). Codes also related to key activities that were identified in the existing literature related to the preparation of turnaround leaders (Duke, 2014). The coding process was divided into two levels. In level one coding, salient passages of text were identified, with descriptive codes being assigned. These codes broadly assigned meaning to the passage and assisted in organizing the corpus of the data. In level two coding, analytic codes that related and applied meaning to these passages were applied. These codes were derived from the literature on preparation programs and inter-organizational partnerships. During level two coding, we wrote memos concerning our interpretation of the data, linking these memos to the coded passages of the text. We generated themes by identifying those codes (and code families) that were most saturated. Three themes emerged from our analysis, which are discussed in detail in the next section.

FINDINGS

Across our data we noted three themes from our qualitative analysis. First, we noted that the participation of district administration in program development required university faculty to re-assess their leadership roles in the program. Previously, the district had deferred to the university to prepare leaders for their schools and thus empowered the university faculty as leadership experts. Through the partnership, however, the district became an active participant and, thus, challenged the university's traditional position as the leader in preparation. Second, we found that the curriculum was seen by the district as a way to influence the shape of the program. The district saw the curriculum as a source of leverage to imbue the program with its own understanding of leadership, as well as to align the preparation experience with the practical realities facing leaders in the district's schools. Third, through the curriculum development process, we noted that partners were continuously faced with the challenge of identifying a shared understanding of leadership, particularly how they defined the concept of turnaround leadership, which undergirded the program. Taken together these findings illustrate the extent to which the partnership forced both the university and district to (re)define their work in regards to leadership preparation and highlights the potential challenges that such partnership arrangements present going forward.

TABLE 8.2 A Priori Coding Scheme for Qualitative Data Analysis

Program Overview

- Motivations for Program—Participant descriptions that explain why the program was created or launched, a need that it met, or a goal.
- Program Objectives—Descriptions of the primary goals for the program (both formal and informal)
- Implementation Challenges—participant's perspectives associated with the challenges of implementing the program given terms of the grant.
- Definition of Turnaround Leadership—participant recollections or references that relate to turnaround leadership, either as the program or the participant's define it.

Preparation for Turnaround Leadership

- Instructional Leadership Activities—specific examples of instructional leadership activities provided to an intern or apprentice (e.g., supervising classroom instruction, observing teachers in their classrooms, writing up teacher evaluations, giving teachers feedback about their practice, etc.)
- Turnaround Leadership Activities—specific examples of the intern/apprentice being provided with opportunities to engage in turnaround leadership activities (i.e., supporting under-performing students, identifying ways to support teacher professional development, improving culture/community in the school, working to improve student attendance, etc.)
- Use of Student Data—specific examples of the program, an instructor, a mentor principal, or an apprentice/intern using student achievement data to support their professional learning (i.e., students provided opportunities to analyze data for trends/gaps, intern collects data as part of school improvement planning process, etc.)

Partnership Development

- Shared interests—participant's descriptions of the shared interests or common goals that prompted the development of the program.
- Challenges—participant's descriptions of the challenges associated with operating/maintaining a partnership program.
- Sustainability—participant's descriptions of the ways that the program can be sustained beyond the initial grant funding.

Partnership Perspectives

- District Administrator–District administrator's comments regarding any concern related to the program or partnership
- University Faculty—University faculty concerns related to the program, its administration, the courses provided, pace of delivery, or student experience.
- Instructors—instructor concerns related to the program, its administration, the courses provided, pace of delivery, or student experience.
- Mentors—mentor's concerns regarding the program, the internship or apprenticeship, expectations of students.
- Students–any concern offered by a student regarding the program, experiences within the program, or processes of the program.

Re-Assessing the Role of the District in Leadership Development

One of the difficulties associated with developing a preparation program in partnership with a large, urban school district is that it requires the university faculty to re-assess the role of the school district within the context of leadership development and the district to recognize leadership development as a dimension of their overarching improvement efforts. In many traditional preparation programs, the university faculty has effectively been "in charge" of leadership development activities for the district—excluding professional development and routine support. To a certain extent, these traditional arrangements have enabled school districts to "outsource" their leadership development to universities without taking full ownership of their responsibility to ensure adequately prepared leaders are guiding their schools. Further, these arrangements have positioned districts as primarily receiving students from universities rather than working in collaboration with universities to prepare them. This positioning implies an inherent power differential. We found significant evidence of this differential in our conversations with university faculty. When asked how faculty related to the district before the partnership, one faculty member noted:

> For years I sat around the table and someone would make the suggestion, "Why don't we bring some practitioners in to test some of our ideas?" and the faculty reaction could be as blatant as, "What do practitioners know? What could they add to what we know?" In other words, you have to have the right kind of faculty, who don't think they have all the answers. In my experience most faculty only teach answers, they don't teach questions or how to ask questions. They themselves give advice and so, it sort of runs counter to what's in the leadership literature, in which you're supposed to listen, and learn, and adapt. Very little of that happens around a lot of faculty tables.

The above comment highlights the extent to which university faculty did not perceive that the district had a role in preparing leaders and were largely dismissive of their knowledge about leadership practice. The idea of questioning what practitioners "know," as well as the participant's characterization of faculty as "teaching answers" simultaneously dismisses practical knowledge and privileges the academy's understandings of the work in schools. This dismissal creates an inherent inequality in the relationship between university and district, making the formation of partnerships between universities and districts problematic.

Data collected through interviews with the district administrators illustrate well the extent to which the power in the partnership we studied was initially skewed toward the university. District administrators perceived that the university was not preparing leaders with the kinds of skills that were needed given the increasing pressure to improve achievement that was being placed on school administrators. As one administrator explained, "For a long time, we have seen assistant principals come from the university without really being ready to go to work or walk into a classroom and recognize poor instruction." The administrators we interviewed perceived that graduates from the university's preparation program had "... big gaps because they had been sort of prepared with this generic kind of leadership model in mind... because the coursework they got was never really developed with input from the district." As one adjunct faculty member characterized it, students entered schools with "romantic notions" of what it meant to be school leaders.

District administrators, adjunct faculty, and mentor principals were increasingly aware that the rising pressure on school leaders to improve student achievement required them to reconsider how leaders were trained and what that training should entail. Indeed, the data suggest that the push to improve the preparation program was not the result of internal volition but rather the product of externally derived threats given poor student achievement in many of the district's schools. As one mentor principal explained, "... the district has been far too passive in preparing leaders. We have taken a lot of what they [the university] gives us and we haven't stepped up and said this is what we need given the pressures we are facing." The result, as one district administrator put it, has been a "constantly weak applicant pool" and ongoing difficulties staffing "schools with strong leaders who understand instruction and help us achieve results." Thus, for its part, the district saw the partnership as an opportunity to renegotiate roles and the resources provided by the partnership, with this being a catalyst to improve leadership development overall.

Leveraging Program Change Through Curricular Development

Within the context of the partnership, we found that the district perceived that the curriculum was a source of leverage over the program and the university faculty. Whereas districts had previously been "outside" of the curriculum development process, the partnership afforded them an opportunity to shape what was taught, how it was assessed, and ultimately how it aligned with the district context. In the words of the district administrator, this proved to be a "powerful incentive" to participate in the development of the program. University faculty characterized the district as "active" and "aggressive" in the development of the program curriculum. The faculty noted that the district often directed conversations or prompted questions about existing preparation practices that were previously taken for granted. These prompts served as opportunities for the district to, as one faculty member described, "interject its preferences in the leadership development experience." Indeed, our data suggest that the development of the program curriculum was an opportunity for the district to ensure that its priorities for leadership development were infused throughout the program and that students were exposed to the kinds of learning experiences that the district felt were important for successful leadership practice.

Data indicate that one of the priorities advanced by the district was to make the preparation experience as practical as possible. District administrators offered numerous statements that critiqued the "theoretical" and "impractical" nature of the preparation program, which preceded the one development by the partners. As one administrator noted,

> ... having the [curriculum] team largely comprised of district administrators was part of the original philosophy around making this program—ensuring that there is a high level of applicability, practical experiences in the program. So, again, from course design to professor selection, I mean it was a concerted effort to make it real world and as practical as we could.

One adjunct faculty member who participated in the curriculum development noted, "We tried to meet the criteria established by the college or whatever criteria there were for that Master's program and then we tried to make a practical side by having the principals there with what we call the [district] way." The introduction of the "district way" throughout the curriculum development prompted significant changes in the program that university faculty did not initially anticipate. As one tenure-line faculty member noted, "The collaboration really forced us to stop and rethink what we thought mattered. We realized we were getting it wrong. It was the most uncomfortable professional experience I've had and yet has been one of the most beneficial in terms of our program, I think." As another faculty member noted, throughout the whole process "the district was at the table and they were very interested in making sure that the curriculum lined up with the work of principals."

The district's emphasis on practicality and applicability significantly altered the direction of the program and changed the role of the university faculty. Whereas faculty had previously developed courses that aligned with state standards and theoretical descriptions of leadership practice, the district's emphasis on practical experiences challenged their understanding and thus elevated the faculty's ideas about what should be taught. As one faculty member explained, "We were suddenly seeing the district as the expert and recognized that they were offering some recommendations that we had not even considered... This changed how we worked together and what we were thinking." Faculty offered several examples of this, ranging from adjusting the order of courses so that it would line up with the "seasons of schooling" to eliminating assignments or exercises that were "too academic." As one administrator noted,

> ...what we did is we actually developed the curriculum, the course, the assessment around action-based learning, which means that they had to be immersed in a problem, they had to go in and solve the problem, and they had to initiate the actual activity in many, many cases. And the instructors that taught these courses, each of these courses, were turnaround leaders themselves, and they were in the very situations that provided them with critical feedback along the way. So the end result of each of the courses met the outcome of the course because those individuals teaching the course were the ones that also developed it and co-developed it with a [university] instructor, with those embedded activities.

Underlying the curriculum changes in the program, we also found that the partnership between the university and district shifted as the district became more actively involved in shaping the program curriculum. Their participation weakened the faculty's stronghold over leadership preparation and also challenged traditional understandings of leadership practice. By shaping what was taught in the program, the district took on greater ownership for leadership development and thus reduced the power of the university faculty to decide how leadership was presented. As one district administrator who participated in the curriculum process explained,

> I think the process was about cultivating a different kind of role for the district from day one. We wanted to be partners in this program because we saw that we could learn from it and also that we could use what we learned to inform our district leadership programs. The university has the expertise but what they lacked was the link that we could make to our principals' work. They didn't really understand that work. They had "book smarts" but not "street smarts." They understand, you know, what instructional leadership is but they don't have to do it so they don't understand how it actually works in schools facing severe sanctions if they don't improve instruction.

The administrator's comments highlight the extent to which the university's role changed as the district became more actively involved in the development of the program. The district's engagement in the program limited the university's role and placed a premium on the value of practicality as an approach to leadership development.

Achieving a Shared Understanding of Turnaround Leadership

The data also indicate that the district's involvement in the development of the program curriculum provided opportunities for the partners to establish a shared understanding of leadership practice, particularly as they understood what it meant to engage in turnaround leadership. Historically, the university faculty shaped how the concept of leadership would be presented in university-based preparation programs. University faculty offered numerous statements which indicate that their understanding of turnaround leadership was initially grounded in existing notions of instructional leadership. As one faculty member explained, "... instructional leadership and turnaround leadership are basically the same except that turnaround leadership places a greater emphasis on improvement." Another faculty member offered a similar statement: "turnaround leadership is taught the same way as you would teach instructional leadership." These comments highlight the extent to which the faculty did not see the district's press for turnaround leadership as being a reflection of the current realities facing school principals. Both comments appeared to minimize that the conception of leadership needed to change.

District administrators were, however, very aware that the demands facing leaders in their schools required a fundamentally different approach to leadership. They saw the university's interpretation of leadership as disconnected from the work of school principals. Indeed, the university's thinking was often, as one administrator described, "out of touch with what it actually means to be a principal," and as another stated, "a poor reflection of the real world." As these comments illustrate, district administrators perceived that university faculty lacked an understanding of the "real world" and perceived their understanding of leadership as "out of touch" with the realities of practice.

In our analysis, data indicated that the curriculum development process provided the partners with an opportunity to revisit their understandings about what turnaround leadership meant. In doing so, they became increasingly aware that faculty from the university and district administrators held fundamentally different understandings about leadership and that these understandings were partly responsible for the disconnect that existed before the program was created. As one faculty member described, "some of our early meetings were like pulling teeth, no one wanted to give up on their views." But as the process unfolded, the faculty member conceded that "the district became increasingly clear in what it felt mattered and that was turnaround leadership so we had to adapt." A district administrator echoed this with, "... it was horrible at first because we saw this gap. It was like a huge gap at first but over time it got smaller. And it ultimately closed because we now talk about turnaround leadership in the same way." As another administrator explained,

> The concept of turnaround leadership is not unique to this district, and certainly not unique to the university. It's something that is out there nationally and there's a lot of interest in it. And, you know, turnaround leadership is a very loose term. So we just took the terminology and we looked at our situation because we are such an urban district, and what we've tried to do is identify best practices that help leaders improve schools. We've identified successes along the way, and we said that since we've been able to identify what it is and what it should look like, and how success should look like, we've been able to model it into this program.

Probing further, we asked the administrator to explain what she felt turnaround leadership entailed. Her explanation was quite thorough, offering a number of different practices in which she perceived turnaround leaders to be engaged. According to her, turnaround leadership involves knowing:

> ...how to interact with adults. How to make some systemic changes in teaching and learning. How to really involve stakeholder involvement in a very deliberate way. How to [provide] peer support with parents, and not just treat them all the same. How to effectively communicate with all stakeholders. How to really take little to no resources and be able to utilize it across a year in an effective way and still get the same results as you would in your non-inner city school or your non-, what we consider our lucky schools, and still get the same positive results. Those are some of the key attributes of a turnaround leader that we've been able to identify.

Taken together, the administrators indicated that the understandings of leadership practice generally, and turnaround leadership in particular, were broader and more holistic than anticipated by faculty.

Data indicate that through the partners' ongoing conversations about what it meant to be prepared for leadership, university faculty increasingly recognized that turnaround leadership and the pressures facing school leaders were fundamentally different from those they had previously considered. As one faculty member explained, "We saw that the world had changed and thanks to those conversations we now talk about leadership very differently. We see it as doing something to improve schools across the board." Another faculty member offered comments which further illustrate the extent to which the district's participation in the program's development changed his understanding. As he noted, "...the program has really provided us with an opportunity to revisit what we believe leadership involves. We saw that we were preparing people to lead but we weren't preparing them to lead with all of the other pressures that they were facing." Indeed, through the process of revising their understanding of leadership practice, we observed that the district and university moved away from differing interpretations toward a shared understanding of what leadership preparation means and what leadership looks like in the contemporary school setting.

DISCUSSION AND IMPLICATIONS

The findings from this study demonstrate the potential that partnerships have for improving university-based preparation programs, as well as the potential impact that such partnerships have on university faculty's traditional roles. Indeed, we see the results as being largely consistent with previous research highlighting the value of partnerships between school districts and universities (Barnett et al., 1999; Darling-Hammond et al., 2010; Orr et al., 2010; Petersen, 1999; Turnbull et al., 2013). Further, much as previous research indicates that partnerships often form when districts acknowledge limitations in their current applicant pools or abilities to provide rigorous training for leaders (Turnbull et al., 2013), the data in this study clearly suggest that the district was motivated by both the limitations of the applicants that it was receiving and the threat of external accountability measures. Indeed, we observed that the district's concern about the capacity of its current principal force to support improvements in student achievement prompted its involvement in the development of the program as well as guided its emphasis on turnaround leadership as a core program element. This, too, is consistent with previous literature about the motivations for partnership formation (Barnett et al., 1999; Whitaker & Barnett, 1999), as well as the specific ways in which partnerships can support the development of turnaround leaders (Duke, 2014). The present study is a particularly important contribution to the existing literature in that it demonstrates how partnerships may be essential to efforts to prepare principals and assistant principals for turnaround leadership given external accountability pressures facing school districts as well as a catalyst to revisit traditional faculty roles and preparation activities.

Furthermore, theoretical understandings of inter-organizational partnerships help us to understand how and why partnerships evolve as they do. First, consistent with previous research (e.g., Bullough & Kauchack, 1997; Schermerhorn, 1979; Thomas et al., 2012), the partners in our study began their work by identifying a set of shared goals and establishing a direction for their collaboration. This appears to be an important prerequisite for preparation programs that engage with multiple partners. Two important questions for partners to consider are: Why are we seeking to change the way we prepare leaders? To what do we hope these preparation experiences will lead? The data from this study indicate that as the partners grappled with these questions, both observed that the influence that the educational leadership faculty historically have had on the direction of preparation changed as the district became an active partner in the development of the program. What is most surprising, though, is that university faculty did not step back from the partnership as their role changed. Rather, they continued working with their colleagues in the district to improve the program and to use it as an opportunity to update their understanding of practice. This, we think, gives credence to those who argue that university-based preparation programs can be enhanced through partnerships (Darling-Hammond et al., 2010; Orr et al., 2010) and challenges those who suggest that university-based preparation programs are so weak that they are in a race to the bottom (Levine, 2005). In addition, while each of the partners highlighted the importance of resources provided by the grant as a catalyst for the partnership, the timing of the study did not permit us to consider how the partnership would continue after these resources were exhausted. Nonetheless, as previous research indicates, partnerships are time and resource intensive (Barnett, et al., 1999; Feldman, 1993; Whitaker & Barnett, 1999). The partnership we studied was launched with an infusion of significant resources. Whether the partnership between the university and district will continue without these resources remains to be seen. Indeed, it would seem that the partnership's continuation will largely depend upon the university's and district's willingness to continue working together to prepare leaders for turnaround schools.

Implications

The findings from this study have three significant implications for leadership, preparation programs, practice, and future research. First, in terms of preparation programs, the findings highlight that leadership programs would be well-served by reaching out to districts as partners, particularly as districts navigate the increasing pressures of the current education accountability environment. The complex environment in which today's school leaders work exceeds the preparatory capacity of universities alone. To be fully effective, universities and districts must work together to ensure that leaders are prepared in ways that allow them to enter struggling schools and make meaningful differences in teaching and learning. This call is not new, as indeed previous research has argued for a similar level of engagement (Borden et al., 2010; Darling-Hammond et al., 2010; Orr et al., 2010), as well as increasing recognition that partnerships foster a level of interdependence that make them unique from other organizational arrangements (Barnett, et al., 1999). What we add to this call is the recognition that many of the challenges facing today's school leaders, such as turning around struggling schools, can only be introduced to aspiring leaders in concert with school districts. Indeed, as Duke (2014) noted in his discussion related to the preparation of turnaround leaders, the types of preparation activities that are required demand engagement from school districts as they are most familiar with the current challenges facing leaders. For example, as Duke (2014) indicated, turnaround leaders must be prepared to analyze the context of low-performing schools and "identify probable causes of low achievement" (p. 82). This requires that students in preparation programs have ready access to student achievement information as well as familiarity with the district's student information system, both of which are more likely when the district is a partner in the preparation program.

Second and relatedly, we also see the findings of the study as challenging how leaders are prepared. As was clear from the data, the district preferred action-based and problem-based learning. Indeed, this point is consistent with research highlighting the potential benefits of using problem-based learning in educational leadership programs (Bridges & Hallinger, 1997). This approach, however, requires educational leadership faculty to reconsider the ways in which preparation program experiences are provided. Indeed, we think engaging districts in planning for preparation experiences provides opportunities for universities to introduce leadership challenges and problems in ways that go far beyond teaching cases or case studies. In effect, the introduction of districts as partners in preparation activities provides opportunities to deeply and meaningfully connect theory and practice. This point has been offered previously (e.g., Ball & Cohen, 1999; Darling-Hammond et al., 2010), and yet preparation programs often continue to recycle activities and strategies that disconnect theory and practice.

Third and finally, the findings offer new opportunities for research on leadership preparation, particularly building on previous work that has sought to define and describe the creation of partnerships between universities and districts (Barnett et al., 1999; Korach, 2010; Petersen, 1999; Whitaker & Barnett, 1999). The current study introduces a new line of research by examining the effects that partnerships have on faculty and students and thus their influence on leadership practice. Such research could assist the field in addressing how and to what extent preparation programs contribute to leadership development. Further, the findings from this study raise important questions about the resources and policy structures that both impede and facilitate partnership programs, which may be particularly relevant given ongoing fiscal challenges and increasing demands for external accountability. Finally, the findings also raise important questions about the ways in which school districts and universities can work more strategically to match preparation program "output" with district "demand." We see this as an important opportunity to understand how university-based preparation programs can fit within the broader context of district human resource systems and practices (Odden, 2011). Indeed, consistent with recent discussions (e.g., Hitt, Tucker, & Young, 2012), we believe that understanding how university-based preparation programs fit within broader district reform efforts and human resource systems is the next step in understanding how preparation programs can be improved. Seeing these programs as autonomous from districts does little to ensure that the leaders they prepare are fully equipped for the complex environment surrounding their leadership practice.

REFERENCES

Ball, D., & Cohen, D. (1999). Developing practice, development practitioners: Toward a practice-based theory of professional education. In L. Darling-Hammond & G. Sykes (Eds.), *Teaching as the learning profession: Handbook of policy and practice* (pp. 3–32). San Francisco, CA: Jossey-Bass Publishers.

Barnett, B. G., Hall, G. E., Berg, J. H., & Camarena, M. M. (1999). A typology of partnerships for promoting innovation. *Journal of School Leadership, 9*(6), 484–510.

Borden, A. M., Preskill, S. L., & DeMoss, K. (2012). A new turn toward learning for leadership: Findings from an exploratory coursework pilot project. *Journal of Research on Leadership Education, 7*(1), 123–152.

Bridges, E. M., & Hallinger, P. (1997). Using problem-based learning to prepare educational leaders. *Peabody Journal of Education, 72*(2), 131–146.

Briggs, K., Cheney, G. R., Davis, J., & Moll, K. A. (2013). *Operating in the dark: What outdated state policies and data gaps mean for effective school leadership*. Dallas, TX: George W. Bush Institute. Retrieved from http://www.bushcenter.org

Brooks, J. S., Havard, T., Tatum, K., & Patrick, L. (2010). It takes more than a village: Inviting partners and complexity in educational leadership preparation reform. *Journal of Research on Leadership Education, 5*(12.4), 418–435.

Bullough, R. B., Jr., & Kauchak, D. (1997). Partnerships between higher education and secondary schools: Some problems. *Journal of Education for Teaching: International Research and Pedagogy, 23*(3), 215–234.

Darling-Hammond, L., Meyerson, D., LaPointe, M., & Orr, M. T. (2010). *Preparing principals for a changing world: Lessons from effective school leadership programs*. San Francisco, CA: Jossey-Bass.

Domina, T., & Ruzek, E. (2012). Paving the way: K–16 partnerships for higher education diversity and high school reform. *Educational Policy, 26*(2), 243–267.

Duke, D. L. (2012). Tinkering and turnarounds: Understanding the contemporary campaign to improve low-performing schools. *Journal of Education for Students Placed at Risk, 17*, 9–24.

Duke, D. L. (2014). A bold approach to developing leaders for low-performing schools. *Management in Education, 28*(3), 80–85.

Feldman, A. (1993). Promoting equitable collaboration between university researchers and teachers. *International Journal of Qualitative Studies in Education, 6*, 341–357.

Fuller, E. J., Young, M. D., & Baker, B. D. (2011). Do principal preparation programs influence student achievement through the building of teacher-team qualifications by the principal? An exploratory analysis. *Educational Administration Quarterly, 47*(1), 173–216.

Fuller, E. J., & Hollingworth, L. (2014). A bridge too far? Challenges in evaluating principal effectiveness. *Educational Administration Quarterly 50*(3), 466–499.

Fusarelli, L. D., & Smith, L. (1999). Improving urban schools VIA leadership: Preparing administrators for the new millennium. *Journal of School Leadership, 9*(6), 534–551.

Grissom, J. A., & Loeb, S. (2012). Triangulating principal effectiveness: How perspectives of parents, teachers, and assistant principals identify the central importance of managerial skills. *American Educational Research Journal, 48*(5), 1091–1123.

Grissom, J. A., Kalogrides, D., & Loeb, S. (2014). Using student test scores to measure principal performance. *Educational Evaluation and Policy Analysis.*

Hallinger, P., & Heck, R. (1998). Exploring the principal's contributions to school effectiveness: 1980–1995. *School Effectiveness and School Improvement, 9,* 157–191.

Hewitt, K. K., Mullen, C. A., Davis, A. W., & Lashley, C. (2012). Making an impact statewide to benefit 21st-century school leadership. *AASA Journal of Scholarship & Practice, 9*(3), 18–31.

Jackson, P. (1991, April). *The enactment of the moral in what teachers do.* Paper presented at the Annual Meeting of the American Educational Research Association, Chicago, IL.

Hitt, D. H., Tucker, P. D., & Young, M. D. (2012). The professional pipeline for educational leadership: A white paper developed to inform the work of the National Policy Board for Educational Administration. Charlottesville, VA: University Council for Educational Administration. Retrieved http://www.ucea.org.

Johnson, M. (1990). Experience and reflections on collaborative research. *International Journal of Qualitative Studies in Education, 3*(2), 173–183.

Kimball, S. (2011). Strategic talent management for principals. In A. R. Odden (Ed.), *Strategic management of human capital in education: Improving instructional practice and student learning in schools* (pp. 133–152). New York: Routledge.

Korach, S. (2011). Keeping the fire burning: The evolution of a university-district collaboration to develop leaders for second-order change. *Journal of School Leadership, 21*(5), 659–683.

Leithwood, K., Harris, A., & Strauss, T. (2010). *Leading school turnaround: How successful leaders transform low performing schools.* San Francisco, CA: Jossey-Bass.

Levine, A. (2005). *Educating schools leaders.* New York: The Education Schools Project.

Mitgang, L. (2013, February). *Districts matter: Cultivating the principals urban schools need.* New York: The Wallace Foundation. Retrieved from http://www.wallacefoundation.org

Murphy, J. F., & Meyers, C. V. (2008). *Turning around failing schools: Leadership lessons from the organizational sciences.* Thousand Oaks, CA: Corwin Press.

Odden, A. R. (2011). *Strategic management of human capital in education: Improving instructional practice and student learning in schools.* New York: Routledge.

Orr, M. T. (2011). Pipeline to preparation to advancement: Graduates' experiences in, through, and beyond leadership preparation. *Educational Administration Quarterly, 47*(1), 114–172.

Orr, M. T., & Barber, M. (2007). Collaborative leadership preparation: A comparative study of innovative programs and practices. *Journal of School Leadership, 16*: 709–739.

Orr, M. T., King, C., & LaPointe, M. (2010). *Districts developing leaders: Lessons on consumer actions and program approaches from eight urban districts*. Education Development Center, Inc.

Orr, M. T., & Orphanos, S. (2011). How graduate-level preparation influences the effectiveness of school leaders: A comparison of the outcomes of exemplary and conventional leadership preparation programs for principals. *Educational Administration Quarterly, 47*(1), 18–70.

Patton, M. Q. (2002). *Qualitative research and evaluation methods*. (3rd ed.). Thousand Oaks, CA: SAGE.

Petersen, G. J. (1999). Collaborative efforts in the preparation of educational leaders. *Journal of School Leadership, 9*(6), 478–483.

Schermerhorn, J. (1979). Inter-organizational development. *Journal of Management, 5*(1), 21–38.

Scribner, J. P., & Machell, J. R. (1999). Interorganizational collaboration in a statewide doctoral program: A lesson in the construction of meaning. *Journal of School Leadership, 9*(6), 511–533.

Thomas, C. N., Hassaram, B., Rieth, H. J., Raghavan, N. S., Kinzer, C. K., & Mulloy, A. M. (2012). The Integrated Curriculum Project: Teacher change and student outcomes within a university-school professional development collaboration. *Psychology in the Schools, 49*(5), 444–464.

Turnbull, B. J., Riley, D. L., Arcaira, E. R., Anderson, L. M., & MacFarlane, J. R. (2013, July). *Six districts begin the Principal Pipeline Initiative.* Washington, DC: Policy Studies Associates, Inc. Retrieved from http://www.wallacefoundation.org

Whitaker, K. S., & Barnett, B. G. (1999). A partnership model linking K–12 school districts and leadership preparation programs. *Planning & Changing, 30*(3), 126–143.

Witziers, B., Bosker, R. J., & Kruger, M. L. (2003). Educational leadership and student achievement: The elusive search for an association. *Educational Administration Quarterly, 39*(3), 398–425.

SECTION IV
CONCLUSION

CHAPTER 9

MOSTLY UNPUNCTUATED DISEQUILIBRIUM

Carolyn J. Riehl
Teachers College, Columbia University

In 2007, the satirical publication *The Onion* described some anticipated features of the very first, soon-to-be-released iPhone. One, they wrote, was "Takes Polaroids." This quip echoes a wide-ranging discourse on change. Prominent theories about diverse phenomena such as new scientific paradigms (Kuhn, 1962), species evolution (Eldredge & Gould, 1972), group behavior (Gersick, 1988), business innovation (Christensen, 1997), and organizational strategy (Romanelli & Tushman, 1994) dispute conventional views of change as gradual and incremental, instead arguing that change often presents in the form of "disruptions" or "punctuated equilibrium"—dramatic episodes of alteration that interrupt periods of comparative calm.

So, one might ask, does the history of the scholarship of education leadership represent incremental change or, like the iPhone, punctuated equilibrium? As Donald Willower noted, "the spirit of the times is a slippery concept" (1996, p. 346). Still, looking back, it is hard to characterize education leadership research, theory, and practice over the past several decades in terms of "equilibrium." In numerous assessments of the field, scholars have portrayed a fairly constant churn of development, disagreement, outright conflict, or contestation (e.g., Willower & Forsyth, 1999). The situation has been stable: flux is constant.

For example, some analysts disparage the period from the 1950s through the mid-1970s as the unproductive "behavioral science era" and celebrate the breaks that were eventually made from it (see Erickson, 1977 for the commentary with the best title; also Erickson, 1979). But others see more value in that time and at least some continuity between it and what followed (Culbertson, 1988; Willower, 1996). Developments in theory and practice regarding instructional leadership, often guided by scholars only loosely connected to the leadership field, have been progressive, flowing gradually from early theoretical framings on leadership and instruction (Bossert et al., 1982; Pitner, 1988), to a late-century effort to build a knowledge base about teaching and learning (Rowan, 1995) and more recent approaches to instructional regimes and leadership of the instructional core (City, Elmore, Fiarman, & Teitel, 2009; Cohen, Raudenbush, & Ball, 2003; Hallinger, 2011). Still, even this has not been a smooth ride, as scholars periodically lament the relative inattention to the political dimensions of leadership and leaders' needs to manage the environment, wavering commitments to diversity and equity, and an over-emphasis on the technical-rational aspects of leadership at the expense of more critical or value-centered approaches to education (e.g., Johnson, 2003; Lopez, 2003; Scribner, Lopez, Koschoreck, Mahitivanichcha, & Scheurich, 1999). Research and practice around standards for educational leadership are another example of contested perspectives. While some laud standards as a way to systematize and professionalize the work of leaders (Murphy, 2005; Young, 2015), others find standards odious, immobile, illusory, and "the hallmark of a dead field (English, 2006).

It is equally hard to identify many clear moments of dramatic and consequential punctuation or disruption, although there have been some attempts. Joseph Murphy, long a leader in the field, gave a conference presentation that led to a volume on "the educational leadership challenge"; in a cornerstone chapter of that book, he called for the re-culturing of the field around three anchors: school improvement, democratic community, and social justice (Murphy, 2002). While much subsequent work has indeed focused on these three themes, substantial prior work did as well. Around that same time, Bill Firestone and I accepted an assignment from Division A of the American Educational Research Association and convened a group of researchers who represented some, but by no means all, of the excellent work being done in the field at the time. We sought to produce a narrative of change for research on education leadership (Firestone & Riehl, 2005). We labeled our collective effort a "new" agenda and hoped it would punctuate the discourse and galvanize attention to some ideas our group thought were particularly promising. While this work was received favorably by at least some (e.g., Honig & Louis, 2007; Levin, 2006), looking back from a decade out, our volume seems to be less of a disruption and more, like Murphy's work and others, a salutary crystallization of some ideas that already had been receiving increased attention.

This long era of "mostly unpunctuated disequilibrium" has, however, been productive; we are not taking Polaroids anymore. Robustness is evident in many ways. For example, while early theoretical framings about leadership have continued to be influential, they have been strengthened with much more theoretical elaboration (Hoy & Miskel, 2005). The field has moved beyond its early, largely prescriptive orientation (Willower, 1996) to a far stronger reliance on empirical work for warranting claims about leadership (Leithwood & Riehl, 2005; Louis, Leithwood, Wahlstrom, & Anderson, 2010; Murphy et al., 2007). Even largely normative orientations such as social justice leadership or leadership for diversity have been pursued through both analytic and empirical work these days (e.g., Brooks, Jean-Marie, Normore, & Hodgins, 2007; Brown, 2006; Furman, 2012).

Prominent philanthropic support, especially from The Wallace Foundation, has helped to provide increased visibility and a stronger evidence base about leadership (Darling-Hammond, LaPointe, Meyerson, Orr, & Cohen, 2007; Leithwood, Louis, Anderson, & Wahlstrom, 2004; Orr, King, & LaPointe, 2010). Epistemological diversity has enabled researchers to follow many different lines of inquiry about leadership, in ways that seem to avoid the "big tent" morass of the past (Donmoyer, 1999). While Willower (1996) opined that "scientific inquiry is our best hope when it comes to understanding the human condition and improving it," (p. 361), others in our field have also embraced the validity of knowledge claims from other kinds of intellectual projects (Collard, 2007; Eacott, 2013; Riehl, 2007).

We now have more varied and sophisticated methodological tools for studying leadership. Erickson (1979) quoted another observer's description of the field at the time: "acres of disjointed, theoretically barren, non-cumulative, and downright shoddy studies... endless, witless administrations of the LBDQ, OCDQ, POS, ABC, and XYZ scales to haphazard collections of teachers and administrators" (p. 10). Now, instead of the once-ubiquitous Leader Behavior Description Questionnaire and convenience samples of practicing administrators sitting in graduate classrooms, we can rely on nationally representative samples of leaders and schools with longitudinal data; quasi-observational techniques such as leadership behavior logs (Camburn, Spillane, & Sebastian, 2010; Spillane & Zuberi, 2009), and rapidly expanding resources of administrative datasets that link information on leadership and school organization with information about students and their performance (Branch, Hanushek, & Rivkin, 2012; Clark, Martorell, & Rockoff, 2009).

Increased demographic diversity by gender, sexual orientation, race, and ethnicity in the ranks of both education leadership professionals and academics has resulted in different approaches to research questions and to practice (Dillard, 1995; Lugg, 2008; Lugg & Shoho, 2006; Murphy, Vriesenga, & Storey, 2007; Murtadha & Watts, 2005). As in many other arenas, there is more attention to global and comparative studies of leadership practice (e.g., Leithwood, 2005). The field is less insular in its disciplinary representation as well. The academic study of education leadership has always drawn on important theoretical perspectives of scholars working primarily outside the field (e.g., Bidwell, 1965; Weick, 1976), but recently there seems to be an uptick in scholars with other primary affiliations directly studying leadership—in some instances because they have unexpectedly fallen upon leadership as a key explanatory variable in school effects studies (e.g., Bryk, Sebring, Allensworth, Luppescu, & Easton, 2010; Clark, Martorell, & Rockoff, 2009; Grissom, Loeb, & Master, 2013).

Finally, there is simply much more to study. With the diversification (or, to some, the breakup) of public schooling in the era of charter schools and high-stakes accountability, there are new venues for leadership in charter management organizations and other intermediary institutions; more challenges in portfolio management of schools at the district level; new systems of governance under mayoral control; and more types of networks of schools. Leaders are asked to manage school turnarounds, as well as school openings and closings, as never before. Education agencies at all levels, from federal to state to district, are working to frame coherent approaches to leadership preparation, certification, deployment, evaluation, and professional development, and as the policy system turns its attention to these targets, the need for authoritative knowledge about leadership increases. As Cohen (1982) suggested, policy begets policy and the increased involvement of the state and federal governments has made more, not less, work for education leaders at all levels—more to do, and more to study.

It is gratifying to see many of these themes reflected and expanded upon in the present volume. In the remainder of this chapter, I offer some comments on this recent work.

LEADERSHIP THEORY AND PRACTICE

Unsurprisingly, a central concern of the education leadership field has been to describe, model, analyze, and codify its object of study by developing theories of leadership practice. Stogdill (1974) noted that there are as many definitions of leadership as there are people defining it, often emanating from very different standpoints and theoretical orientations. But currently many characterizations seem to converge in echoing that offered by Yukl

(2006), who defines leadership as "the process of influencing others to understand and agree about what needs to be done and how to do it, and the process of facilitating individual and collective efforts to accomplish shared objectives" (p. 8). In this sense, leadership is viewed as relational, consensual, collective, and pragmatic—quite a bit different from authoritarian, power-dominant models of leadership of earlier times (Morrison, 2013).

One long-standing concern with theory in the field of education leadership is that much of it has been primarily analytic or normative in character. While it is entirely reasonable to develop a leadership theory on rational/analytic or normative grounds, in the current era of "evidence-based practice" this is often seen as an insufficient basis for knowledge development. The problem is exacerbated when audiences take theories that, still under construction, are largely normative or analytic and treat them as if they already have been empirically validated, jumping on the proverbial bandwagon before there's a strong evidentiary justification for doing so. This has been a risk with early work on leading schools as communities, for example (Sergiovanni, 1994), as well as with transformational leadership (Morrison, 2013), distributed leadership (Mayrowetz, 2008), social justice leadership (Brown, 2006), and even some versions of instructional leadership (Hallinger, 2011).

In addition, many now describe leadership as a constellation of functions, pursued through a variety of actions (e.g., Leithwood & Riehl, 2005; Sebastian & Allensworth, 2012). This raises the potential for different combinations of functions and discrete actions to be assembled into a wide variety of leadership models, theories, or styles (Hallinger, 2011; Leithwood & Duke, 1999). This, in turn, creates confusion as to whether the models ought to be adopted wholesale or piecemeal, and how to make sense of their overlapping concepts and approaches, either in practice or in research on practice (Robinson, Lloyd, & Rowe, 2008). This can create problems when trying to aggregate or compare findings across studies.

Many researchers have tried to sort things out. Marks and Printy (2003; cf., Printy, Marks, & Bowers, 2009) examined the relationship between instructional and transformational leadership, while Brooks, Jean-Marie, Normore, and Hodgins (2007) explored how social justice leadership and distributed leadership interact. Leithwood, Patten, and Jantzi (2010) acknowledged that the search for the mediating factors through which leadership operated was resulting in some models that were oversimplified and others that were too complex to be useful. They suggested a heuristic framework of four metaphorical "paths" along which leadership influences learning: rational (classroom and school variables affecting the technical core), emotions, organizational, and family. Each path incorporates numerous potential mediating behaviors, and leaders with intimate knowledge of their own context can employ the practices most likely to matter. Hallinger

(2011) proposed yet another framework—"leadership for learning"—that he claimed gathered elements of multiple other leadership models into a useful synthesis.

In this volume, Nordengren handles these two problems adroitly. He looks across a range of what he calls "collective models of educational leadership" to locate common theories of action that explain the empirical evidence linking leadership practices to student outcomes. The four models he examines are instructional leadership, transformational leadership, teacher leadership, and distributed leadership; these are included because they incorporate "collectivity" or teams of leaders working together on shared units of work with common goals. Having located 26 studies with multiple leaders and student outcomes represented, Nordengren employed systematic review strategies and determined the studies that reliably connected leadership with learning had three elements: a clear theory of action for how leadership led to changes in classroom practice affecting students; a perspective on "leadership routines" or the practices and actions comprising leadership, and methodological tools up to the task of this complex analysis.

Three theories of action were dominant in studies linking collective leadership to learning. These were action pathways for building school improvement capacity, fostering a school culture of shared purpose, and pursuing the redesign of teachers' work. These theories of action, says Nordengren, are enacted in diverse ways that shared three common features: developing a common language for the work, operating multiple levers of change simultaneously, and placing a collective focus on instruction, the core technology of schools.

The point of view reflected in this chapter reflects a technical rationality focused on producing measurable student achievement outcomes. This doesn't seem entirely misplaced or inappropriate; it is natural to want students and schools to do well, and learning-focused leadership is an improvement on the managerialism for which school leaders have been criticized (Bush & Glover, 2014). Some, however, suggest that the contemporary anxiety about school outcomes and accountability is a pernicious manifestation of the neoliberal production of "docile subjects" (Davies & Bansel, 2007, p. 249), whose needs and desires are reconfigured around ideologies of economic productivity. As this argument goes, education has become a pawn in a larger game of measurement, markets, and procurement. By this reasoning, an effective education leader ought at least to raise questions about these developments and discuss their impact with stakeholders.

Leadership theory is also enhanced by taking a more comprehensive, comparative look at global patterns. Spurred initially by the indictment about economic non-competiveness offered by *A Nation at Risk*, and soon thereafter by the international benchmark assessments in the TIMSS study series, researchers in the United States have paid attention to how schooling in America compares to other countries, not only with regard to student achievement but also in terms of how it is organized and led (e.g., Lee, 2010; Mourshed, Chijioke, & Barber, 2010; Sahlberg, 2007). This has largely been a salutary effort; comparative studies have not only introduced new insights from other countries but have also reminded us of the need to contextualize any understandings of leadership.

In the current volume, the chapter by Arar and Oplatka on women's participation in education leadership in the Arab world offers an illuminating perspective and an urgent challenge. In light of well-publicized disparities in health, education, and economic opportunity for girls and women around the world, patterns of women's participation in education in Arab states have global, not just local, impact. Much of what Arar and Oplatka describe will probably seem eerily familiar to anyone schooled in the history of women in education leadership in the United States (Riehl & Lee, 1996). In this country, women were "stuck" in teaching jobs for long times; they experienced a very slow rate of growth in representation in leadership. Once they started to obtain leadership positions, a safe approach seemed to be to adopt male-patterned approaches to leadership. Teachers—especially men—had strong feelings about working for women. Over time, the qualities that women seemed to uniquely bring to leadership—emotional, relational leadership styles, along with a strong emphasis on the tasks of teaching due at least in part to many years in the classroom waiting for an administrative position—have become part of our normative model of leadership, expected of both men and women.

Many of these changes in the United States and other developed countries were wrought in concert with broader changes in women's position in society on the heels of the second feminist movement beginning in the 1960s. As Arar and Oplatka report, women in the Arab world experience even more cultural constraints to this day. The numerical data are startling: they report that in Saudi Arabia in 2014, women were 58% of college students but only 14% of the labor force, and of the women in paid employment, fully 85% were working in education, and not at the leadership level. Not only do Arab women in education have longer career paths to leadership, much as in the United States historically, but they also suffer from lower self-esteem, a concern that may hinder their leadership efficacy. The situation is similar, though not quite as dramatic, in other Arab countries in the Middle East and North Africa and among Arabs in Israel.

Arar and Oplatka make two points that are especially intriguing. First, they ask whether and how progress for women in education leadership in these countries can influence the character and progress of Arab society more broadly. That is a sobering comment on the interpenetration of cultural context and education leadership. It's fairly easy and reasonable to surmise that women's increased participation in education leadership in the United States has had some salutary effects on schooling, but extrapolating from that to more general effects on our cultural milieu seems to be quite a stretch. If this is even a possibility in the Arab states, it is a heady responsibility and possibility.

Second, they cite the work of Moghadam, who has written about the role of neoliberalism in non-Western cultures:

> Neoliberalism and patriarchy feed off each other and reinforce each other in order to maintain the vast majority of women in a situation of cultural inferiority, social devaluation, economic marginalization, "invisibility" of their existence and labor, and the marketing and commercialization of their bodies. All these situations closely resemble apartheid. (2009, p. 148)

As noted above with regard to the United States, working to improve achievement outcomes in schools may also implicate one in a less sanguine project in the current policy environment where the emphasis on markets and success is closely linked to veiled efforts to privilege some segments of society at the expense of others. In the Arab world, for women educators to challenge patriarchy may call into question the foundations of contemporary education reform in other ways as well, creating a situation that requires courage and delicacy to resolve.

LEADERSHIP OUTCOMES AND EFFECTS

The observation that leadership accounts for a quarter of the school-based variation in student achievement has been stated, restated, and cited so often (e.g., Brown, 2006; Goff & Finch, this volume; Leithwood, Louis, Anderson, & Wahlstrom, 2004; Leithwood, Day, Sammons, Harris, & Hopkins, 2006; Marzano, Waters, & McNulty, 2005) it has run the risk of becoming an urban myth. This estimate of leadership effects is problematic in at least two ways. First, it simply might not be accurate anymore. The estimate, as reported in two separate publications (Leithwood & Riehl, 2005; Waters, Marzano, & McNulty, 2003), was based on studies of school effectiveness from which leadership effects were only inferred and on a meta-analysis that calculated a pooled effect size using methods that may no longer meet analytic standards and that drew from many studies that were not peer-reviewed. Second, trying to pin down a single, authoritative effect size for leadership tends to trivialize a very complex phenomenon. Education leadership is enacted by many different kinds of individuals; it comprises many functions and actions that operate contingently in a wide variety of contexts. Capturing all of this variability in a single effect size seems implausible.

On the other hand, given the dizzying array of studies attempting to measure leadership effects on student learning through quantitative research, grasping at a single number has its appeal. Intrepid readers can, however, start to wade through the growing number of studies by differentiating among those based in the United States context versus other countries (which seem to use different analytic models and produce different results) and separating studies testing direct effects from those exploring indirect, mediated, or reciprocal effects (Witziers, Bosker, & Krueger, 2003; Supovitz, Sirinides, & May, 2010; Heck & Hallinger, 2010, 2014; Robinson, Lloyd, & Rowe, 2008). Doing so, it quickly becomes clear that an area of scholarship that was once vilified as naïve and trivial (Erickson, 1979), and that later on was so thin it could only generate weak findings about leadership effects via school mission and climate (Hallinger & Heck, 1996), has now earned the right to conclude "leadership matters," though how much and in what ways is still quite open to specification.

The exponential growth in administrative data sets combining school, student, and leader information, along with researchers' facility with sophisticated causal modeling techniques, and in some cases the use of sensitive data collection tools for gathering evidence about what leaders actually do, may lead the search for leadership effects in some very interesting directions. For example, Branch, Hanushek, and Rivkin (2012) explored principal productivity with regard to standardized test achievement using longitudinal data on principals and schools in Texas. They made fortuitous use of rich administrative data; they used sophisticated fixed-effects models, acknowledging a variety of potential issues with measurement error and specification error. Focused on "principal value-added" based on student achievement growth, net of prior achievement, student mobility, and principal and student demographic characteristics, they found that the more effective principals added even more value in schools with higher rates of poverty. Grissom and Loeb (2011) combined administrative records with survey data from parents, teachers, and school leaders and concluded, somewhat contrary to many theories about leadership, that principals' organizational management skills were positive predictors of student achievement. These studies suggest that as methodological sophistication grows, and as research on leadership attracts more scholars outside the field, it will be important to ensure that the conceptual models used to design studies and explain findings take good advantage of the strongest theorizing done about leadership over the past several decades. The meta-analysis by Hendriks and Scheerens (2013) is a good example of research that combines careful treatment of quantitative results with a perspective on leadership that avoids both over-stating and under-stating the importance of leadership for student outcomes.

In the present volume, Goff and Finch comment on a set of quantitative studies of school leadership; though not all of the studies link leadership to student outcomes, they nonetheless illustrate the range of approaches that could be used to study leadership effects. The authors begin with the premise that the leadership field is poised to take advantage of rich data sets and powerful causal analysis techniques, and they suggest the benefits of these resources will only accrue if they are matched by appropriate and rigorous research designs. They group the studies they reviewed into four broad categories based on each study's contribution to causal inference, change over time, comparisons between groups, and descriptive studies. Goff and Finch further place the causal inference studies into a category labeled "Tier I" because they make "unambiguous contributions to the field." They gathered the other studies, covering longitudinal change, group comparisons, and description, into "Tier II" because their designs tended to raise more questions and produce results that couldn't be fully interpreted.

For Goff and Finch, cross-sectional designs raise all sorts of red flags because they typically are inadequate for teasing out causal directions, especially reciprocity, and for specifying the mechanisms of indirect effects of leadership. These are particularly thorny matters in research covering the interactions among perceptions and behaviors of multiple actors such as principals, teachers, and students. To drive this point home, Goff and Finch subject a data set on leadership and teacher trust to multiple iterations of cross-sectional and longitudinal analysis to show that even the most complex statistical test cannot fully compensate for a faulty temporal design.

Three things stand out about this chapter. First is the fairly obvious implication that anyone wishing to take an active part in producing, using, and evaluating advanced quantitative studies of leadership will need to be well-schooled in a specialized set of methodologies. This may create something akin to a generation gap for leadership researchers, depending on when and how they learned quantitative methods. The ante is raised even more if leadership researchers, who may know the substantive body of knowledge inside and out, find themselves competing with economists and others, trained in advanced causal methods but lacking deep knowledge of leadership, for the opportunity to utilize rich administrative data sets.

Second, Goff and Finch make occasional mention of how a quantitative analysis they reviewed was enhanced by being linked to a parallel qualitative analysis or to the refinement of measures and models through some kind of qualitative component. In mixed methods research, qualitative methods need not only be the handmaiden of quantitative analysis, and it will be interesting to see if and how the sophisticated quantitative measures described by Goff and Finch might ever be used to support qualitative interpretations.

Finally, Goff and Finch have said relatively little about other aspects of research design that can confound studies of leadership, namely sampling frames, measurement models, observational and survey data collection strategies, and the need to be transparent about exactly how the limitations of analytic methods—whether qualitative or quantitative—may reduce confidence in the findings. And while they allude to the importance of being guided by appropriate and well-informed conceptual models, the point bears repeating: just as studies employing high-powered quantitative tools can be done in by the weak link of a poor temporal design, so studies using powerful samples, methods, and temporal designs can be undone by incomplete or inaccurate theories about leadership and its correlates.

Perhaps not surprisingly, one of the richest articulations of the complexity of leadership, and why it is so hard to measure its effects using any kind of method, is found in this volume's chapter on Qualitative Comparative Analysis (QCA) by Caves, Meuer, and Rupietta. Doing research with qualitative methods has been an important strategy for gathering evidence about the pathways of leadership effects on student learning (Leithwood & Riehl, 2005), and methods texts like Miles and Huberman's (1994) influential sourcebook have guided countless researchers in developing explanations for patterns found in naturalistic data. But qualitative studies, especially when they are restricted to single case studies, are often discounted because they can lay few claims to generalizability, and—although this is not always explicitly noted—they do not provide opportunities to examine counterfactuals in order to establish causality without question. As Caves, Meuer, and Rupietta explain, QCA attempts to overcome these limitations and proffers some real analytic strengths for "small-n" research.

As the authors argue, leadership is a multidimensional and highly contingent phenomenon; it simply unfolds differently in different contexts, and what works well in one setting might not work at all in another. As others have also argued, the charge for education research is to model and explain how interlocking arrays of conditions and actions operate locally (e.g., Easton, 2010; Bryk, Gomez, & Grunow, 2011). While this may be inconvenient for researchers using other analytic strategies, it is just what QCA was developed to handle in its use of set theory and Boolean logic. In particular, explain the authors, it accommodates four important aspects of leadership that can be very difficult to untangle. First, QCA can help distinguish between factors that are sufficient and those that are necessary for linking leadership with outcomes. As they explain, this helps differentiate those qualities of leadership that must be present for positive outcomes to be realized from qualities that present one possible pathway to positive outcomes. Second, the method is able to parse "conjunctural causation" by identifying different combinations of factors that work in concert. This is quite different from a traditional regression equation that "controls" for individual variables to estimate the effects of others. Third, QCA can handle "equifinality"—the presence of multiple pathways to the same destination, a quality that is natural and common to leadership (Riehl, 2007). And fourth, it can identify "asymmetric causality," the analysis of how the presence of a factor can have an impact very different from its absence, another dimension by which leadership can be characterized.

Using a hypothetical example, Caves, Meuer, and Rupietta show that data collection for a QCA examination of leadership can be straightforward, utilizing information practitioners themselves might gather, and the actual analysis involves the application of fairly simple logic rather than complicated mathematical calculations. Based on a systematic method of reduction instead of merely eyeballing the data, patterns emerge that illustrate the essence of complex pathways.

It is easy to imagine scenarios that could lend themselves to an analysis using the QCA approach. For example, it would be fascinating to employ QCA with the studies reviewed by Nordengren and see if the findings would be consistent with his. As another example, what kind of leadership is needed under changing conditions, and how might it differ from leadership in conditions that are more settled? Larry Cuban asserted some time ago that leadership is about change while management is about stability; these terms refer to different sorts of actions and priorities on the part of leaders. Leithwood, Day, Sammons, Harris, & Hopkins (2006, p. 5) opined that 'there is not a single documented case of a school successfully turning around its pupil achievement trajectory in the absence of talented leadership.' But what should that "talented leadership" look like? Must it reside in one individual or be more distributed and collaborative? And we know that some routines and practices in schools offer substitutes, or possibly shortcuts, for leadership (Conley & Enomoto, 2005; Pitner, 1986; Spillane, Parise, and Sherer, 2011), How might all of these factors come together in different contexts? QCA might be just the analytic strategy that's needed to meet this challenge.

POLICIES ABOUT LEADERSHIP

It's difficult to ascertain what came first—promising advances in the study of leadership, or the policy system's gravitation towards leadership as a target for reform activity. Either way, policy makers have devoted much attention recently to leadership, and researchers have contributed scholarship to support their efforts. State level attempts to build "coherent systems" of preparation, certification, and evaluation of school leaders have been stimulated by federal education legislation, and local districts have revamped their approaches to "talent development." Not all of these new policy initiatives around leadership are fully fleshed out as yet (e.g., Fuller & Hollingworth, 2014). As Nordengren (this volume) notes, there is a paradox in juxtaposing the understanding that leadership effects are probably largely indirect alongside "the expectation of policymakers and the public that leaders can fix failing schools." There are probably numerous ways for the policy system to deal with this, for example by aligning and distributing accountability proportionately to reflect the nested, interactive nature of leadership influence back and forth among teachers, building administrators, and others. In any case, as Morrison (2013) argues, it is quite possible that expecting to discover, much less mandate, leadership effects on learning is a fool's errand when school leaders are asked to serve as functionaries in hierarchical systems of standards and accountability, bringing reform ideas from the outside into the school in ways that may preclude durable school improvement.

This latter point begs the larger and more fundamental meta-question of how and why leadership matters. What do the functions and practices and mechanisms of leadership add up to, beyond a technical theory of action? Is leadership "working" because it is part of the machinery of more tightly coupled control systems extending from the statehouse to the principal's office to the classroom? Or is leadership effective because it serves other, more authentic processes of continuous improvement and system learning, which many consider the only sustainable form of change (Copland; 2003; Fullan, 1995)? As research on leadership becomes methodologically more sophisticated, it will be important for these kinds of questions to be addressed, lest the research devolve into an under-theorized search for limited effects along a narrowed causal pathway.

BUT WHAT'S A LEADER TO LEAD?

One topic that has received limited attention in this volume is the matter of schools themselves and their probable lifespan as environments for learning. In some ways, there appears to be an unquestioned assumption that education will continue to take place largely within the confines of schools as formal organizations. Daft (2004) defined formal organizations as goal directed social entities with deliberately structured and coordinated activity systems and an identifiable boundary (p. 11). Traditional schools are bounded in space, mostly in the form of classrooms housed in buildings. They are bounded in time by daily schedules and yearly school calendars, and bounded in other ways by regularities regarding teacher qualifications, student-teacher ratios, grade level organization, administrative hierarchies, the routines of pedagogy, and so on. But will that always be the case?

In December 1997, *Educational Administration Quarterly* published a theme issue on "what will replace the comprehensive high school?" The answers that might be given to that question today could hardly have been anticipated nearly 20 years ago. Increasingly, new technologies are conjuring new imagined futures for learning (J. S. Brown, 2006). Will there be anything resembling "teaching" as we know it today, and will the environments in which these activities take place look anything like school? These questions have obvious implications for education leadership. Not only will leaders likely need to work with adults and children involved in constellations of activities that fall outside the traditional classroom instruction model, they also may need to manage environments that are more distributed, networked, virtual, information-rich, personalized, and far less scripted than most schools are today. In these brave new contexts, the leader's first job may be to manage traditional schools out of business, but the need for leadership might continue to expand. How are we preparing leaders for such a transition?

The Cooper and Rollert contribution to this volume poses a related question about how to prepare leaders to lead non-traditional schools. Alternative schools appear to be growing in number, currently representing about 14% of all secondary schools in the United States. In their chapter, Cooper and Rollert resist an oversimplified distinction between traditional and alternative schooling, noting that "schools across the spectrum from traditional to alternative differ considerably in regards to context and student needs." The logic of their argument appears to be that since the students in alternative schools are different in various ways from those who thrive in traditional settings, the learning environments must be different as well, primarily in terms of their high degree of personalization, flexibility, and culture of care. Echoing similar arguments about culturally responsive education, they make the case that "good leadership" won't suffice in these alternative settings; leaders must explicitly be equipped with knowledge and skills to understand students' social and emotional needs, provide appropriate curriculum and instruction, lead and manage a distinctive school culture and climate, offer and coordinate wrap-around services for students. They must also know how to attract and support appropriate staff for such schools, as well as monitoring and evaluating program effectiveness.

Two observations flow from this chapter that seem worthy of concern. First, alternative schools have been around for decades, but the evidence base on leadership for them is woefully thin; this chapter is based largely on a literature review covering three resource guides, two research reports, and two evaluation guides. If, as I surmise, environments for learning are going to expand and diversify in the future, we need to do a much better job of exploring the leadership ramifications by gathering solid evidence, including evidence from design research with learning environments that are just being created.

Second, a growing evidence base would likely generate even more complexity around leadership than currently exists, and our descriptive and analytic models will need to reflect it. The variations in how leaders address the four common functions of setting direction, developing people, developing the organization, and managing the instructional program will likely multiply, and those might not even be appropriate functional categories for the future.

A similar observation arises from the Luter chapter on improving urban inner-city education. Luter begins by making the point that the literature on education leadership has not sufficiently taken into account the newer strategies of place-based education reform and their tensions with more conventional approaches to improvement. Urban education policy has cycled through comprehensive school reform and school choice as major mechanisms for driving improvement. Each has created tensions within and around individual schools and has had only limited effectiveness in improving urban education. Given a growing recognition of the effects of neighborhoods on children and their education, place-based education strategies are likely to become more prominent, including community schools, community organizing efforts, and comprehensive neighborhood development strategies such as Promise Neighborhoods. As yet, Luter claims, there is little research knowledge about three dimensions of these emerging alternatives: how place-based comprehensive community initiatives are implemented, the role of individual schools and school systems in place-based reform, and how the education sector can balance conflicting policy demands occasioned by place-based reform and other traditional education policies, especially for accountability.

Community schooling and other place-based education reforms have a long history, and apart from a limited but insightful spate of analysis of such efforts back in the 1990s (Crowson & Boyd, 1993; 1996; Dryfoos, 1994), the leadership challenges of these initiatives are indeed poorly understood. Locally based, cross-sector initiatives for education reform, service delivery to children and youth, and community development are becoming more prominent across the United States, often established under the umbrella concept of "collective impact" (Henig, Riehl, Rebell, & Wolff, 2015). These initiatives pose at least three major challenges: how to develop a comprehensive theory of action that guides meaningful action toward expressed goals; how to negotiate the considerable complexity of urban politics, often delineated across lines of race, social class, and the distances between elite community leaders and grassroots community organizations and citizens; and how to manage the equally complex organizational dynamics of securing participation, providing leadership, facilitating communication, obtaining and sharing resources, monitoring implementation and service delivery, and resolving conflicts among partners, many of whom can bolt at will. School leaders may find themselves in especially vulnerable positions in these collaborations, which are often organized precisely to fix what the school systems have not been able to fix. And, as Luter makes clear, place-based reform isn't always consistent with other education policy initiatives.

The full-service "bubble" of the 1990s revealed that education leaders were not well prepared, or especially inclined, to lead these kinds of comprehensive initiatives. As Crowson and Boyd (1993) artfully termed it, "designing arks for storms and seas unknown" proved to be a difficult undertaking. This time around, there is more governmental and philanthropic support for place-based education reform in many settings, along with strong justifications for doing so, but the implementation hurdles are daunting. Education leadership researchers and practitioners will have much to contribute by designing, observing, and theorizing about these efforts.

THE INTEGRATION OF LEADERSHIP THEORY, RESEARCH, AND PRACTICE

Perhaps the most distressing but ultimately also the most hopeful contribution to this volume is the chapter by Lochmiller, Chesnut, and Stewart on preparing education leaders in an era of school turnarounds. This chapter describes a partnership that developed between a university and a school district, specifically for the purpose of preparing turnaround leaders for the local district and improving both the rigor and relevance of their training. Sound reasoning guided the partnership; as the authors note from their review of literature, such partnerships can increase the coherence between preparation and professional practice, and they also become productive employment pipelines. They are especially helpful and effective when districts seek out the universities because of a felt need for something the university can provide; and they seem to have benefits for individual students as well as programs.

Lochmiller and his colleagues describe how, in the past, the school district had deferred to the university for decisions about leader preparation. In effect, the district took a passive role and outsourced the training function for its leaders—not unusual at all, since this has been the typical arrangement with pre-service education, although new approaches like this one are challenging the model (e.g., Orr, King, & LaPointe, 2010; Sanzo, Myran, & Clayton, 2011). But once the district became more actively involved, they began to challenge the university's control, privilege, and authority. In reconciling the positions of university and district representatives, all participants had to develop what Lochmiller et al. term a "shared understanding" of leadership. They discarded the "romantic notions" about leadership promoted by the university, critiqued the "theoretical and impractical" nature of the traditional training, and promoted "the district way." As one university professor described, "It was the most uncomfortable professional experience I've had and yet has been one of the most beneficial in terms of our program."

The authors explain that as a result of the partnership, the preparation program began to incorporate more problem-based learning, changed the sequence of courses, and eliminated assignments that were "too academic." Together the partners focused on the district's view of turnaround leadership, especially ensuring new leaders knew how to interact with adults, how to make systematic changes in teaching and learning, how to involve stakeholders in change, how to effectively communicate, and how to utilize limited resources well. As a result, reported one informant, the partnership provided "opportunities to deeply and meaningfully connect theory and practice."

In all fairness, this brief account probably omits many salient details, and in any event it is commendable that the university faculty approached the opportunity to partner with its local school district in such a spirit of openness and humility. Nonetheless, the case is distressing in its lack of a critical examination of what might be meant by connecting practice, research, and theory, not to mention policy, which to some observers comprise the "building blocks" of leadership (Bush & Glover, 2014). To an outsider, it seems as if the university simply absorbed the district's pragmatic views of what new leaders need to know and be able to do (recalling that the district was anticipating some kind of state accountability sanctions, suggesting that their notions of effective leadership might have needed some revision). Many university-based preparation programs could probably be admonished for being out of touch with real practice, for not respecting the perspectives and needs of professionals, and for not giving their students enough opportunity to engage with real problems of practice, although some critiques may be overblown (e.g., Levine, 2005). But that doesn't mean that research, theory, and "book smarts" are necessarily irrelevant to practice.

John Q. Easton, former director of the Institute for Education Sciences at the U.S. Department of Education, has spoken eloquently of researchers' obligation to "shine a light" on problems of practice and then to work with practitioners as they craft solutions; this characterized the relationship between the Chicago Public Schools and the Consortium on Chicago School Research under his tenure there. Knowledge can and must flow from practice to research and theory, not simply the other way around (Shulman, 2007). Ever since Kurt Lewin uttered his famous phrase in 1945, it has often been repeated that "there's nothing so practical as a good theory." And there are many good examples of practical theories in the field of education leadership that have already proven their worth to practitioners, including—to name just a few—theories about the futility of reforms that ignore the importance of institutional legitimacy (Tyack & Cuban, 1995), theories about sensemaking and the cognitive aspects of leadership (Coburn, 2005; Spillane, Reiser, & Reimer, 2002), and theories about schools as professional learning communities (Kruse, Louis, & Bryk, 1994). In fact, what we may need are not fewer theories and less research, but more of both—on topics of real concern to leadership practitioners. To that end, efforts to support the inquiry practices of leaders and teachers working in schools (Riehl, Larson, Short, & Reitzug, 2000; Talbert, 2011) may offer the most promise for building fruitful relationships between academics and practitioners. By introducing this topic for consideration, Lochmiller, Chesnut, and Stewart have made a valuable and hopeful contribution to this volume of work.

REFERENCES

Bidwell, C. (1965). The school as a formal organization. In J. G. March (Ed.), *Handbook of organizations* (pp. 972–1018). Chicago, IL: Rand McNally.

Bossert, S. T., Dwyer, D. C., Rowan, B., & Lee, G. V. (1982). The instructional management role of the principal. *Educational Administration Quarterly, 18*(3), 34.

Branch, G. F., Hanushek, E. A., & Rivkin, S. G. (2012). Estimating the effect of leaders on public sector productivity: The case of school principals *NBER Working Paper Series #17803*. Cambridge, MA: National Bureau of Economic Research.

Brooks, J. S., Jean-Marie, G., Normore, A. H., & Hodgins, D. W. (2007). Distributed leadership for social justice: Exploring how influence and equity are stretched over an urban high school. *Journal of School Leadership, 17*(4), 378–408.

Brown, J. S. (2006). New learning environments for the 21st century: Exploring the edge. *Change: The Magazine of Higher Learning, 38*(5), 18–24.

Brown, K. (2006). "New" educational injustices in the "new" South Africa. *Journal of Educational Administration, 44*(5), 509–519.

Brown, K. M. (2006). Leadership for social justice and equity: Evaluating a transformative framework and andragogy. *Educational Administration Quarterly, 42*(5), 700–745.

Bryk, A. S., Gomez, L. M., & Grunow, A. (2011). Getting ideas into action: Building networked improvement communities in education. In M. Hallinan (Ed.), *Frontiers in sociology of education* (pp. 127–162). New York, NY: Springer.

Bryk, A. S., Sebring, P. B., Allensworth, E., Luppescu, S., & Easton, J. Q. (2010). *Organizing schools for improvement: Lessons from Chicago*. Chicago, IL: The University of Chicago Press.

Bush, T., & Glover, D. (2014). School leadership models: What do we know? *School Leadership & Management, 34*(5), 553.

Camburn, E. M., Spillane, J. P., & Sebastian, J. (2010). Assessing the utility of a daily log for measuring principal leadership practice. *Educational Administration Quarterly, 46*(5), 707.

Christensen, C. M. (1997). *The innovator's dilemma: When new technologies cause great firms to fail.* Cambridge, MA: Harvard Business Press.

City, E. A., Elmore, R. F., Fiarman, S. E., & Teitel, L. (2009). *Instructional rounds in education: A network approach to improving teaching and learning.* Cambridge, MA: Harvard Education Press.

Clark, D., Martorell, P., & Rockoff, J. (2009). School principals and school performance *CALDER Working Paper No. 38.* Washington, DC: Urban Institute.

Coburn, C. E. (2005). Shaping teacher sensemaking: School leaders and the enactment of reading policy. *Educational Policy, 19*(3), 479–509.

Cohen, D. K. (1982). Policy and organization: The impact of state and federal educational policy on school governance. *Harvard Educational Review, 52*(4), 474.

Cohen, D. K., Raudenbush, S. W., & Deborah Loewenberg, B. (2003). Resources, instruction, and research. *Educational Evaluation and Policy Analysis, 25*(2), 119–142.

Collard, J. (2007). Constructing theory for leadership in intercultural contexts. *Journal of Educational Administration, 45*(6), 740.

Conley, S., & Enomoto, E. K. (2005). Routines in school organizations: Creating stability and change. *Journal of Educational Administration, 43*(1), 9–21.

Copland, M. A. (2003). Leadership of Inquiry: Building and sustaining capacity for school improvement. *Educational Evaluation and Policy Analysis, 25*(4), 375–395.

Crowson, R. L., & Boyd, W. L. (1993). Coordinated services for children: Designing arks for storms and seas unknown. *American Journal of Education, 101*(2), 140–179.

Crowson, R. L., & Boyd, W. L. (1996). Achieving coordinated school-linked services: Facilitating utilization of the emerging knowledge base. *Educational Policy, 10*(2), 253–272.

Culbertson, J. A. (1988). A century's quest for a knowledge base. In N. J. Boyan (Ed.), *Handbook of research on educational administration* (pp. 3–26). New York: Longman.

Daft, R. L. (2004). *Organization theory and design* (8th ed.) Mason, OH: South-Western.

Darling-Hammond, L., LaPointe, M., Meyerson, D., Orr, M. T., & Cohen, C. (2007). *Preparing school leaders for a changing world: Lessons from exemplary leadership development programs.* Stanford, CA: Stanford University, Stanford Educational Leadership Institute.

Davies, B., & Bansel, P. (2007). Neoliberalism and education. *International Journal of Qualitative Studies in Education, 20*(3), 247–259.

Dillard, C. B. (1995). Leading with her life: An African American feminist (re)interpretation of leadership for an urban high school principal. *Educational Administration Quarterly, 31*(4), 539.

Donmoyer, R. (1999). The continuing quest for a knowledge base: 1976–1998. In J. Murphy & K. S. Louis (Eds.), *Handbook of research on educational administration* (2nd ed.; pp. 25–43). San Francisco, CA: Jossey-Bass Publishers.

Dryfoos, J. G. (1994). *Full-service schools: A revolution in health and social services for children, youth, and families.* San Francisco, CA: Jossey-Bass.

Eacott, S. (2013). Towards a theory of school leadership practice: A Bourdieusian perspective. *Journal of Educational Administration and History, 45*(2), 174.

Easton, J. Q. (2010). *Out of the tower, into the schools: How new IES goals will reshape researcher roles.* Presidential Talk, Annual Meeting of the American Educational Research Association, Denver, May 2.

Eldredge, N., & Gould, S. J. (1972). Punctuated equilibria: An alternative to phyletic gradualism. In T. J. M. Schopf (Ed.), *Models in paleobiology* (pp. 82–115). San Francisco, CA: Freeman Cooper.

English, F. W. (2006). The unintended consequences of a standardized knowledge base in advancing educational leadership preparation. *Educational Administration Quarterly, 42*(3), 461.

Erickson, D. A. (1977). An overdue paradigm shift in educational administration, or how can we get that idiot off the freeway? In L. L. Cunningham, W. G. Hack, & R. O. Nystrand (Eds.), *Educational administration: The developing decades* (pp. 114–143). Berkeley, CA: McCutchan.

Erickson, D. A. (1979). Research on educational administration: The state-of-the-art. *Educational Researcher, 8*(3), 9–14.

Firestone, W., & Riehl, C. (Eds.) (2005). *A new agenda for research in educational leadership.* New York: Teachers College Press.

Fullan, M. (1995). The school as a learning organization: Distant dreams. *Theory Into Practice, 34*(4), 230.

Fuller, E. J., & Hollingworth, L. (2014). A bridge too far? Challenges in evaluating principal effectiveness. *Educational Administration Quarterly, 50*(3), 466.

Furman, G. (2012). Social justice leadership as praxis: Developing capacities through preparation programs. *Educational Administration Quarterly, 48*(2), 191.

Gersick, C. J. G. (1988). Time and transition in work teams: Toward a new model of group development. *Academy of Management Journal, 31*(1), 9–41.

Grissom, J. A., & Loeb, S. (2011). Triangulating principal effectiveness: How perspectives of parents, teachers, and assistant principals identify the central importance of managerial skills. *American Educational Research Journal, 48*(5), 1091–1123.

Grissom, J. A., Loeb, S., & Master, B. (2013). Effective instructional time use for school leaders: Longitudinal evidence from observations of principals. *Educational Researcher, 42*(8), 433–444.

Hallinger, P. (2011). Leadership for learning: Lessons from 40 years of empirical research. *Journal of Educational Administration, 49*(2), 125–142.

Hallinger, P., & Heck, R. H. (1996). Reassessing the principal's role in school effectiveness: A review of empirical research, 1980–1995. *Educational Administration Quarterly, 32*(1), 5.

Heck, R. H., & Hallinger, P. (2010). Collaborative leadership effects on school improvement: Integrating unidirectional- and reciprocal-effects models. *The Elementary School Journal, 111*(2), 226.

Heck, R. H., & Hallinger, P. (2014). Modeling the longitudinal effects of school leadership on teaching and learning. *Journal of Educational Administration, 52*(5), 653–681.

Hendriks, M. A., & Scheerens, J. (2013). School leadership effects revisited: A review of empirical studies guided by indirect-effect models. *School Leadership & Management, 33*(4), 373.

Henig, J. R., Riehl, C. J., Rebell, M. A., & Wolff, J. R. (2015). *Putting collective impact into context: A review of the literature on local cross-sector collaboration to improve education.* New York, NY: Teachers College Press.

Honig, M. I., & Louis, K. S. (2007). A new agenda for research in educational leadership: A conversational review. *Educational Administration Quarterly, 43*(1), 138.

Hoy, W. K., & Miskel, C. G. (2005). *Educational administration: Theory, research, and practice* (7th ed.). Boston, MA: McGraw-Hill.

Johnson, B. L., Jr. (2003). Those nagging headaches: Perennial issues and tensions in the politics of education field. *Educational Administration Quarterly, 39*(1), 41–67.

Kruse, S., Louis, K. S., & Bryk, A. (1994). Building professional community in schools. Issues in Restructuring Schools, Issue Report No. 6, pp. 3–6. Madison, WI: University of Wisconsin, Center on Organization and Restructuring of Schools.

Kuhn, T. S. (1962). *The structure of scientific revolutions.* Chicago, IL: University of Chicago Press.

Lee, Y. (2010). Views on education and achievement: Finland's story of success and South Korea's story of decline. *KEDI Journal of Educational Policy, 7*(2), 379–401.

Leithwood, K. (2005). Understanding successful principal leadership: Progress on a broken front. *Journal of Educational Administration, 43*(6), 619–629.

Leithwood, K., Day, C., Sammons, P., Harris, A., & Hopkins, D. (2006). *Seven strong claims about successful school leadership.* Nottingham, England: National College for School Leadership.

Leithwood, K., & Duke, D. L. (1999). A century's quest to understand school leadership. In J. Murphy & K. S. Louis (Eds.), *Handbook of research on educational administration,* (2nd ed.; pp. 45–72). San Francisco, CA: Jossey-Bass Publishers.

Leithwood, K., Louis, K. S., Anderson, S., & Wahlstrom, K. (2004). *How leadership influences student learning.* New York: The Wallace Foundation.

Leithwood, K., Patten, S., & Jantzi, D. D. (2010). Testing a conception of how school leadership influences student learning. *Educational Administration Quarterly, 46*(5), 671.

Leithwood, K. A., & Riehl, C. (2005). What do we already know about educational leadership? In W. Firestone & C. Riehl (Eds.), *A new agenda for research in educational leadership* (pp. 12–27). New York: Teachers College Press.

Levin, H. M. (2006). Can research improve educational leadership? *Educational Researcher, 35*(8), 38–43.

Levine, A. (2005). *Educating school leaders.* Washington, DC: The Education Schools Project.

Lopez, G. R. (2003). The (racially neutral) politics of education: A critical race theory perspective. *Educational Administration Quarterly, 39*(1), 68–94.

Louis, K. S., Leithwood, K., Wahlstrom, K. L., & Anderson, S. E. (2010). *Investigating the links to improved student learning: Final report of research findings.* Minneapolis, MN: University of Minnesota, Center for Applied Research and Educational Improvement.

Lugg, C. A. (2008). "Why's a nice dyke like you embracing this postmodern crap?." *Journal of School Leadership, 18*(2), 164–199.

Lugg, C. A., & Shoho, A. R. (2006). Dare public school administrators build a new social order? Social justice and the possibly perilous politics of educational leadership. *Journal of Educational Administration, 44*(3), 196–208.

Marks, H. M., & Printy, S. M. (2003). Principal leadership and school performance: An integration of transformational and instructional leadership. *Educational Administration Quarterly, 39*(3), 370–397.

Marzano, R. J., Waters, T., & McNulty, B. (2005). *School leadership that works: From research to results.* Aurora, CO: ASCD and McREL.

Mayrowetz, D. (2008). Making sense of distributed leadership: Exploring the multiple usages of the concept in the field. *Educational Administration Quarterly, 44*(3), 424.

Miles, M. B., & Huberman, A. M. (1994). *Qualitative data analysis* (2nd ed.). Thousand Oaks, CA: SAGE Publications.

Moghadam, V. M. (2009). *Globalization and social movements: Islamism, feminism, and the global justice movement.* Lanham, MD: Rowman and Littlefield.

Morrison, A. R. (2013). Educational leadership and change: Structural challenges in the implementation of a shifting paradigm. *School Leadership & Management, 33*(4), 412–424.

Mourshed, M., Chijioke, C., & Barber, M. (2010, November). *How the world's most improved school systems keep getting better.* New York: McKinsey & Company. Retrieved from: http://www.mckinsey.com/Client_Service/Social_Sector/Latest_thinking/Worlds_most_improved_schools.aspx.

Murphy, J. (2002). Reculturing the profession of educational leadership: New blueprints. In J. Murphy (Ed.), *The educational leadership challenge: Redefining leadership for the 21st century* (101st Yearbook of the National Society for the Study of Education, Part I, pp. 65–82). Chicago, IL: National Society for the Study of Education.

Murphy, J. (2005). Unpacking the foundations of ISLLC standards and addressing concerns in the academic community. *Educational Administration Quarterly, 41*(1), 154–191.

Murphy, J., Vriesenga, M., & Storey, V. (2007). Educational Administration Quarterly, 1979–2003: An analysis of types of work, methods of investigation, and influences. *Educational Administration Quarterly, 43*(5), 612–628.

Murtadha, K., & Watts, D. M. (2005). Linking the struggle for education and social justice: Historical perspectives of African American leadership in schools. *Educational Administration Quarterly, 41*(4), 591–608.

Orr, M. T., King, C., & LaPointe, M. (2010). *Districts developing leaders: Lessons on consumer actions and program approaches from eight urban districts.* Newton, MA: Education Development Center, Inc.

Pitner, N. J. (1986). Substitutes for principal leader behavior: An exploratory study. *Educational Administration Quarterly, 22*(2), 23–42.

Pitner, N. J. (1988). The study of administrator effects and effectiveness. In N. J. Boyan (Ed.), *Handbook of research on educational administration* (pp. 99–122). New York: Longman.

Printy, S. M., Marks, H. M., & Bowers, A. J. (2009). Integrated leadership: How principals and teachers share transformational and instructional influence. *Journal of School Leadership, 19*(5), 504–532.

Riehl, C. (2007). Research on educational leadership: Knowledge we need for the world we live in. In F. W. English & G. C. Furman (Eds.), *Research and educational leadership: Navigating the new National Research Council guidelines* (pp. 133–168). Lanham, MD: Rowman and Littlefield Publishers, Inc.

Riehl, C., & Firestone, W. (2005). What research methods should be used to study educational leadership? In W. Firestone & C. Riehl (Eds.), *A new agenda for research in educational leadership* (pp. 156–170). New York: Teachers College Press.

Riehl, C., & Lee, V.E. (1996). Gender, organizations, and leadership. In K. Leithwood, J. Chapman, D. Corson, P. Hallinger, & A. Hart (Eds.), *International handbook of educational leadership and administration* (pp. 873–919). Boston, MA: Kluwer Academic Publishers.

Riehl, C., Larson, C. L., Short, P. M., & Reitzug, U. C. (2000). Reconceptualizing research and scholarship in educational administration: Learning to know, knowing to do, doing to learn. *Educational Administration Quarterly, 36*(3), 391–427.

Robinson, V. M. J., Lloyd, C. A., & Rowe, K. J. (2008). The impact of leadership on student outcomes: An analysis of the differential effects of leadership types. *Educational Administration Quarterly, 44*(5), 635–674.

Romanelli, E., & Tushman, M. L. (1994). Organizational transformation as punctuated equilibrium: An empirical test. *Academy of Management Journal, 37*(5), 1141.

Rowan, B. (1995). Learning, teaching, and educational administration: Toward a research agenda. *Educational Administration Quarterly, 31*(3), 344.

Sahlberg, P. (2007). Education policies for raising student learning: The Finnish approach. *Journal of Education Policy, 22*(2), 147–171.

Sanzo, K. L., Myran, S., & Clayton, J. K. (2011). Building bridges between knowledge and practice. *Journal of Educational Administration, 49*(3), 292–312.

Scribner, J. D., Lopez, G. R., Koschoreck, J. W., Mahitivanichcha, K., & Scheurich, J. J. (1999). The building blocks of educational administration: A dialogic review of the first three chapters of the "Handbook." *Educational Administration Quarterly, 35*(4), 477–499.

Sebastian, J., & Allensworth, E. (2012). The influence of principal leadership on classroom instruction and student learning: A study of mediated pathways to learning. *Educational Administration Quarterly, 48*(4), 626.

Sergiovanni, T. J. (1994). Organizations or communities? Changing the metaphor changes the theory. *Educational administration quarterly, 30*(2), 214–226.

Shulman, L. S. (2007). Practical wisdom in the service of professional practice. *Educational Researcher, 36*(9), 560–563.

Spillane, J. P., Parise, L. M., & Sherer, J. Z. (2011). Organizational routines as coupling mechanisms: Policy, school administration, and the technical core. *American Educational Research Journal, 48*(3), 586.

Spillane, J. P., Reiser, B. J., & Reimer, T. (2002). Policy implementation and cognition: Reframing and refocusing implementation research. *Review of Educational Research, 72*(3), 387–431.

Spillane, J. P., & Zuberi, A. (2009). Designing and piloting a leadership daily practice log: Using logs to study the practice of leadership. *Educational Administration Quarterly, 45*(3), 375.

Stogdill, R. M. (1974). *Handbook of leadership: A survey of theory and research.* New York: The Free Press.

Supovitz, J., Sirinides, P., & May, H. (2010). How principals and peers influence teaching and learning. *Educational Administration Quarterly, 46*(1), 31–56.

Talbert, J. E. (2011). Collaborative inquiry to expand student success in New York City schools. In J. O'Day, C. S. Bitter, & L. M. Gomez (Eds.), *Education reform in New York City: Ambitious change in the nation's most complex school system* (pp. 131–156). Cambridge, MA: Harvard Education Press.

Tyack, D., & Cuban, L. (1995). *Tinkering toward utopia: A century of educational reform.* Cambridge, MA: Harvard University Press.

Waters, T., Marzano, R. J., & McNulty, B. (2003). *Balanced leadership: What 30 years of research tells us about the effect of leadership on student achievement.* A working paper. Denver, CO: Mid-continent Research for Education and Learning.

Weick, K. E. (1976). Educational organizations as loosely coupled systems. *Administrative Science Quarterly, 21,* 1–19.

Willower, D. J. (1996). Inquiry in educational administration and the spirit of the times. *Educational Administration Quarterly, 32*(3), 344.

Willower, D. J., & Forsyth, P. B. (1999). A brief history of scholarship on educational administration. In J. Murphy & K. Seashore Louis (Eds.), *Handbook of research on educational administration* (2nd ed.; pp. 1–23). San Francisco, CA: Jossey-Bass Publishers.

Witziers, B., Bosker, R. J., & Krueger, M. L. (2003). Educational leadership and student achievement: The elusive search for an association. *Educational Administration Quarterly, 39*(3), 398–425.

Young, M. D. (2015). New national standards for leadership practice and preparation. *School Administrator, 72*(3), 35.

Yukl, G. A. (2006). *Leadership in organizations.* Upper Saddle River, NJ: Prentice Hall.

ABOUT THE CONTRIBUTORS

Khalid Arar (PhD) is a Senior Lecturer at the Center for Academic Studies and co-head of MA degree studies in Education Administration at Sakhnin Academic College. His studies focus on issues of diversity, equity and ethnicity in education in general and in educational leadership and higher education in particular. His most recent book *Arab women in management and leadership* (2013) New York: Palgrave, with Tamar Shapira, Faisal Azaiza and Rachel Hertz Lazarowitz). Correspondence to: Dr. Khalid Arar, email: khalidarr@gmail.com .

Bruce G. Barnett is a Professor in the Educational Leadership and Policy Studies Department at the University of Texas at San Antonio. Previously, he has worked at the Far West Laboratory, Indiana University, and the University of Northern Colorado. Besides developing and delivering master's, certification, and doctoral programs, his professional interests include: Educational leadership preparation programs, particularly cohort-based learning and school-university partnerships, Mentoring and coaching, Reflective practice, Leadership for school improvement, Realities of beginning principals and assistant principals, and International trends in leadership preparation and development.

Bruce's work in these areas appears in a variety of books, book chapters, and journals including *Educational Administration Quarterly*, *Journal of Educational Administration*, *International Journal of Urban Educational Leadership*, *Journal of Research on Leadership Education*, *Journal of School Leadership*, *Journal of Staff Development*, and *Leading and Managing*. For well over a decade, he has become involved in international research and program development, co-authoring books on school improvement; researching mentoring and coaching programs operating around the world; and presenting workshops in Australia, New Zealand, England, Hong Kong, Ireland, and Canada. From 2008-2013, Bruce served as the Associate Director of International Affairs for the University Council for Educational Administration. One of the current projects being implemented is the International School Leadership Development Network, a collaboration of colleagues around the world examining leadership preparation and development in different cultural contexts.

Alex J. Bowers is an Associate Professor of Education Leadership at Teachers College, Columbia University, where he works to help school leaders use the data that they already collect in schools in more effective ways to help direct the limited resources of schools and districts to specific student needs. His research focuses on the intersection of effective school and district leadership, data driven decision making, student grades and test scores, student persistence and dropouts. His work also considers the influence of school finance, facilities, and technology on student achievement. Dr. Bowers studies these domains through the application of Intensive Longitudinal Data analysis (ILD), such as data visualization analytics, multi-level and growth mixture modeling, and cluster analysis heatmap data dashboards. He earned his Ph.D. in K12 Educational Administration from Michigan State University, and previous to teaching and education research, spent a decade as a cancer researcher in the biotechnology industry, with an M.S. in Biochemistry, Microbiology and Molecular Biology, and a B.S. in Biochemistry.

Katherine Caves is a post-doctoral researcher in the KOF Swiss Economic Institute at ETH Zurich. She earned her PhD in 2015 from the University of Zurich's Department of Business Administration. Her research focuses on the economics of education, specifically the use of multiple methodologies for addressing key questions in the field. Currently, Katherine is part of the Center for the Economics and Management of Education and Training Systems (CEMETS) where she works with various cities, states, and countries on labor market-oriented education systems reforms.

Colleen Chesnut is a Research Associate at the Center for Evaluation & Education Policy at Indiana University. Her research focuses on education policy issues related to equity for English language learners, leadership development, and school law. Her recent research has focused on job-embedded learning in leadership preparation programs and legal analyses of education policies related equity for diverse students. Her research has been published in *West's Education Law Reporter, Teachers College Record*, and in edited volumes.

Kristy Cooper is Assistant Professor of K-12 Educational Administration at Michigan State University. She completed her doctorate in Education Policy, Leadership, and Instructional Practice at the Harvard Graduate School of Education in 2011. Her research examines systematic approaches to increasing student engagement in classrooms—with the ultimate goals of enhancing student learning, improving students' affective experiences in schools, and increasing high school graduation rates. Cooper also studies instructional improvement, teacher leadership, and alternative high schools. Her research has appeared in the *American Educational Research Journal, Urban Education, The High School Journal*, and *Phi Delta Kappan*. She is also a co-author on the 2009 book *Inside Urban Charter Schools*. A Nationally Board Certified teacher, Cooper has six years of teaching experience in Los Angeles.

Maida Finch is an assistant professor at Salisbury University in the Education Specialties department, where she teaches classes on literacy theory, research methods, and quantitative analysis. She also supervises student teaching interns. Dr. Finch's research investigates questions that hold promise for resolving complex problems of education policy and practice. The topics of her research are diverse including education labor markets, teaching and learning, and policy development and effects.

Peter Goff is an assistant professor at the University of Wisconsin-Madison in the department of Educational Leadership and Policy Analysis, where he teaches classes on quantitative analysis, research methods, and k-12 finance policy. Dr. Goff's research examines the policies and practices surrounding the strategic management of human capital (SMHC). Using a combination of experimental, quasi-experimental, and descriptive methods, his work explores SMHC policies at the school, district, and state-level, with a particular focus on the two-sided selection process that arises during hiring. His current research projects examine student assignment practices, the impact of within-school teacher mobility on instructional growth, and gender bias in the leadership labor market.

Chad Lochmiller is an Assistant Professor in the Department of Educational Leadership & Policy Studies in the School of Education at Indiana University. His research focuses on education policy issues related to school finance, human resources, and leadership development. His recent research has focused on leadership preparation programs and strategies that can be used to make preparation experiences more rigorous and better aligned with the needs of school districts. His research has been published in the *Educational Policy Analysis Archives, Journal of Research on Leadership Education, Journal of Cases in Educational Leadership, Journal of School Leadership*, and in edited volumes.

D. Gavin Luter is receiving his PhD student in Educational Leadership and Policy Studies at the University at Buffalo, State University of New York, and will be joining Wisconsin Campus Compact as Executive Director in June 2015 based at the University of Wisconsin Extension. He formerly also served as Coordinator of Educational Programs at the UB Center for Urban Studies where he oversaw a project-based learning enrichment effort in an urban K-8 school centered on bolstering student critical consciousness. He also led the education planning component of a US Department of Housing and Urban Development Perry Choice Neighborhood Mini-Education Pipeline strategy. As a practitioner / scholar, he has experience working in and with educational non-profits, school systems, and universities to both run programs and build systems-wide service coordination and reform capacity. This work links back to his main research interest of how universities can catalyze school and neighborhood transformation. Recent scholarly work has included implementation of a comprehensive place-based school reform initiative, an examination of a university-assisted community schools intervention, and as Guest Editor of a themed issue of the Peabody Journal of Education, "*Higher Education's Role and Capacity to Assist with Public School Reform.*"

Johannes Meuer is a Senior Researcher in the Department of Management, Technology, and Economics at ETH Zurich. Johannes received his PhD from the Rotterdam School of Management. His work has been published in *Research Policy, Organization Studies*, and *The Academy of Management Proceedings*. Johannes' current research focuses on organizational design and configuration theory, on innovation theories with a particular focus on organizational innovation, and on the application of set-theoretic methods in organization studies and the combination of set-theoretic and econometric methods.

Chase Nordengren's (chasen@uw.edu; chasenordengren.net) teaching and research focuses on the application of mixed methods to the study of complex problems in educational organizations. As an IES pre-doctoral fellow with the University of Washington's College of Education, Chase received his Ph.D. in Leadership, Policy, and Organizations in K-12 Systems in 2015. His dissertation uses mixed methods social network research to identify and follow the work of informal teacher leaders in an elementary school through their patterns of advice-giving, information-sharing and support, drawing on distributed models of instructional leadership. Future work will continue to explore how emergent methods in educational research can drive quantitative and qualitative understandings of the relationship between educational organizations and student learning.

Izhar Oplatka is a professor of Educational Administration and Leadership at The School of Education, Tel Aviv University, Israel. Prof. Oplatka's research focuses on the lives and career of school teachers and principals, educational marketing, emotions and educational administration, and the foundations of educational administration as a field of study. His most recent books include The legacy of educational administration: A historical analysis of an academic field (2010, Peter Lang Publishing); The essentials of educational administration (2015, Pardes Publisher, in Hebrew); Organizational Citizenship Behavior in Schools (2015, Routledge, with Anit Somech). Prof. Oplatka's publications have appeared in varied international journals including Educational Administration Quarterly, Journal of Educational Administration, Educational Management Administration & Leadership, Comparative Education Review, Teacher College Record, Canadian Journal of Education Administration and Policy, International Journal of Leadership in Education, Journal of Education Policy, School Leadership & Management, Urban Education, International Journal of Educational Management, and so forth.

Carolyn Riehl, Associate Professor of Sociology and Education Policy at Teachers College, Columbia University, focuses her scholarship on leadership and organizational dynamics in education, policy and the management of instruction, and research design and methods. Her work reflects a broad concern for how practice, policy, theory, and research can inform each other to support both careful analysis and pragmatic improvement, especially in settings where students traditionally have been poorly served. She has been a high school English teacher and has held faculty appointments at the University of Michigan, Eastern Michigan University, and the University of North Carolina at Greensboro. Her current research projects include a field study of teachers' instructional planning and use of data in elementary schools and a study of cross-sector collaborations for education reform.

Kate Rollert is a third-year doctoral student at Michigan State University pursing a dual degree in Educational Policy and Administration. Her research interests lie in urban education systems, school accountability, urban teacher preparation programs, and policies that increase the supply and quality of teachers in under-resourced, urban schools. Kate is currently researching urban teacher attrition in Detroit Public Schools and writing an article on school accountability in Dallas Public Schools. She also teaches a course on human diversity, power, and opportunity in social institutions. Prior to her doctoral studies at Michigan State University, Kate taught AP

Biology and Chemistry in Dallas, Texas. She has a Masters of Education from Southern Methodist University and a Bachelor of Science from Western Michigan University's Lee Honors College.

Christian Rupietta is a post-doctoral researcher at the University of Zurich Department of Business Administration. His current research focuses on the economics of education and innovation, in particular on knowledge diffusion in vocational education and training systems, on configurational theory in human resource management and organizational design, and the integration of econometric and set-theoretic methods.

Alan R. Shoho is the Dean of the School of Education and Professor of Administrative Leadership at the University of Wisconsin-Milwaukee. Prior to UWM, he was at the University of Texas at San Antonio where he was a Professor and Associate Vice Provost for Academic and Faculty Support for 21 years. He was an American Council of Education (ACE) Fellow during 2012/2013 academic year at the University of North Carolina at Charlotte. His research focuses on aspiring principals and assistant principals, high school social processes, and organizational cultures. In 2010, he served as the President for the University Council for Educational Administration. Dr. Shoho earned his Ed.D. at Arizona State University, M.Ed. at the University of Hawaii, and his B.S.E.E. in Electrical Engineering at California State University at Fullerton.

Molly Stewart is a Research Associate at the Center for Evaluation & Education Policy at Indiana University. Her research interests are in K-12 state and federal policy design, policy implementation and monitoring, and school choice and education markets. Her recent research and policy analysis projects look at how the implementation of market and quasi-market education policies differ from the theoretical assumptions built into their designs, and how future policy designs can build on lessons learned from those differences. She is also interested in building accessible, user-friendly, and information-rich tools for parents who are interested in exploring educational options.